Pragmatism and sociology

Pragmatism
and
sociology

EMILE DURKHEIM

Translated by

J. C. WHITEHOUSE

Senior Lecturer in French in the School of Modern Languages
University of Bradford

Edited and introduced by

JOHN B. ALLCOCK

Lecturer in Sociology in the School of Interdisciplinary
Human Studies, University of Bradford

With a preface by

ARMAND CUVILLIER

CAMBRIDGE UNIVERSITY PRESS

Cambridge

London   New York   New Rochelle
Melbourne   Sydney

Published by the Press Syndicate of the University of Cambridge
The Pitt Building, Trumpington Street, Cambridge CB2 1RP
32 East 57th Street, New York, NY 10022, USA
296 Beaconsfield Parade, Middle Park, Melbourne 3206, Australia

Originally published in French as *Pragmatisme et sociologie* by
Librairie Philosophique J. Vrin, Paris, 1955
and © Librairie Philosophique J. Vrin, 1955

First published in English by Cambridge University Press 1983 as
Pragmatism and sociology

Printed in Great Britain at
the University Press, Cambridge

Library of Congress catalogue card number: 82-14630

British Library Cataloguing in Publication Data

Durkheim, Emile
Pragmatism and sociology.
1. Pragmatism—Addresses, essays, lectures
I. Title   II. Allcock, John B.
III. Pragmatisme et sociologie. *English*
144'.3   B832

ISBN 0 521 24686 5

Contents

Contents

Acknowledgements

My interest in pragmatism was aroused about ten years ago by Cliff Slaughter, and in the interval during which this project has been brewing a large number of people have rendered assistance or encouragement in one form or another. It is clearly not possible to record my debt to all of them personally. Several individuals or groups stand out, however, as meriting particular thanks.

I would have abandoned the project on several occasions had it not been for the timely encouragement of Tony Giddens, Steven Lukes, Bill Pickering and Ernest Wallwork.

Roger Fellows and Tom Lane have made bibliographical suggestions which have been of unusual value.

The staff of the Brotherton Library at the University of Leeds have been very helpful, and have tolerated cheerfully the disorder I created for them.

Early drafts of the Introduction have been read as papers to the Sociology Staff/Graduate Seminar at Bradford, and to the *Groupe d'études durkheimiennes* at its meeting during the Ninth World Congress of Sociology at Uppsala. Valuable comment was made by various colleagues on these occasions.

Finally, I would like to acknowledge the patient assistance of Beverley Toulson and Vera Hawley, who have typed and revised the entire script without once complaining about my handwriting.

J.B.A.

Note on the translation

The general style and manner of expression of this work of Durkheim's are largely determined by its form as lectures, or rather as reconstituted lectures based on notes taken by students. The sense of the material, as is usually the case with Durkheim, seems fairly clear, and its only defects as a text are the tendency to recapitulation and repetition inevitable in a course of lectures, and a certain woodenness of expression. Cuvillier's decision to leave the text as it stood in this regard has been respected here, and this translation simply attempts to reproduce as directly as possible the sense and general form of the original. (See p. xii of the Preface.)

There has been an earlier translation by Charles Blend of some of the material, namely, Lectures I–V, XIII and XIV. These were published in Kurt H. Wolff (ed.), *Emile Durkheim, 1858–1917: A Collection of Essays, with Translations and a Bibliography*, Columbus, Ohio, Ohio State University Press, 1960. Blend also seems to have adopted the method of faithful and literal translation. In preparing this new version, full attention has been paid to his work. Given the style and nature of the French original, it is inevitable that the two translations should coincide to a large degree, but differences of interpretation, emphasis and expression are also clearly detectable.

It was our hope that access to the original documents from which Cuvillier's edition was prepared might have been possible. Acquaintance with this material could have served the aim of minimizing the distortion which could arise from successive editings of the work. An approach was made to M. Paulhac, of Vrin et Cie., but in spite of his kind co-operation this has not been possible. It appears that after the completion of the 1955 edition the sets of notes, together with Durkheim's file of cards described in the Preface (see below, p. xi), passed into the possession of Professor Cuvillier. Unfortunately, he died several years later, and his estate was divided among his relatives. In this process the relevant documents have once more been lost. We have therefore been compelled to rely entirely upon the Cuvillier edition.

An additional word of explanation seems appropriate in connection with the notes. As Cuvillier explains in his Preface (see below, p. xiii), two systems of references were adopted in the published French text. These systems have been adhered to in our translation. Some alterations have been made, however, in producing this edition, and it is appropriate to mention these here. First, the notes have been checked throughout. References have been given to English-language editions of works where these exist, for the convenience of the reader. Secondly, in some places it has been necessary to supplement and correct the references. The bibliographical references given in Cuvillier's edition were frequently scanty, and occasionally misleading or wrong. All additions or corrections to the footnotes or the text, in this English edition, are indicated by square brackets [ ].

J.C.W.

J.B.A.

Preface to the French edition of 1955

Marcel Mauss, analysing Durkheim's unpublished work in *L'Année Sociologique* for 1925,[1*] wrote as follows:

Similarly, the loss of the entirely new series of lectures which Durkheim gave in the academic year 1913–14, just before the war, is a sad one. His aim was to introduce students to pragmatism, a form of philosophical thought, which was still new at that time. The lectures were intended for his son, André, then a student of his. He wanted to fill a gap in the education of the young men of that period; and he took the opportunity, not only of introducing them to pragmatism, but also of clearly defining the relationships, and the areas of similarity and difference, which he saw between this system and the fundamental ideas which in his view were emerging from the new discipline of sociology. He established his own position with regard to Bergson, James, Dewey and the other American pragmatists. Not only did he summarize their teaching powerfully and conscientiously, he also drew off from it that which, in his view, needed to be kept. He paid great attention to Dewey, for whom he had a lively admiration. The lectures were very successful, and made a great impression on a wide audience, particularly (and this was Durkheim's sole aim) on certain keen young minds. Unfortunately, the manuscript text of the lectures, the high point of Durkheim's philosophical work, is lost. All that remained of it, in files found at his home, was a few notes and references, chiefly to extracts from the books of the American pragmatists, particularly Dewey's. A certain number of these references are numbered, often in blue pencil in the order in which the documents were quoted in the fair copy of the manuscript and in the summaries of lectures he carried with him, but often never even opened when teaching.

We have no idea why or how all other traces of them have disappeared. It may be that Durkheim gave the text of the lectures to his son, André, and that André passed it on to a friend who like him was subsequently killed. Durkheim perhaps relied on notes that André took during his lectures, and the latter may have lent these to someone else.

If these papers are in the possession of a friend or of anyone else of good will who has a right to them, we beg that person, whoever he may be, to pass them on to us. If, by a stroke of luck, the manuscript is found, the collaboration of former students who followed the lectures will one day make it possible to give some

*The notes to the Preface are on pp. 106–8.

xi

idea of the work. For the present, all that we can do is to point out how important it is.

Mauss's appeal was not unproductive. We know that some of those who had attended the lectures gave him their notes. Unfortunately, it has proved impossible to find them amongst his papers in the *Musée de l'Homme*. The references he mentioned must have been destroyed with all Durkheim's other papers by the Germans during the occupation in the Second World War.

By a fortunate chance, we have been able to acquire, through the good offices of MM. Vrin the publishers, two sets of student's notes. One of these was complete save for perhaps one lecture, the other more fragmentary. It seemed possible to use them to reconstitute Durkheim's lectures as far as we could. It must however be fully understood that what we offer the reader here is not Durkheim's own text, since his manuscript, if it ever existed, has not yet been found. What we have, it must be repeated, is only a *reconstituted text*, which we have tried to establish as faithfully as possible on the basis of the two sets of notes. These have often enabled us to cross-check from one version to another, bringing texts together, with a high degree of certainty; and we are convinced that, in certain passages at least, an identical or almost identical text in both versions has really caught for us the authentic echo of Durkheim's voice.

In these lectures there is no doubt that the reader will find some repetitions and careless turns of phrase which would certainly have been suppressed in a version intended for publication. It will be noted in particular that at the beginning of a lecture the main ideas or conclusions of the preceding lecture are often briefly recapitulated. This, however, was one of Durkheim's favourite expository techniques in his teaching, and can be seen in his other published lectures such as those on *Moral Education*, *The Evolution of Educational Thought* and the *Leçons de Sociologie* recently published in Istanbul.[2] We have deliberately refrained from correcting these slight faults and have applied the rule formulated by Durkheim himself when he published the series of lectures by O. Hamelin on Descartes. He pointed out that Hamelin had written them 'as lectures, imagining himself before his future audience':

This means [he explained] all kinds of turns of phrase and expository techniques which a lecturer needs, but which are not as necessary in a book: frequent summaries, clearly established links between a lecture and the one preceding it, the clear marking of divisions, and so on ... One wonders whether it would not be a good idea to edit the text so as to rid it of all this pedagogical apparatus. It did however seem to us that it was not our task to take the author's place and give him a different language . . . In general, such efforts on the part of an editor, even when they are as discreet as possible, are more than likely to be arbitrary, and we have therefore decided to eschew them. Under the guise of seeming to correct one or two unimportant imperfections, we should run the risk of taking from the work something of its own character. It was conceived as a course of lectures, and it should be presented to the public in that form.[3]

In the case of the texts of the authors quoted in the lectures, particularly those of James, Dewey and Schiller, it has not been difficult to re-establish all of them, even without the bibliographical references mentioned by Mauss, as the quotations discovered in the manuscripts, even though often abridged or incorrect, were sufficiently precise and explicit to enable us to trace the originals. Sometimes, moreover, one or other of our versions, and indeed sometimes both, contained both the exact reference and the quotation.

The reader should therefore not be surprised to find that this work contains two series of references, one contained within the text and including those we found in the manuscripts, and the others shown in the notes and containing those which we ourselves have been able to find.

In general, *the notes are ours, as are the titles and sub-titles incorporated into the text* in the interests of clear presentation.

Many of those who heard these lectures have confirmed Marcel Mauss's statements about the impression that they produced on those attending them in 1913–14. Nor, it seems to us, is their interest any the less today. Their value at the time when they were given was that by comparing them with the teachings of the pragmatists, one could arrive at a better understanding of the ideas and, one might say, the philosophy of Durkheim. Added to this is now their real present-day relevance. Pragmatism now seems rather dull and out-of-date, but certain of its basic ideas reappear in philosophical systems which are claimed to be new. With regard to these, Durkheim's criticisms are still totally valid.

To take the first point first. It is quite clear that the ideas in these lectures both complement and, so to speak, are a continuation of the theory of knowledge mapped out in *The Elementary Forms of the Religious Life*. As Durkheim points out at the beginning of these lectures, there was at the time virtually no other theory of truth than pragmatism. Kantianism and neo-Kantianism were both already outmoded. There was also, of course, Hamelin's idealism. We know the friendship that existed between Durkheim and the author of *Les Eléments principaux de la représentation*, whose lectures on the system of Descartes he had published, and the high opinion he had of his ideas.[4] Hamelin's synthetic idealism, however, had the disadvantage of presenting knowledge as presupposing a given, already existing external object.[5]

In contradistinction to this, what Durkheim held on to from pragmatism is the idea that *thought creates truth* and that consequently truth is neither something fixed nor already existing, but something living and human. But the way in which pragmatism interpreted that idea, which was correct in itself, seemed to him ultimately *purely and simply to impoverish truth* by making it into something arbitrarily variable, devoid of any objectivity and negating the idea of 'necessary' truths.

Students of Durkheim have often been mistaken here, which is possible if Durkheim is not seen here as protesting vigorously against the consequences of pragmatists' teachings, which he calls 'the amorphousness of truth' (see below, p. 69). If this were the case, the danger might seem to be that in linking truth to life and action Durkheim fell into the trap of a kind of utilitarianism which subordinated thought to practice, the latter being at most interpreted in terms of the social dimension. This is the danger seen by M. Parodi:[6]

The doctrines of such writers as Pierce, Dewey and James in America, and Schiller in England, which are fairly vague, have the common characteristic of regarding truth or error as entirely relative to action and of being meaningful only by virtue of their consequences, their usefulness or their convenience. It is undeniable that the same notion is found in Henri Poincaré, in M. Bergson and subsequently in a large number of his contemporaries. It can even be found in Durkheim, since for him categories have a social origin, are adapted to the demands of collective life and their function is consequently mainly that of enabling us to act in the properly human milieu. Durkheim himself notes, as M. Bergson might, 'the close relationship between the three ideas of tool, category and institution'.[7]

But Durkheim himself alludes specifically in these lectures (Eighteenth Lecture p. 86) to this possible misunderstanding. He rejects pragmatism as 'a logical utilitarianism' which does not explain the 'hard' character of truth. Probably, just as the moral good appears both 'desirable' and obligatory, the truth, as pragmatism says, brings us a certain 'satisfaction' (pp. 48–9). At the same time, however, it 'imposes itself', both as a matter of law and as a matter of fact, with an obligatory and constraining character. It is often painful (p. 74). In Durkheim's view, only a sociological theory of truth can explain this double nature.

Durkheim will not accept that truth can be defined in terms of its practical efficacy alone, or that it does not correspond to reality. He goes so far as to contrast the characteristics of thought and those of action (pp. 79–81). He is almost too harsh in judging this transatlantic teaching, which he accuses of being not so much a doctrine of action as 'an attack on pure speculation and theoretical thought' (p. 64). Against Dewey, he maintains vigorously that truth, of whatever kind, always has a speculative function. The expression 'of whatever kind' is important, for not all truth, Durkheim tells us, is of a purely rational order. Along with scientific truths, there are and always will be truths which he describes as 'mythological'. But even these are quite different from pure fantasies or mere instruments of action. If they too can in one sense be said to be 'truths', it is because they express, in local and temporal forms, realities which are unchallengeable, because they are seen to be rooted in the social. It is a mistake to believe that society can live in total illusion or total fantasy. These 'mythological truths' have thus a certain rational quality, since they correspond to a *real intellectual need*, a *need to understand*. They are cosmologies which express the way in which a society, at a given point in its history, both imagines the universe and also sees itself; and since for Durkheim society is part of nature and its 'highest manifestation', the categories which serve the intelligence of society are also those which act as frameworks for knowing the universe.[8] Thus, the true function of thought is very different from a practical one. Pragmatism was right to say that it is thought which creates reality, but was unable to interpret that formula properly. The role of consciousness is to create being (pp. 23 and 82). This is true even at the psycho-organic level where, according to Durkheim,[9] the sum of all discrete sense-impressions results in a level of consciousness which can be described as 'the organism knowing itself'. It is even more true at the psycho-social level, where it is clearer than elsewhere that the function of thought is 'to create a being which would not exist without it', to 'make', as the pragmatists say ('the making of reality' is the title of a chapter of Schiller's), that higher reality which is society (p. 85).

It is curious to see in this way Durkheim's sociological realism finally resolve itself into a theory of knowledge which is at the same time idealistic and realistic.[10] According to this, just as society constitutes 'an organism of ideas', as Espinas had already maintained, so too thought and truth are homogeneous with reality. The final section of these lectures is in fact a critique which is no longer restricted to pragmatism, but also includes Bergson, and which is directed at the idea that rational thought could be outside reality and life. The 'life force' itself, retorts Durkheim (p. 95), is deeply differentiated, and contains in embryonic form many immanent variations, so that in this respect conceptual thought merely shares in a property of the real.

There is a second area in which these lectures help us to a better understanding of Durkheim's thought. He has been accused of confusing the collective consciousness, the repository of all intelligence and truth, with 'the world of eternal Ideas', with the universal *Logos*, even with God, and also with having established, behind what is ostensibly a sociological theory of morality, a 'semi-sociological, semi-metaphysical meta-morality' claiming to 'draw from an existing theoretical knowledge a morality which imposes ends and prescribes rules of conduct', and which subsequently leads to an inability to recognize the impossibility 'of both knowing and prescribing at the same time'.

As early as 1939, the *Revue de Métaphysique et de Morale* was defending him against the first of these accusations, which it saw as gratuitous:

Durkheim's theory of knowledge, which is barely an outline of a theory and clearly questionable, certainly attempts to reduce the universal to the collective, but in no way tries to move in the opposite direction and reduce the collective to an *a priori* universal ... Opinion on his explanation may differ; but it does not seem possible to deny that it is a purely positive one. For the moment, the existence in his work of a *metaphysic*, and still less of a *theology*, remains unproven.[11]

M. Davy, in his introduction to *Professional Ethics and Civic Morals*,[12] has similarly replied to the second criticism, pointing out that the two major themes of Durkheim's thought, knowledge and society, may from certain points of view be opposites, but they are nevertheless by no means incompatible. On the contrary, they complement each other; and according to Durkheim, they exist in harmony and act together. In our view, the lectures which we are now publishing offer striking support for that view, for they provide a means of replying definitively to objections based on a fundamental misunderstanding of his ideas, and thus a way through to the understanding of their fundamental meaning.

Anyone attempting to establish an axiology, whether it be concerned with truth or moral values, is faced with 'the false demand of reason' rejected by André Lalande in 1907, by which he meant the need to prove everything, even first principles, particularly in normative questions.[13] The fact of the matter is, however, that fundamental to any 'normative science', any system of morality or logic, any 'theory of knowledge', there are one or more principles which are incapable of proof or demonstration in the proper sense of the word, if not of all rational justification. Thus, only 'lived experience' can provide us with these principles, or rather these 'foundations' for an axiology. There are, however, many ways of understanding what is meant by 'lived experience'.

We can see that in Durkheim's case recourse to the social is precisely the solution to the difficulty. It certainly does not mean that in his view society is a thing *in se*, eternally fixed and unchanging, or a static 'supreme good'. What it *does* mean is that Durkheim was clearly aware, although of course expressing his ideas differently, of the need which contemporary philosophers have so keenly felt of *establishing the ground for man's basic values in his lived existence*, of 'grounding' them, as it were. It is not a matter of demonstrating them deductively or inductively, for this would involve us in a vicious circle, but of showing them as *entailed in that very existence*, which for Durkheim, at least at the level of ideal values, is a *social existence*. Thus it is quite mistaken to see any 'metaphysic' in this. Durkheim consistently takes the opposite path, and embraces the criticism which pragmatism makes of all those theories of largely Platonic origin which treat truth as something 'quasi-divine' (p. 66), in which truth is lost in the 'distant realms of an intelligible world or a divine understanding' (p. 97). In Durkheim, recourse to the social is an indication of his deep and lively sense of the *existential* conditions of choice.

M. Lalande reminds us that Durkheim praised Paul Janet's observation that the 'foundations' of morality are 'the obligations accepted by everybody, or at least by those with whom one argues and for whom one speaks'.[14] Durkheim himself recognized that any morality implies at least one principle which does not derive from knowledge – a value judgement to the effect that life is worth living.[15] The same holds in the case of truth, as in the sphere of moral values. In these lectures Durkheim stresses this parallel. Just as it is illusory, he says, to proceed as most philosophers do, by means of pure conceptual construction when we want to find out what morality is, if we wish to find out what truth is, we must not decide *a priori* what it is to be in its ideal form, but must study *living truths*, truths *recognized as such by men in society*, and analyse their characteristics (pp. 72 and 84).

We can now see why Durkheim, as Marcel Mauss notes, is so sympathetic towards pragmatism, while at the same time expressing such serious reservations about it. Pragmatism chiefly sees its task as that of making truth less 'rigid', of 'softening' it as James says (p. 66), of showing that it is a human product and hence shifting and changing; in short, of 'linking thought to existence and life' (p. 16).

Thus pragmatism shows us the excessive narrowness of classical rationalism, but also enables us to renew it, for it opens the way for us to accept a theory (namely, the sociological theory of knowledge) which will not see reason as a rigid and immutable faculty, but as linked to the history and the very life of humanity (pp. 67–8). Durkheim himself says that what he most appreciates in pragmatism is 'its heightened sense of human reality, the feeling for the extreme variability of everything human' (p. 71).

At this point we should consider a third misunderstanding which has occurred – and has been propagated – in connection with Durkheim's teaching. Certain of those commenting on his work maintain that he saw the social and the institutional as identical, and consequently failed to perceive all that is living and 'effervescent' in social life. This is an even stranger misreading of him than those we have already discussed. There can be no possible doubt that Durkheim saw institutions as constantly changing (p. 70) and, above all, saw society as a historical reality in which 'new forces' come constantly into being and 'never remain the same', but develop and grow in syntheses which are 'rich in boundless possibilities' and essentially creative (pp. 24 and 70). Misunderstandings of this kind can only be explained if they are seen as linked to that kind of sociological 'typology' which is essentially non-temporal, and is the prey, in the words of one eminent historian, to a basic 'antihistoricism'. It would be perverse to heap the consequences of such an error on Durkheim's head.

But Durkheim's thought, although it never retreats into ontological questions, and comes strangely close to certain perspectives in modern philosophy, is by no means simply the appeal to 'lived experience' that it is nowadays often seen as being. In the first place, Durkheim does not see that lived experience as being subjective, the inner experience of the individual (which in the last analysis would open the way to a flood of arbitrary and gratuitous interpretations which would negate all objective values). It is collective experience, the experience of man *in society*. In addition – and this should be particularly noted – that collective experience should be *the object of rational thought*. In the first edition of *The Rules of Sociological Method* Durkheim declares that 'the only designation we can accept is that of "rationalist"',[16] – and in *The Elementary Forms of the Religious Life* he speaks of 'the rationalism that is immanent in a sociological theory of knowledge'.[17] This indicates a resolute opposition to pragmatist ideas, and he takes a vigorous stance against this war on reason declared by a doctrine of foreign origin, which goes against all the traditions of French thought. Nowadays in France such language would lead to charges of xenophobia and chauvinism, but Durkheim does not mince his words. It is a matter of (he says) 'national importance' (p. 1) regarding this question, that we have a true picture in which the whole spirit of French culture is at stake. It is interesting to imagine what his reaction might have been, on reading in James's work, that pragmatism is 'fully armed and militant' against rationalism (p. 1); or even, in *The Varieties of Religious Experience*, that 'the sciences of nature know nothing of spiritual presences, and on the whole hold no practical commerce whatever with the idealistic conceptions towards which general philosophy inclines'.[18]

No one has stated more explicitly than Durkheim the 'ideal' nature of human values,[19] nor has anyone affirmed more resolutely that, in one sense, the ideal is indeed 'both of and in nature' and that consequently 'it is subject to examination'.[20] There is no doubt, as Durkheim says, a sort of 'popular philosophy' which precedes science, which contains both a philosophy of truth and a philosophy of moral values. Sociology, although it can never completely replace it, aims at systematizing this spontaneous 'philosophy' (p. 89). The 'science of morals' is no more than the rationalization of the spontaneous collective experience of the human conscience. Similarly, a theory of knowledge would be the rationalization of the collective representations and beliefs of humanity, of those lived truths just discussed which, when analysed, would enable us to identify real as distinct from abstract truth.

Fourthly, we must mention (rather more briefly) the role of the individual as Durkheim saw it. Here too there have been many misunderstandings of various kinds. The (quite relative) antithesis between the *individual* and *society* can be disposed of as illusory and as a *false problem*.

From more or less all sides, Durkheim has been accused of 'deifying' society, misunderstanding the role of the individual, discrediting the subject and individual awareness and thus coming close to totalitarian doctrines. A German sociologist recently spoke[21] of the 'strangling' (*Erdrosselung*) of the personality by Durkheim in the interests of the social. With regard to the individual/society antithesis, the eminent English sociologist Morris Ginsberg recently devoted an article[22] to an examination of its real theoretical and practical importance. His lectures on *Professional Ethics and Civic Morals* show us how little moral or social justification there is for the second charge. In them, Durkheim describes the gradual emergence of the individual personality as the most constant fact of history. 'There is no rule more soundly established', he wrote.[23] Insufficient attention has also been paid to those passages in *The Elementary Forms of the Religious Life*[24] in which Durkheim seems to admit that the categories of reason are, in a certain sense and in a certain form, 'immanent in the life of the individual'; and that the role of social life has been chiefly to enable him to become aware of that fact. Here, in the lectures on pragmatism, it is noteworthy that at first, following Ribot's theory, he even recognizes in body-awareness the basis of self-awareness and the germ of thought and knowledge (p. 82). Furthermore, Durkheim then not only retains the pragmatist notion of the diversity of minds (p. 24), but also takes pains to justify it sociologically, showing how 'intellectual individualism' develops with the arrival of rational and scientific thought, which itself is a correlative of the increasing complexity of societies (p. 91 ff). He is led to conclude that 'truth is only ever achieved by individuals' (p. 97).

As we have already suggested, however, these lectures do not only help us to understand Durkheim better. They are also of current interest, in that they offer a critique which anticipates certain contemporary philosophical positions which, although they are quite independent of pragmatism, nevertheless have certain undeniable affinities with it as far as their inspiration is concerned.

In our time, it has seemed possible to solve certain epistemological problems, particularly with regard to sociology, in one or the other of two ways. On the one hand, we encounter what has been called 'hyper-empiricism'[25] which, given a more or less dialectical twist, invokes the truism that 'experience is always human' and sees that experience as identical with both man's individual and his social praxis.[26] On the other hand, we find 'pluralism' which denies in particular the unity of the social and multiplies the distinctions between the forms, levels, strata and so on of reality. Under the cloak of a war against dogmatism and 'the passive contemplation of eternal ideas'[27] this pluralism is a recrudescence of the hostility, which we have already noticed in pragmatism (which refused to be called a 'doctrine'), towards any attempt to achieve clarity and distinctness in the world of ideas, and towards any position avoiding intellectual dishonesty.

We can look at these three points rapidly. As for 'hyper-empiricism', James had already described his own teaching as 'radical empiricism' (p. 33) as well as pragmatism; and, apart from the exaggeration implied by the prefix 'hyper', it is difficult to see the difference. What about the 'always human' nature of experience we hear about today? Pragmatism was so aware of it that James returns again and again to the 'human' nature of truth (pp. 18, 53 etc.); and another eminent representative of that system, F. C. S. Schiller of Oxford, had called his version of it humanism. As to the indissoluble link between experience and praxis, his declared position is basically a doctrine which sees experience and action as identical; and more than one pragmatist – and Dewey in particular – stressed the social as well as the individual nature of such action. But it was precisely Durkheim's rationalism which prevented him from accepting this philosophical position. With Hamelin, he would have described it as 'the negation of all knowledge';[28] it also prevented him from participating in a 'demolition of concepts',[29] which he could only see as harmful. Indeed, the opposite was the case; and he energetically defended the use of them and their value (pp. 32, 46, 82, 96–7 and 103–5). He had also cut through the fraudulence of the so-called 'happy-go-lucky' attitude (James even used the term 'anarchist')[30] which claims to rely only on pure experience, and yet really delights in the most arbitrary conceptual constructions. He has no scruples about accusing it of contradiction. 'In particular one must criticize the *abstract nature* of their argument', he said of the pragmatists, 'for it clashes with the general orientation of their thought, which they say is empirical. The proofs they offer are most commonly of a *dialectical* nature, and everything is reduced to a purely logical construction' (p. 65). This criticism could be applied to others of our contemporaries.

Nor is Durkheim taken in by the *pluralism* of the pragmatists. By calling itself pluralist, pragmatism (particularly in James, where the title of the French translation of his *A Pluralistic Universe, Philosophie de l'expérience*, hides its real import) was already revealing its weakness. Thought is acknowledged to be incapable of overcoming the diversity and contradictions inherent in reality. This, however (according to the empiricist position) is precisely its task, unless one sees it as a mere reflection of that reality. That failure of philosophical thought was seen quite clearly by Durkheim when he criticized pragmatism for lacking 'those basic characteristics which one has a right to expect of a philosophical doctrine' (p. 65). A taste for subtle and arbitrary distinctions and the multiplication of differences and points of view is not a purely contemporary phenomenon. Plato had already criticized the sophists of his time for the same failing when he said that 'the attempt to separate all existences from one another is a barbarism, and utterly unworthy of an educated and philosophical mind'.[31] Nor is the discovery which we believe we have made of the 'mutual connectedness' and 'reciprocal immanence' which is reminiscent of those mythological beliefs of which Durkheim speaks (p. 86) exclusively an achievement of our age. It is in mythology that one finds that totality which is 'wholly contained in each of its parts', and that 'reciprocity of perspectives'[32] that an American sociologist recently described as 'not easy to understand' and as having been 'nowhere ... elucidated clearly'.[33] In different, plainer words, James has already given us a picture of what he calls a 'strung-along' universe (p. 27) in which all parts compenetrate, hold together, are interrelated in all sorts of ways and are themselves constantly changing. Here too, however, it has not escaped Durkheim's notice that this so-called 'pluralism' is as ambiguous as the empiricism to which the attempt has been made to relate it. In reality, it is simply a disguised form of monism (pp. 35–6), the monism of general confusion. It accepts only a single and uniform plane of being and experience and therefore 'levels' everything. With regard to useful and subjective experience it diminishes values, it fails to recognize that fundamental dualism between the individual and the social, and between the empirical and the rational (pp. 43 and 68) which alone, in Durkheim's view, gives a basis for our action on the world. On what basis, indeed, can one claim to transform something, if one believes that everything is to be put on the same level and if there is no difference between values and crude existence (p. 64)?

It is not difficult to see that in this last connection there is also a similarity between pragmatism and the other systems we have in mind. They are indeed systems, but hide the fact that they are systems, humbly claiming to be 'attitudes' or 'general orientations' of thought (p. 10). An attitude which will not 'domesticate' itself, as we are repeatedly told,[34] is really very like that which Durkheim criticizes in James, when the latter claims to remain 'free' in the face of the truth (p. 2). It is a convenient one, and means that one need not provide a coherent synthetic account of one's ideas (pp. 9–10 and notes), which has no scruples about other systems (pp. 12 and 65) or the need to avoid contradictions (p. 65). It is in short a system of thought which is as 'strung-along' as the universe which it claims to enable us to grasp.

It seems reasonable to think that Durkheim, whilst paying tribute to what is valid in pragmatism, detected in it that tendency to undermine the intellect which is still developing in our time and that he undertook the task of maintaining, with the help of sociology, the traditions of French philosophy: fidelity to clear and distinct thought.

A. Cuvillier

N.B. Our colleague and friend, M. René Maublanc, *professeur agrégé de philosophie au lycée Henri Quatre*, who was unable to put his personal notes at our disposal as he had sent them to Marcel Mauss, contacted his contemporaries at the *Ecole [Normale Supérieure?]* who had followed Durkheim's lectures with him. The notes of the two lectures by Durkheim on *Certainty* and *Concepts* which do not deal directly with pragmatism, but are relevant to the theory of knowledge, were provided by M. Marcel Tardy, the editor of *Le Monde*, who has kindly authorized us to reproduce them here. Our cordial thanks are due to both these gentlemen.

Editorial introduction to the English translation

That pragmatism is not usually accorded a significant place in the history of sociology can be readily verified by a glance through the range of works on the topic. Many discussions of the history of the discipline either omit altogether any reference to the pragmatists, or at most are content to pass over their contribution with only the slightest of comment.[1]*

The reason for this neglect is suggested by one of the few authors who do pay any attention to pragmatism, Don Martindale. In his discussion of the *Nature and Types of Sociological Theory*, the writing of James and Dewey appears to earn its place for three reasons. First, he quotes (not altogether without approval) the view of Ruggiero, that 'Pragmatism is the logical conclusion and therefore the *reductio ad absurdum* of empiricism.'[2] It is a philosophical blind alley into which an unsuspecting few were led, only to find themselves locked in an embrace of death with a kind of proto-fascistic ideology of business.[3] Secondly, as one of the philosophical ancestors of 'behaviourism', the pragmatic tradition is reckoned to be of some importance in the history of *psychology*. Thirdly, as associates of, or influences on, G. H. Mead and C. H. Cooley, James and Dewey can be regarded as contributors indirectly to the development of *social psychology*.[4]

An account such as this, although each of its points may be serious contenders for our consideration, by no means adds up to an adequate assessment of the importance of pragmatism *for* sociology. The major drawbacks in Martindale's approach are twofold: they tend to direct attention away from the genuinely *sociological* import of the pragmatic perspective, and they confine that perspective, both in its genesis and its effects, to North America. Contrary to both of these points, however, a consideration of the pragmatic tradition as a whole is of vital import-

*The notes to the Introduction are on pp. 108–14.

xxiii

ance to our understanding of the development of sociology both in Europe and the United States. Indeed, pragmatism can be regarded as one of the most vital of the roots from which modern sociology has grown.[5]

This general neglect of the part played by pragmatism in the growth of sociology is reflected in a widespread ignorance of Durkheim's work on pragmatism. Although his interest in the subject has been known for some considerable time now, this knowledge has not yet permeated generally throughout the sociological fraternity, neither has this information been at all integrated into our understanding of his work.

The edited text of his lectures on pragmatism appeared in French in 1955,[6] and a selection of these lectures was included in the commemorative volume on Durkheim which Kurt H. Wolff edited in 1960.[7] Although a further broad hint regarding the importance of William James in Durkheim's thought was given with the translation (in 1955) of the latter's essay on 'Individual and collective representations',[8] little progress has been made in this direction. Those commentators on his work who do give any recognition to his interest in pragmatism often fail to relate this to a more general consideration of the development of his sociological thought.[9]

Possibly one reason for the neglect of Durkheim's critique of pragmatism lies in the consensus which prevailed for a long time regarding the overall interpretation of his work, according to which Durkheim was chiefly important as one of the 'founding fathers' of modern functionalism. From this viewpoint, the lectures on pragmatism can appear as nothing more than a fortuitous and rather odd aberration – a kind of intellectual 'sport' – since they can bear little relation to the kind of problems central to a 'functionalist' approach. More recent studies of Durkheim, however, have tended to take both a broader and a more sophisticated approach to the interpretation of his sociology.[10] As we set out to show in succeeding pages, *Pragmatisme et sociologie* reveals an involvement with some of the main themes of Durkheim's work, enabling us to give the lectures a more central place in the structure of his contribution to the development of the science.

This introductory essay addresses itself to two aspects of Durkheim's encounter with pragmatism. First, we will attempt to suggest why he should have chosen to attempt to provide a sociological response to the movement. Secondly, we will try to indicate the place of the lectures on pragmatism within the general development of his sociology.

Editorial introduction to the English translation

Before turning directly to a consideration of Durkheim's lectures on pragmatism, it will be useful to devote some time to considering the way in which pragmatist ideas came to be established in French intellectual life at the time. Both the speed of communication of these ideas, and the manner in which they came to be presented to the French public, are relevant to an understanding of Durkheim's response to the movement.

The penetration and spread of pragmatist ideas in France was relatively rapid.[11] The seminal essay by Charles Sanders Peirce, 'How to make our ideas clear', was first published in the *Popular Science Monthly* in 1878; a translation of this was contained in the *Revue Philosophique* of January 1879. The writing of William James was widely available in France within a few years of its publication in English and, for reasons which we will be examining below, he quickly built up an entensive following among the French. The greater part of his work – and certainly the most important elements of it – were available in French to the students who attended Durkheim's lectures in 1913.

One of James's first philosophical publications was a letter to the *Critique Philosophique* in 1878.[12] This was followed by articles in the same journal in 1880 and 1881.[13] The editor of this periodical was Charles Renouvier, with whom James developed a warm friendship in later years. James's text-book *Psychology: Briefer Course* of 1892 appeared in France in 1909: parts of *The Will to Believe* of 1897 were published there as articles in the *Critique Philosophique* in subsequent years, and eventually appeared in book form. The first part of his *Talks to Teachers on Psychology* (1899) also was published in translation in 1909. *The Varieties of Religious Experience* (the Gifford Lectures of 1901–2) shows the increasing interest in James's thought, through the reducing gap between English- and French-language editions: the French version was issued in 1906. Parts of *A Pluralistic Universe* (with the curious title, *Philosophie de l'expérience*) were presented to a French audience only one year after being issued in America (1909 and 1910). The topicality of Durkheim's lecture course is suggested by the appearance of *Pragmatism* in 1911, and a French version of *The Meaning of Truth* in 1913.

The popularity of James is somewhat exceptional, as is indicated by the fact that neither Schiller's nor Dewey's works were readily accessible to a French audience at the time of Durkheim's course. We may permit ourselves to ask, how did James secure such a substantial foothold in French intellectual life?

In the winter of 1869–70, following the intense study necessary to gain him his medical degree, and after a period of illness, James lapsed into a profound and bitter depression. The life-line which drew him out of this wretched condition was the reading of a volume of essays by Charles Renouvier.[14]

Correspondence between James and Renouvier appears to have begun in the winter of 1872, but their relationship did not really develop with any warmth until 1876. In that year James contributed a review (under the title 'Bain and Renouvier') to the *Nation*, and he sent a copy of this to the Frenchman.[15]

The two men seem to have found common ground; and each enthusiastically acclaimed in the other's work the echoes of his own. James immediately took it upon himself to introduce Renouvier's work to an American audience, using his essays as texts in one of his courses at Harvard.[16] Renouvier, of course, was directly responsible for the inclusion of James's articles in the *Critique*, translating the first of these himself.[17] The two men met for the first time during James's visit to Europe in the summer of 1880.[18] It is clearly through the personal patronage of this established figure of French philosophy that James secured his *entrée* into French philosophical discourse. This relationship, based on a mutual appreciation of each other's calibre, rather than on the close similarity of their views (such as characterized James's relationship to Bergson) continued until the death of Renouvier in 1903.

The second important point of contact with French intellectual life to which we need to devote our attention is James's correspondence with Etienne Boutroux. He was a figure of rather slighter stature than Renouvier, but he is of considerable importance in establishing a relationship between Durkheim and James. How the two men first made contact we are unable to say, but it was Boutroux who was selected to write the preface to the French translation of *The Varieties of Religious Experience*, which Perry has described as 'highly sympathetic'.[19] James responded by sending a copy of his *Pragmatism* in 1907. The upshot of the exchange between the two men was, amongst others, a chapter on 'William James et l'expérience religieuse' in a book on science and religion published by the elder philosopher in 1908.[20]

Boutroux's conclusions were mildly critical, but he clearly regarded James as a major intellectual force. Correspondence between the two flourished during 1908 and 1909, and we know that during this period

Boutroux also read James's *A Pluralistic Universe* and *The Meaning of Truth*.[21]

In the following year Boutroux became President of the French Academy of Moral and Political Sciences; and it must have given him great pleasure to be able to announce in that year the election of James as a foreign Associate to the Academy. The younger man was able to reciprocate by the arrangement of a course of lectures at Harvard to be given by his French colleague.[22]

In the United States, Boutroux stayed for a while with James's family, and was clearly most impressed by the personality, as well as the intellect, of his host. The latter's hospitality was repaid during James's final visit to Europe, on the eve of his death, in 1910. The warmth of the relationship between the two men is conveyed in the 'fraternal and affectionate adieux' of the final letters,[23] and the extent of their intellectual mutuality by the short biography which Boutroux wrote within a few months of his friend's death. Although this betrayed in Boutroux a philosophical inheritance quite foreign to that of James, it also measured the depth of his respect for the younger man.

Finally, in considering the personalities which connected William James with the French thought of his day, we turn to Henri Bergson. It is clear from both a reading of their works and the correspondence between the two men that James was intellectually far closer to Bergson than to either Boutroux or Renouvier.[24]

A reference in James's *Principles* suggests that he read Bergson's *Données immédiates de la conscience* immediately after its publication in 1889.[25] Perry observes that this 'appears ... to have made little impression on him', and he also informs us that Bergson sent James a copy of his *Matière et mémoire* at the time of its publication in 1896. However, for some reason unknown to us, it was not until James reread both of these works together in 1902 that he began to realize their significance. 'Nothing I have read in years', he wrote to a friend, in 1903, 'has so excited and stimulated my thought.' He immediately wrote to Bergson, with fulsome thanks and praise, sending him copies of his own works. The Frenchman replied with similar warmth of appreciation, and their correspondence flourished over the succeeding years, leading to a meeting of the two during James's holiday in Europe in May 1905. The French translation of his *Varieties* was then under way, and it seems that Bergson took a lively interest in the enterprise, although through illness he was unable to oblige with the preface which he had originally been asked to contribute.

The relationship, which Perry has described as 'a remarkable example of friendship without submergence of individual differences', continued to mature up until the date of James's death in 1910, each taking a close interest in the development of the other's thought. James devoted one of his Hibbert Lectures, of 1908, to an exposition of Bergson's ideas;[26] and during the visit to Europe to deliver these lectures, the two arranged a further meeting (October 1908). Their final conversation took place shortly before James's death, during the last European trip of May 1910. It is clear from the record of these meetings that each enjoyed the other's company as much as his philosophy. Bergson's final service to his older friend was a substantial introduction to the French edition of *Pragmatism*, 1911.

Whereas we consider Renouvier for his importance in presenting James to a wider French public through his editorship of the *Critique*, and Boutroux for his close personal sponsorship of James's ideas (and particularly for his association with the American's theories about religion), it is simply for Bergson's personal pre-eminence in the history of French ideas of the period that he merits our attention. Bergson was not only a philosopher, he was also a major public figure. Indeed, his very popularity detracted from his professional stature in the eyes of many of his academic colleagues, who had considerable reservations about his metaphysics. The nature of his following in this period has been summed up by H. Stuart Hughes:[27]

Bergson's lectures became major events. Tourists and society ladies flocked to them, as to one of our sights of the capital. And Bergson did not disappoint his audience ... People left the auditorium with a sense of 'liberation'. They felt uplifted in the spirit as in the mind. Of all the intellectual innovators of the 1890s, Bergson was the one with the greatest *charisma*, the one whose direct personal influence was the most compelling.

This essay is not an appropriate place in which to review Bergson's philosophy. What is important for our purposes, however, is to note that in this pre-war period, Jamesian pragmatism was closely associated with the thought of this highly influential and popular figure. When Bergson became so openly identified with James, in his introduction to *Pragmatism* in 1911, the magnitude of the forces confronting Durkheim's own philosophical position became clear.

The rapid spread of James's version of pragmatism in France contrasts in an initially puzzling manner with the sluggishness of the French response to Dewey. Whereas the former was freely available in translation to a French readership at the time of Durkheim's lectures the latter was known, or so it would appear, mainly by reputation, and through secondary accounts of his work. Although his publications were regularly summarized and abstracted in the *Revue de Métaphysique et de Morale* and the *Revue Philosophique*, it was not until 1909 that any of his writings were translated, when part of the 1900 edition of *The School and Society* appeared in the journal *L'Education*.[28] Further articles became available in 1912 and 1913, and also in 1913 a French edition of *The School and the Child* was published in Geneva.

Several of the early reviews of Dewey's papers in the *Revue Philosophique* were prepared by the editor, the *doyen* of French psychology, Théodule Ribot: but no evidence has emerged of any close relationship or friendship or patronage between the two.[29]

Writing shortly before Dewey's death, Durkheim's former pupil Dominique Parodi attests to Dewey's reputation in France, and the esteem in which he was held. Yet the account which he gives of the establishment of that reputation only begins in the 1920s, after Durkheim's death.[30] During the interwar period several other articles and books by Dewey were made available in French, and appreciation of his thought spread beyond a relatively narrow circle of professional philosophers. His standing in France during this period is suggested by the invitation extended to him in 1923 to become a corresponding member of the *Institut de France*, and by the honorary degree of *Docteur de l'Université* conferred upon him by the University of Paris in 1930.[31] To the audience attending Durkheim's course on pragmatism in 1913 however, Dewey was almost certainly seen as a minor luminary in comparison with William James.

The reasons for this state of affairs are probably fairly straightforward. First, Dewey was rather later than James in the building of a reputation in his native country. In spite of his prodigious productivity, and his rapid emergence as a controversial public figure as well as a notable philosopher, he was seventeen years younger than James.

Secondly, whereas James addressed his reader in prose of almost startling vividness, Dewey laboured throughout his life under the burden of a style which was convoluted and difficult. As a French critic remarked in 1908, his writing was full of '*tours, détours et retours*'.[32] In the long term Dewey may be remembered as the better philosopher, but his popularity was certainly hindered by the opacity and deviousness of his writing.

Probably as significant as either of these two factors in retarding the availability of Dewey to a French readership was the fact that before the First World War he had not developed the personal contacts within the French philosophical establishment which could sponsor the dissemination of his ideas. Whatever the reasons for Dewey's relative obscurity, however, it is plain that in this period, pragmatism was identified first and foremost with William James. The name of Dewey was probably little better known than that of C. S. Peirce, and undoubtedly less familiar to the French philosophical reader than that of F. C. S. Schiller, whose *Studies in Humanism* had been translated by Jankélévitch in 1909.[33]

DURKHEIM CONFRONTS PRAGMATISM

In the academic year 1913–14, Durkheim gave at the Sorbonne the course of lectures which has been collected and published as *Pragmatisme et sociologie*. Why should Durkheim have chosen, quite out of the apparent habit of his writing and teaching, to deal so thoroughly with this subject? It is to this question that we will now turn our attention.

The generally accepted reasons for this interest are those which Durkheim himself sets out in the introductory lecture to his course.

The problem raised by pragmatism is indeed of a very serious nature. We are currently witnessing an *attack on reason* which is truly militant and determined. Consequently, the problem is of threefold importance.

1   In the first place, it is of *general* importance. Pragmatism is in a better position than any other doctrine to make us see the need for a reform of traditional rationalism, for it shows us what is lacking in it.

2   Next, it is of *national* importance. Our whole French culture is basically an essentially rationalistic one ... A total negation of rationalism would constitute a danger: it would overthrow our whole national culture. If we had to accept the form of irrationalism represented by pragmatism, the whole French mind would have to be radically changed.

3   Lastly, it is of specifically *philosophical* importance. Not only our culture but the whole of the philosophical tradition ... is inspired by rationalism. If pragmatism were valid, we would have to embark upon a complete reversal of this whole tradition.[34]

There is no need for us to elaborate on this indictment in its clarity and succinctness: but a number of additional factors might have appeared to Durkheim to make the need for an appraisal of pragmatism particularly pressing.

First, as we have indicated in the foregoing section, the spread of pragmatist ideas in France had been rapid, and had been sympathetically received by a number of eminent figures in French philosophy. Pragmatism, therefore, appeared not only as an ideal or possible 'threat' to French rationalism, but as a threat which was very actual indeed, and rapidly gaining ground.

Secondly, as Durkheim himself remarked, against the onslaught of this self-confessed enemy of rationalism there appeared to be no serious intellectual champions in the field. 'Pragmatism ... is almost the only current theory of truth.'[35] Not that traditional French rationalism lacked potential champions: several critics had come forward to do battle with advancing pragmatism in the years before Durkheim's lectures. But as Emmanuel Leroux remarked several years later, 'all of the books devoted to pragmatism [in France] have remained to this date deplorably superficial'.[36]

The need for an answer to pragmatism must have impelled Durkheim with particular vigour in view of his close personal association with some of its principal friends and supporters in France, especially Renouvier and Boutroux.[37]

As we have already indicated, to Renouvier belongs the credit for introducing James to a French audience and ensuring an awakening of interest there in his philosophy. Coming from one of the major figures of French philosophy during the second half of the nineteenth century, the prestige of his *imprimatur* on James's work must have been considerable. Renouvier was, as is widely known, one of the major formative influences on the young Durkheim during this period of study at the *Ecole Normale Supérieure*.[38] It is worth noting that this period in Durkheim's life coincided with the introduction of James to a French readership (1879–82), although we have no direct evidence of Durkheim's familiarity with James during these years. The first reference to James which we find in Durkheim's work is a detailed discussion of his *Principles of Psychology* in an article entitled, 'Individual and collective representations' of 1898.[39] This article can be regarded as something of a turning-point in Durkheim's work, depicting as it does a shift from a central interest in the *conscience collective* of the *Division of Labour* to a concern for *représentations collectives*. There is some evidence that he derived this notion of representation from Renouvier.[40]

In the case of Boutroux, the bridge between James and Durkheim becomes more tangible. Boutroux had been one of Durkheim's teachers at the *Ecole Normale Supérieure*, and was also a member of the tribunal to which Durkheim presented his doctoral thesis at the Sorbonne in 1892.[41] The publication of Boutroux's *Contingency of the Laws of Nature*, in 1874, had laid a foundation for his reputation in French philosophy, and clearly his views had a considerable impact upon the development of Durkheim's own methodological perspective.[42]

It was not, however, in the field of scientific method that Boutroux can be regarded as having exposed Durkheim to Jamesian notions, but in the field of religion. From 1902, Boutroux became director of the *Fondation Thiers*, and in this period his mind came increasingly to occupy itself with the problems of relating a religious and a scientific perspective. It appears to be as a consequence of this interest that Boutroux was invited to write the preface to the French edition of James's *Varieties*, in 1905. In view of the sympathetic nature of his presentation of James's ideas, it is not surprising to find a considerable debt to James evident in his own writing on religion.[43]

Although Durkheim had intermittently taken an interest in religion over a number of years, it was only in this period following the publication of James's *Varieties of Religious Experience* that the ideas began to take shape which were to come to fruition in his own major work on the subject.[44] We know, from the evidence of *The Elementary Forms of the Religious Life*, that he became familiar with both Boutroux's book and James's *Varieties* during the course of his studies of religion.[45]

The preceding account, however, cannot explain entirely Durkheim's decision to confront pragmatism. The reasons which we have set out here suggest only an *external* compulsion – almost as if Durkheim were compelled against his will to lay aside his 'real' interests in sociology, and to make a *sortie* into philosophy as a kind of conscripted 'national service'. If this were the case, then there would be little reason for the sociologist to follow Durkheim in his labours, for the result would be quite incidental to the comprehension of Durkheim's *sociological* works. A close examination of his lectures, however, will show us that another view is required.

First, there is some evidence to suggest that the topic of pragmatism was of active interest among the Durkheim circle for several years before the course of 1913–14. Parodi had published an article on James in 1908, and both he and Célestin Bouglé contributed papers to a symposium on *La signification du pragmatisme*, organized by the *Societé Française de Philosophie*, in the same year.[46] In a lecture at the *Ecole des Hautes Etudes Sociales* in 1912 or 1913, Parodi had concerned himself in part with a comparison between the approaches to religion adopted by James and Durkheim.[47] This suggests that, far from being a sudden diversion of his attention into an area apparently unrelated to his earlier intellectual interests, the lectures on pragmatism represent Durkheim's contribution to a discussion which had been current among his close associates over a considerable period of time. (Certainly this view is borne out by Durkheim's intimacy with the literature on his subject, which is obvious from the lectures themselves.)

Far from being a digression, or an aside, from the mainstream of

Durkheim's thought, the confrontation with pragmatism is quite central to it. The lectures must be construed as underlining the central concerns of Durkheim's sociology. It is commonly said that the *Division of Labour* sets out all the main sociological themes which occupied Durkheim in the development of his sociology – that it can be seen as Durkheim's sociological 'manifesto'. Much in this manner, the lectures on pragmatism can be seen to recapitulate these themes at the end of his labours.

THE PLACE OF THE LECTURES ON PRAGMATISM IN DURKHEIM'S SOCIOLOGY

Durkheim's involvement with pragmatism did not begin with the lectures. In the essay on 'Individual and collective representations' of 1898[48] he had already demonstrated his familiarity with Jamesian psychology. *The Elementary Forms of the Religious Life* (1912) can scarcely be understood apart from a consideration of James's *Varieties of Religious Experience*, since both the introduction and the conclusion to the book contain extensive, and only partly acknowledged, discussion of the pragmatic approach to religion. The extent of Durkheim's reading of the pragmatists as revealed in the lectures (particularly his reading of James) indicates that he had been following an interest in their ideas for a considerable period of time.[49] This temporal factor is not only of passing interest, for it points the way to the continuity of subject-matter linking the study of pragmatism to the rest of Durkheim's work. There are two principal lines along which this continuity will now be traced; namely, the sociology of knowledge and the sociology of morals.[50] In fact they flow into a single stream in his studies of pragmatism.

Possibly the most serious limitations of Durkheim's sociology of knowledge, as it has hitherto been understood, stem from the fact that his discussion is confined to *primitive* societies. (The two works upon which an understanding of his sociology of knowledge is usually based are *The Elementary Forms of the Religious Life* and *Primitive Classification*, which he prepared in association with Marcel Mauss.)[51] In this context Durkheim is almost constrained by the nature of his subject-matter into an excessive hypostatization of 'society' and an oversimplification of 'knowledge'. It is not difficult to appreciate how this comes about. The societies to which Durkheim devotes his attention are characterized, in his own well-known phrase, by 'mechanical solidarity'. In these simple, undifferentiated societies, the individual confronts directly the massive uniformity of a homogeneous set of 'collective representations', with their attendant repressive sanctions. The homogeneity of the social world is here mirrored in the integrity of its mental world, in that essentially mythological systems of 'representations' hold undisputed sway in the minds of men. Both 'knowledge' and 'society' are relatively simple entities, therefore, whose relationship can be conveyed by a number of relatively simple hypotheses.

Three important limitations can be seen to follow directly from this simplification of 'knowledge' and 'society'. First, the kind of 'knowledge' with which Durkheim deals is not of a technical or practical nature, but rather it is what might loosely be called 'speculative'. He is not concerned with the knowledge which men have about hunting animals, making tools or growing crops in primitive societies: he is interested in their classification of natural species, their ideas about ontology and their general beliefs about causation in nature, and so on. These may not be unrelated to men's practical activities – but their connection lies outside of Durkheim's apparent interest. His investigations into the knowledge of primitive man are premissed upon, and shaped by, an understanding of the religion of primitive man.

The intimate and necessary implication of knowledge with religion, in Durkheim's work, leads us to the second limitation in his sociology of knowledge. From this viewpoint, knowledge becomes almost confined to the problem of *regulation* in society. Although Durkheim lays out in detail the importance of the division of labour for the creation and maintenance of social solidarity, in those societies which are *not* characterized by a developed division of labour the burden of solidarity falls upon the sharing of 'collective representations'. Knowledge, then, in this religious form, has to do with the adaptation of man to his *social* world rather than to his material world.

It is a short step from this point to the third aspect of the limitations of a Durkheimian theory of knowledge. He appears to be quite unconcerned with the *development of knowledge*, and hence with the question of the way in which a sociology of knowledge might relate to the study of social change. Knowledge is a 'given' factor in society, to all intents and purposes. Because of the three reasons suggested here, looked at exclusively from the point of view presented in the *Elementary Forms* and *Primitive Classification*, Durkheim's contribution to a sociology of knowledge must appear to be very one-sided; and, furthermore, it seems to be congruent with a relatively unsophisticated and static 'functionalism'.

An examination of the approach to the sociology of knowledge which Durkheim intimates in the lectures on pragmatism must challenge this view, and lead to a more subtle and rounded appreciation of Durkheim's grasp of the problems involved. In the lectures, his attention shifts from primitive societies, dominated by mythological forms of representation, to the problems of the position of *science* in more recent and complex social orders. Immediately the tendency to hypostatize both 'society' and 'knowledge' abates, and his discussion of the sociology of science reveals that he is aware of, and deeply concerned by, competition between alternative modes of knowledge and the ways in which knowledge develops.

The suggestions outlined in *Pragmatism and Sociology* do not, of course, add up to a fully formed sociology of science: they are no more than 'programme statements', identifying significant problems which merit sociological investigation, rather than essays in empirical sociology. The first issue to which Durkheim directs his attention is the Comtean problem of the unification of diverse sciences – the problem, as he puts it, of the 'intellectual anarchy' of the age of revolution.[52] Here the interest of Durkheim's discussion centres precisely upon the similarities and differences between scientific and mythological thought – the characteristics of intellectual culture in structurally complex or simple societies.

Durkheim finds that, in one respect at least, mythological truths are fundamentally the same as those of science. In spite of the fact that we believe that scientific truths 'express the world as it is', 'nevertheless, scientific representations are themselves also collective representations'.[53] But as collective representations, scientific views of the world bring with themselves certain problems. Scientific judgements refer to fragments of the world, and of our experience within it. Scientific fields have become so very specialized that within a world dominated by the scientific mentality we also need a *conscience collective* which will unite and authorize these various separate and fragmentary truths.

Durkheim therefore challenges the Comtean view of science in general, and of sociology in particular. The solution which Comte had envisaged to the fragmentation of knowledge was principally an *intellectual* one – the positive philosophy. In Durkheim's eyes, however, the problem of the unity of scientific thought is seen as a *sociological* one; and far from standing as the supreme regulator of the *conscience collective*, science itself is in need of social regulation. The concepts with which science deals are 'collective representations': as such they are the product of the collective life of scientists, and in turn they exercise a constraint upon the operation of the scientific mind.[54] Science is thus a 'moral community' – and it is a moralizing force in society. Science itself, however, 'lacks the mental material with which it is possible to reconstitute communal consciousness' of a more general kind, within which the truths of individual sciences might find a recognized place.[55]

Although this is the role which Comte marked out for sociology, it is a part which Durkheim believes that sociology is ill-equipped to play; for 'its means of investigation are difficult, since direct experimentation is impossible'. 'Under such conditions it is easy to understand why ideas expressing social matters in a really objective way are still rather rare.' Consequently, sociology can 'only express fragmentary hypotheses, and these have so far had scarcely any effect on popular consciousness'.[56]

If scientific images of the world are unable to provide us with the basis of a unified consciousness in the modern world, then we must expect the continuation in force of mythological modes of thinking, or their modern analogues, which in the decline of properly religious beliefs will continue to serve the same purpose. Notions such as 'democracy', 'progress' or 'the class struggle' can be seen in this light.[57]

There is, and there always will be, room in social life for a form of truth which will perhaps be expressed in a very secular way, but will nevertheless have a mythological and religious basis. For a long time to come, there will be two tendencies in any society: a tendency towards objective scientific truth and a tendency towards subjectively perceived truth, towards mythological truth.[58]

There is no opportunity in a paper such as this to explore further the detail of Durkheim's argument. It is plainly possible to discern at this point, however, that Durkheim's sociology of knowledge has begun to extend even beyond a sociology of science and into a theory of ideology.[59]

The importance of *Pragmatisme et sociologie* as a contribution to Durkheim's sociology of knowledge has a very different character from the impact which this work must have upon our understanding of his sociology of morals. In the former case, a reading of the lectures gives us an indication that Durkheim's consideration of the subject was rather wider and more flexible than had previously been supposed. They give us further insight into what Durkheim considered a sociology of knowledge might look like. But these lectures add little if anything to our knowledge of Durkheim's sociology of morals, either of a substantive, methodological or theoretical nature. Their relevance is far more fundamental than this: for what in fact they do is to direct our attention towards *the centrality of morality to the entire structure of Durkheim's sociology.*

What is the substance of Durkheim's critique of pragmatism? In a nutshell, his attack is based upon the premise that the weakness of pragmatism is a *moral* weakness. What he finds in pragmatism is no less than *intellectual anomie*, in that there is insufficient regulation of that which passes for truth in society. This point is the fulcrum of his entire discussion of pragmatism: and incidentally it points the way to a reappraisal of the general drift of Durkheim's sociology. For Durkheim, the sociology of knowledge in general, and of science in particular, is necessarily subordinated to the sociology of morals.

If we admit, for the sake of argument, that we live in a world of experience along the lines conceived by the pragmatists, we are still faced with the question of the status of our mental representations of that experience, whether to these we allocate the term 'truth' or not. The burden of the pragmatist exposition here must fall, as Durkheim recognizes, upon the concept of 'action'. The crucial test of truth is the action which leads to a state of 'satisfaction', in which the unease of the crossroads situation is dispelled.[60] The pragmatist directs our attention away from 'veracity' to the process of 'verification' – a series of actions in which the trustworthiness of our ideas are tested, or (in the words of Schiller) in which we see how much 'work' they can accomplish. '*Truth is simply* [and here Durkheim quotes from James's *Pragmatism*] a collective name for verification processes just as *health, wealth, strength*, etc. are names for other processes connected with life.[61] But in what, insists Durkheim, lies the *criterion* or measure of 'satisfaction' or 'verification'? There are two aspects to this problem that are dealt with by Durkheim.

First, there is a logical confusion in the pragmatist position between the notions of 'truth' and 'reality'. The typical pragmatist treats them as essentially the same question, but they must be distinguished logically. 'Satisfaction' has presumably a psychological, or as Schiller would have said, a 'personal' reference;[62] then how do we ascertain that the constructions that we make are not purely illusory? Is the knowledge which we have, which meets these personal satisfactions, 'incommunicable, untranslatable', or can it become a part of the 'common treasure of humanity'? What, then, is the basis upon which this personal truth becomes acceptable 'impersonally'?[63]

At this point, Durkheim's argument takes a characteristic, and possibly even an expected, twist, as he introduces the basic thesis of his reply to the pragmatists: 'What will bring about and strengthen agreement more than anything else is the action of society ... A yardstick for measuring truth gradually takes shape which society tends to sanction and guarantee.'[64] In short, the answer to pragmatism lies in part in a sociology of knowledge.

In summarizing the pragmatist position, Durkheim clearly has a great deal of respect for the way in which, in its attempt to 'soften' the truth, 'to take from it its absolute and almost sacrosanct character', it prepares the way for a historical and sociological study of the changing forms and bases of human knowledge. Yet he is constantly offended by the fact that 'pragmatism ... claims to explain truth psychologically and subjectively'.[65] The particular advantage of a sociological approach over the pragmatist point of view, however, is clear. 'Men have always recognized in truth something that in certain respects imposes itself on us, something that is independent of the facts of sensitivity and individual impulse. Such a universally held conception of truth must correspond to something real.'[66] Pragmatism, however, misses the point here, 'by failing to recognize the duality that exists between the mentality which results from individual experiences and that which results from collective experiences'.[67] Without this recognition of the social element in knowledge, pragmatism succeeds in becoming no more than a form of 'logical utilitarianism'.[68]

In reply to this 'logical utilitarianism', Durkheim enumerates three major elements which he regards as necessary to a notion of 'truth'. First, truth carries with it 'a *moral obligation*'. 'Truth cannot be separated from a certain moral character. In every age, men have felt that they were obliged to seek truth. In truth there is something which commands our respect and a moral power to which the mind feels properly bound to assent.'[69]

Secondly, pragmatists have failed to recognize the *necessary* character of truth. The criterion of 'satisfaction', or the 'advantageous' character of truth, as conceived by the pragmatic theory, cannot account for the fact that the truth is *not* always desirable. The man who is confronted by the truth may be required to 'transform his entire mental organization' by a truth which is disconcerting, disorganizing and painful. It is frequently our dogmas and our illusions which 'satisfy' rather than the truth, which we *nevertheless* must recognize for what it is.[70]

Thirdly, Durkheim underlines the need for us to recognize the *impersonality* of truth, for unless we are able to determine both a truth that is acceptable transpersonally, and to state non-subjective criteria according to which we acknowledge the veracity of knowledge, then there is a danger that the 'logical utilitarianism' of the pragmatists will degenerate into a complete 'logical subjectivism'. The only way out of this impasse, in the view of Durkheim, is through the discovery of 'an authority capable of silencing the differences between individuals and of countering the particularism of individual points of view.'[71]

All of Durkheim's major works contain extensive discussion of one or more aspects of morality: and when one turns one's attention from his writing to his teaching, it is clear that the greater part of Durkheim's career as a teacher was bound up with the investigation of moral phenomena.

Finally, in our examination of the place of the lectures on pragmatism in Durkheim's sociology, it is necessary to turn our attention briefly to his epistemology. This issue arises naturally from the consideration of both his sociology of science and his sociology of morals.

It is often recognized that a great deal of Durkheim's writing is relevant to questions of epistemology; but there are two important respects in which this discussion tends to be deficient, and where attention to these lectures could be valuable. First, Durkheim's epistemological reflections have, in large measure, been assumed to lie concealed within his sociological work, so that the task of the critic has been to discover these and render them explicit. Secondly, the range of his concerns in this area has typically been thought to be rather narrow.

The tendency to portray Durkheim as having only an *implied* epistemology is clearly exemplified in Paul Hirst's book. In his *Durkheim, Bernard and Epistemology* he attempts to extract from *The Rules of Sociological Method* the submerged epistemological implications of Durkheim's argument. 'The form of Durkheim's theory of knowledge, and, in particular, its logical order (in contrast to its expositional order which is haphazard and confused), ... is a form dictated by his point of departure and by the structure of his discourse as a whole.'[72] The task of the critical reader must therefore be to reconstitute this theory for himself.

In a similar vein, Jean Duvignaud, introducing the collected edition of Durkheim's contributions to the *Année Sociologique*, describes its role under Durkheim's leadership as that of 'the epistemological laboratory of French sociology'.[73] The surface appearance of engagement with the comparative study of a succession of empirical issues conceals an essential sub-structure of epistemological exploration, which undergirds the whole enterprise of the journal. 'To this it [ie. the *Année Sociologique*] owes its extreme importance.'

This position echoes that taken by Talcott Parsons nearly forty years earlier. Parsons is certainly to be given credit for his early recognition of the importance of Durkheim's efforts to wrestle with a theory of knowledge, but: 'These considerations do not ... amount to explicit epistemological discussion, which Durkheim did not attempt until the *Formes élémentaires*.'[74]

The interest of the lectures on pragmatism lies partly in the fact that they show us that Durkheim had developed his ideas in this area to a far greater degree of articulation and clarity than that which is acknowledged by these commentators on his work. There is in *Pragmatism and Sociology* a measure of epistemological reflection with which most readers of Durkheim are not familiar, and which provides the justification for Mauss's description of these lectures as 'the crowning achievement of Durkheim's philosophical work'.[75]

Durkheim's philosophical work on a theory of knowledge is not only more explicitly developed than he is usually given credit for; it is also much wider in its range. Two main questions have hitherto dominated discussion of Durkheim's epistemology. The first of these is the problem of the nature of 'social facts'. His attempt to build a secure foundation for sociology depended in large measure on his identification of a distinctive and unambiguously specified object of social knowledge. Secondly, he is known for his contribution to what is more properly termed the sociology of knowledge, rather than epistemology in its technical sense, through his examination of the social origins of categories of thought. Debate on the first of these issues usually centres on the *Rules*, whereas in relation to the second critical attention is mainly focussed upon the *Elementary Forms* and *Primitive Classification*.

In *Pragmatism and Sociology*, however, we see Durkheim grappling with quite different problems, such as the nature and function of concepts, and the role of speculative thought. Questions of truth and validity occupy the centre of the stage on this occasion.

The assimilation of these lectures into our understanding of Durkheim's work will undoubtedly result in a greater appreciation of his philosophical standing. A similar process has already taken place in relation to his sociology of morals. Increasing familiarity with the essays collected in *Sociology and Philosophy* and his course of lectures on *Moral Education* brought home the firmness of Durkheim's grasp of both the Kantian heritage of moral philosophy and the utilitarian tradition. The lectures presented here can leave us in no doubt that in his attempt to produce a defence of and a revision of classical rationalist epistemology, Durkheim was similarly in command of his material.

A rounded assessment of Durkheim's epistemology has yet to be undertaken.[76] Mauss's judgement, quoted above, stands in lively contrast to both that of Parsons, who observed that 'Durkheim's sociological epistemology involves inextricable philosophical difficulties'[77] and that of Hirst, who concludes his own discussion with the remark that Durkheim's epistemology is 'impossible'. 'Durkheim's work is a unity, a unity not of science but of epistemological contradiction ...'[78]

Unfortunately there is insufficient space to explore these matters here. Two things, however, are certain: their further exploration will involve considerable controversy and, whatever the balance of that assessment may turn out to be, a close reading of *Pragmatism and Sociology* will be necessary for all those who wish to engage themselves with these problems.

JOHN B. ALLCOCK

The origins of pragmatism*

What led me to choose the subject of these lectures? Why did I call them *Pragmatism and Sociology*? First, because pragmatism is almost the only current theory of truth, and is of topical interest. Secondly, because it has, in common with sociology, a sense of *life* and *action*. Both are children of the same era.

I do part company totally, however, with the conclusions of pragmatism. It is therefore useful to indicate the respective positions of the two doctrines. The problem raised by pragmatism is indeed of a very serious nature. We are currently witnessing an *attack on reason* which is truly militant and determined.[1] Consequently, the problem is of threefold importance.

1   In the first place, it is of *general* importance. Pragmatism is in a better position than any other doctrine to make us see the need for a reform of traditional rationalism, for it shows us what is lacking in it.

2   Next, it is of *national* importance. Our whole French culture is basically an essentially rationalistic one. The eighteenth century is a prolongation of Cartesianism. A total negation of rationalism would thus constitute a danger, for it would overthrow our whole national culture. If we had to accept the form of irrationalism represented by pragmatism, the whole French mind would have to be radically changed.

3   Lastly, it is of specifically *philosophical* importance. Not only our culture, but the entire philosophical tradition, right from the very beginnings of philosophical speculation (with one exception, which we shall discuss shortly) is inspired by rationalism. If pragmatism were valid, we should have to embark upon a complete reversal of this whole tradition.

It is true that in the philosophical tradition, two currents are generally distinguished: the rationalist and the empiricist. Nevertheless, it is easy to see that empiricism and rationalism are basically only two different ways of affirming reason. Each in its own way insists on something

*Notes to the First Lecture, of 9 December 1913, are on pp. 114–15.

1

which pragmatism tends to destroy, the *cult of truth*; and both admit the existence of *necessary judgements*, though they differ in the way they explain this necessity. Empiricism bases its explanation on the nature of things, rationalism on reason itself, on the nature of thought. Both, however, recognize the necessary and obligatory nature of certain truths, and the differences between them are subsidiary to their agreement on this fundamental point. It is precisely this obligatory force of logical judgements, this necessity of true judgements, that is denied by pragmatism, which affirms that the mind remains free with regard to truth.

In this respect, pragmatism comes close to the single exception already referred to, sophism, which also denied all truth. This resemblance is not arbitrary, and is admitted by the pragmatists themselves. Thus, Schiller proclaims himself a 'Protagorean' and recalls the axiom of Protagoras that 'man is the measure of all things'.[2]

We should not forget, however, that sophism played a useful part in the history of scientific thought, and can be said to have produced Socrates. In the same way, pragmatism can serve to arouse philosophical thought from the new 'philosophical slumber' into which it has tended to fall since the shock it received from Kant's criticism. Its value is, as has already been mentioned, that it shows up the weaknesses of the old rationalism, which needs to be reformed if it is to meet the demands of modern thought and take into account certain new points of view introduced by modern science. The problem is to find a formula which will both preserve what is essential in rationalism and answer the valid criticism that pragmatism makes of it.

Nietzsche[3]

In a recent book, René Berthelot maintains that the first form of pragmatism is to be seen in Nietzsche: or rather, that Nietzsche represents a radical and integral pragmatism.[4] Here the author indicates his belief that he can link pragmatism with German romanticism and establish that it was of German inspiration. We, however, see it rather as belonging to the Anglo-Saxon tradition of thought.

We should first examine the common ground between Nietzsche's thought and pragmatism. Nietzsche refuses to accept that any kind of moral idea has an absolute character, the character of universal truth. The ideal, he maintains, is beyond truth and falsehood. '"This is – now my way," says Zarathustra. "Where is yours?" Thus did I answer those who asked me "the way." For *the* way – it doth not exist.'[5]

In his view, logical or moral norms are a lesser concern. His aim is to free completely both conduct and thought. Speculative truth cannot be either impersonal or universal. We can only know things by means of processes which distort them and, to a greater or lesser degree, transform them into our own thoughts. We build them in our own likeness: we give them a location in space, we assign them to genera and species, and so forth. But none of this exists, not even the link of cause and effect. We replace reality with a whole system of symbols and fictions, in a word, of illusions: 'How could we ever explain! We operate only with things which do not exist, with lines, surfaces, bodies, atoms, divisible times, divisible spaces – how can explanation ever be possible when we first make everything a conception, our conception!'[6]

But why do we establish such fictions? Because, Nietzsche answers, they are useful to us for living. They are false, but must be thought to be true so that beings like us can maintain themselves. What has helped us to live has survived; the rest has disappeared:

No living being would have been preserved unless the contrary inclination – to affirm rather than suspend judgement, to mistake and fabricate rather than wait, to assent rather than deny, to decide rather than be in the right – had been cultivated with extraordinary assiduity. – The course of logical thought and reasoning in our modern brain corresponds to a process and struggle of impulses, which singly and in themselves are all very illogical and unjust; we experience usually only the result of the struggle, so rapidly and secretly does this primitive mechanism now operate in us.[7]

Thus, for Nietzsche, those judgements which are acknowledged to be true and those which are rejected as false are determined by *utility*. The idea that *what is true is what is useful* is the very principle of pragmatism.

There are, however, some profound differences between Nietzsche's thought and pragmatism. It should be noted that what Nietzsche does not say is that what is useful is true. What he does say is that what *seems* true has been established as a result of its utility. In his view, the useful is false. There is, he says, one form of truth which is quite other than that described as true by the men of the 'herd', a morality other than the 'slave morality', a logic other than common logic. There is a truth which only liberated spirits can attain. The artist is the very type of this spirit, freed from all rules and capable of adapting himself to all the forms of reality and of understanding *intuitively* what is hidden beneath appearances and fiction.

There are no such ideas in pragmatism, for which there is no 'surface of things' quite separate from the basis on which they rest. Things as they appear to us are the surface. That is what we live on, and what reality is. There is no reason to look beneath appearances. We must deal only with the world as it appears to us, without worrying about knowing whether there is anything else. William James himself presents his doctrine as 'radical empiricism', and his method of argument often consists of ridiculing reasoning and logic. For him, the only important things are those which appear in immediate experience: thought only ever moves on a singular plane, not on two different planes.

The proof is that even when pragmatism seems to admit something that goes beyond, something above the world of phenomena, it does not really leave that world. This is plainly apparent in James's *religious tendencies*, which are very real. He sees supernatural beings, the gods, as existing in nature, as real forces, near to us, which we cannot observe directly, but whose *effects* are revealed to us at certain times, in certain experiences. Consequently we can discover them gradually, just as we have discovered many physical forces (such as electricity) which were unknown for a long time but which nevertheless existed. Thus, everything takes place on the plane of phenomena, which is very far from Nietzschean thought.

It is true that at certain periods in his life Nietzsche denied the existence of a substratum hidden under appearances, and also admitted that appearances were all that existed. He thus saw the role of the artist as that of freeing himself from these and creating in their place a world of varied, moving and independently developing images; and thought too, once its logical framework had been broken, would also be able to develop freely.

Pragmatism, however, had no more place within it for this second explanation than for the first. It claims neither to study reality deeply nor to go beyond it and set up in its stead a world of mental creations. The dominant features of pragmatism are a realistic sense and a practical sense. The pragmatist is *a man of action*, who consequently sees things as important. He does not act in a dream and, unlike Nietzsche, never speaks like a prophet or a visionary. He knows neither anguish nor uneasiness. Truth, for him, is something *to be achieved*.

Romanticism

Certain characteristics common to both *pragmatism* and *romanticism* should also be noted; in particular the sense of the complexity, richness and variety of life as we know it. Romanticism was partly a revolt against the simplistic aspects of late eighteenth-century rationalism and social philosophy.

This sense of the complexity of human affairs, this feeling of the inadequacy of eighteenth-century philosophy, is also encountered in the embryonic sociology found in the works of Saint-Simon and Auguste Comte, who both understood that social life was made up not of abstract relationships, but of extremely rich material. A feeling of this kind does not necessarily lead to either mysticism or pragmatism. Comte in particular was a rationalist in the highest degree, who nevertheless wished to found a sociology which would be richer, more complex and less formalistic than the social philosophy of the eighteenth century.

The Anglo-Saxon milieu: Peirce

In order to understand pragmatism there is no need to go back to ideas as old as these, or to German philosophy. One needs only to put it back into its original setting, the Anglo-Saxon milieu.

The first thinker to use the word 'pragmatism' was the American scholar Peirce.[8] It was he who put forward for the first time the ideas which pragmatists claim as their own, in an article published in January 1878 in an American journal.[9] It appeared in translation in the *Revue Philosophique* of January 1879 under the title 'Comment rendre nos idées claires'.[10]

It could be summarized as follows. Peirce asks why we think. He answers: because *we doubt*. If we were in a perpetual state of certainty, we should not need to think and to attempt to resolve our doubts. 'The action of thought is excited by the irritation of doubt, and ceases when belief is obtained.'[11] Moreover, belief is expressed by *action*: belief that does not produce action does not exist, and action must take on the character of the belief that gives rise to it. The state of belief is a state of equilibrium and hence of rest, and that is why we seek it. The essential mark of belief is thus 'the establishment of a habit ... Our habit has the same bearing as our action, our belief the same as our habit, our conception the same as our belief.'[12] In this way, *doubt* gives rise to the *idea*; and the idea gives rise to *action* and, having *belief*, is expressed by organized movements, by *habit*. The whole sense of the idea is to be found in the sense of the habit that it determines.

Hence this rule: 'Consider what effects, that might conceivably have practical bearings, we conceive the object of our conception to have. Then, our conception of those effects is the whole of our conception of the object.'[13] If, in two cases that we take to be different, the effects are the same, the fact is that we are in the presence of a false distinction: the object is the same. We could take the arguments between Catholics and Protestants over transubstantiation as an example of this. The latter see in the Eucharist a symbol, the former a real presence. The final effect, in each case, is the same: the consecrated wafer is food for the soul. Whether or not it is really the flesh and blood of Christ is henceforth relatively unimportant. The debate is merely a matter of words.[14]

And yet all this is only a very early intimation of pragmatism. Indeed, Peirce does not use the word in the article in question, and did not use it until 1902, in his article in J. M. Baldwin's *Dictionary of Philosophy and Psychology*.[15] He did however say later[16] that he had been using it in conversation for a long time.

There is obviously some degree of kinship between the thesis Peirce put forward in his earlier article and pragmatism. Both doctrines are in agreement, in that each of them establishes a connective link between idea and action, each refuses to concern itself with all purely metaphysical questions and verbal discussions and each finally poses only problems of practical interest whose terms are borrowed from the world of senses.

But there is an essential difference. Peirce's article contains no theory of *truth*. The problem of truth is not posed at all. The author asks how we can succeed in *clarifying* our ideas, not what conditions are required if the idea of a thing is to give a true representation of its sensory effects. What is more, Peirce admits, following the classical theory, that truth imposes itself with a kind of 'inevitability' before which the mind can only bow.[17] Thus, truth is an opinion that possesses intrinsic rights, and all investigators are *obliged* to accept it. This is the exact opposite of the pragmatist principle.

Consequently, when William James's works were later published, Peirce refused to ally himself with him, and insisted on pointing out the differences between them. Peirce did not repudiate rationalism. For him, if action has any value, it is because it is a way of advancing *reason*. In 1902, in his article in Baldwin's *Dictionary*, he admitted that he had not stressed this point sufficiently and explicitly dissociated himself from James's interpretations. In his article in the *Monist* of 1905, 'What pragmatism is', he even invented a new term, 'pragmaticism', which he said was 'ugly enough to be safe from kidnappers',[18] in order to avoid any confusion between his own argument and that of James. In another article, 'The issues of pragmaticism',[19] he calls his own doctrine a 'philosophy of Common Sense'. Given these facts, it is rather curious that James has continued to call himself his disciple, has saluted him as the father of pragmatism and has never pointed out these differences.

6

The origins of pragmatism

It would be more accurate to see William James[20] as the true father of pragmatism. In 1896, he published *The Will to Believe*,[21] which appeared in a new edition in 1911. In that book, he makes a distinction between purely theoretical questions which are connected with science alone – a field in which, although we do not yet see with perfect clarity, we can ultimately expect illumination, for science will one day be able to provide us with the elements necessary for our beliefs – and those practical questions which engage our life. When we are dealing with the latter, we cannot wait, but must choose and commit ourselves, even if we are uncertain: and by so doing, we obey personal factors, extra-logical motivators such as temperament, surroundings and so on. We yield to our urges; one hypothesis seems more alive to us than others; we concretize it and convert it into actions.

Here, James is thinking in particular of religious belief, of which moral belief is in his view only an aspect. This is Pascal's 'wager'; although truth cannot be demonstrated in this area, nor clearly perceived, it is necessary to commit oneself and act appropriately. It is here that we find the major starting-point for pragmatism. This kind of preoccupation with religion is to be found in the work of all the pragmatists, and it was in this form that pragmatism first appeared in James. The consequence is that, for James, truth has a *personal* character and *truth* and *life* are inseparable. Another great pragmatist, F. C. S. Schiller of Oxford, even if he does not go as far as James and say that it is necessary to have an attitude towards religious questions, does maintain that truth must not be 'depersonalized' or 'dehumanized', and calls his pragmatism *humanism*.

Nevertheless, the term 'pragmatism' had so far not been used by James. He did not use it before his study 'Philosophical conceptions and practical results',[22] which appeared in the *University Chronicle* at Berkeley, California, on 9 September 1898. The essential themes of pragmatism were to be developed in this work.

The pragmatist movement*

Thus is was in America, between 1895 and 1900, that pragmatism first appeared. Although it is a recent phenomenon, the history of its origin is rather difficult to trace. This is because it came into being undetectably, like a slow, underground movement spreading only gradually beyond the circle of private conversations. James defines it as one of those changes 'that opinion undergoes without being aware of it'.

As already stated, Peirce used the word only in private talk. James, using a term that others had used before him, was the first to apply it to an established group of ideas. For several years he limited himself to the presentation of his ideas in various articles in journals, the earliest of which date from 1895. The most important of these, written prior to 1898, he collected in a volume entitled *The Meaning of Truth*,[1] of which the French translation, *L'Idée de vérité*, appeared in 1913. In 1906, James gave a series of lectures in which he developed his thought more fully. These were published in 1907, with the title *Pragmatism*.[2] The French translation appeared in 1911. In 1909, he was bold enough to go to Oxford, the citadel of Hegelianism, to expound his doctrine, presenting it in a perspective that most strikingly brought out its contrast with Hegelian thought. He entitles this group of lectures *A Pluralistic Universe*,[3] and in 1910 they were translated into French under the rather inappropriate title *Philosophie de l' expérience*. His *Essays in Radical Empiricism*, a collection of articles, the first of which, 'Does consciousness exist?'[4] had appeared in 1904, were published in 1910. A summary of this article in French,[5] which is important because it raises the question of whether there exists a specific dualism in the universe, provided the substance of an important communication to the Congress of Philosophy in Rome in 1905.

Following a parallel path, John Dewey[6] had begun a campaign in a series of articles in which he moved gradually towards pragmatism. These articles are listed on page 575 of the *Revue de Métaphysique* of

*Notes to the Second Lecture, of 16 December 1913, are on pp. 115–17.

1913.[7] There is no work of Dewey's which gives his overall position, only partial studies such as the *Studies in Logical Theory*, a collective venture to which he contributed only the first four chapters,[8] or his little book *How We Think*.[9] It was around Dewey that the *Chicago* or *instrumentalist school* grew. His chief disciple is A. W. Moore.[10]

These ideas were not long in crossing the Atlantic. As early as 1902, a group of young philosophers at Oxford came together to wage a campaign against both materialistic evolutionism and the theories of Hegel. Under the title *Personal Idealism* they published a collection of articles, of which the most important was F. C. S. Schiller's[11] 'Axioms as postulates'. In the following year, Schiller collected his own main articles in his book *Humanism*.[12]

In Italy, the review *Leonardo*[13] carried pragmatism to extreme, even paradoxical, lengths.

In France, pragmatism appears chiefly in the neo-religious movement described as 'modernist'. Edouard Le Roy claims to base his religious apologetics on principles borrowed from pragmatism.[14]

It should be pointed out, however, that the pragmatists are a little too apt to claim some thinkers who are far from accepting all their theses. In this way James recruits Henri Poincaré, and also Henri Bergson[15] (from whom he also borrows certain arguments), simply because Bergson introduced pragmatism in France in a preface,[16] in which he speaks of it in somewhat general terms, and suggests his reservations about it.

THE ESSENTIAL THESES OF PRAGMATISM: CRITICAL PART

There are thus three chief protagonists of pragmatism: Dewey, Schiller and James.

Dewey is a logician, and always attempts to be rigorous. However, he is often heavy, the development of his thought is laborious and is sometimes not very clear. James himself admits that he does not always fully understand him. Dewey, he says, 'recently gave a series of lectures entitled "Pragmatism": they were dazzling flashes of light amongst Cimmerian darkness'.[17]

Schiller and James, on the contrary, write very clearly. But both do this in a different way. Schiller forges straight ahead. He is not afraid of paradox and, far from trying to reduce the impact of his ideas, aims at exaggerating them and astonishing the reader. He makes his deductions with an unexpected and surprising logic of a brusque and intransigent kind. James too shows a certain liking for paradox, even in his psychological theories. He expresses ideas which would be more easily acceptable if they were expressed in a different way. He first presents his theses in a sharply defined way, but in discussion he is skilled at rounding off the corners, whilst keeping his basic principles, and one ends up wondering whether one perhaps agrees with him. The title of his book on pragmatism clearly indicates the way his mind tends to work. Although in it he shows pragmatism as a real revolution at the centre of philosophical thought, he calls it *Pragmatism: A New Name for Some Old Ways of Thinking.*[18] As circumstances permit, he presents his doctrine sometimes in one light and sometimes in another. This diversity detracts to some extent from the unity of pragmatism (one American writer recently counted some thirteen varieties of it) and makes a general exposition no easy task.[19]

In addition, none of the pragmatist philosophers has given us such an overall exposition.[20] We have only articles scattered in periodicals, which have sometimes been collected in books, lectures and 'popular' talks. There are no lectures in which the speaker explores the heart of his subject before a specialized audience. What we have are lectures for the general public, in which only the salient points of certain questions are presented. Each one is self-contained, and matters which in one are central are secondary concerns in another, and vice versa. This changes the whole appearance of the doctrine, and it is not easy to discern the major ideas in it. This rather elusive aspect of pragmatism means that some of those opposed to it have been able to accuse it of contradicting itself.

And yet it is not impossible to discover its basic theses and to find a common ground in them. That is what I shall try to do here, without claiming to give a historical explanation, even if it means pointing out the particular nuances that are proper to each author. In *The Meaning of Truth*,[21] James declares that he shares Peirce's ideas. Schiller recognizes James[22] as his master. Dewey, although he expresses some reservations, differs from James mainly on particular points.[23] There is, therefore, an identical orientation in all three. My intention is to make this clear and, in particular, to demonstrate the major criticisms that the pragmatists direct against rationalism.

Pragmatism is not presented as a fixed system. James is quite precise on this point. Pragmatism, he says, is not a system, but a discussion, a movement, which may later take a clearer shape. It is, in his view, less a definitive pattern of ideas than a general impulsion in a certain direction. It can be described in three ways:[24] (1) as a method, a general attitude of the mind; (2) as a theory of truth; and (3) as a theory of the universe.

1   As a *method*, pragmatism is simply the attitude or general cast to be adopted by the mind when faced with problems. That attitude consists of directing our attention towards 'results, consequences, facts': 'The pragmatic method ... is to try to interpret each notion by tracing its respective practical consequences'.[25] This is still Peirce's pragmatism, which tries above all to get rid of verbal discussions and useless problems, and is marked by a characteristic choice of questions and manner of dealing with them.

2   There is so far nothing particularly exclusive to pragmatism in that. It is as a *theory of truth* that pragmatism is of particular interest, and it is from that point of view that we shall study it. We shall discuss pragmatism as a *theory of the universe* only in so far as is necessary to understand it as a theory of truth. In this connection, the method has been indicated by James himself. The strength of pragmatism, he says in *The Meaning of Truth* (pp. 57–9), is the failure of earlier theories, and in particular the inadequacy of rationalism, which has led us to seek a different understanding of truth. Unfortunately, James's discussion of rationalism is for most of the time mixed up with the exposition of his own idea of truth. It is important to separate them, however, because we must above all understand why the pragmatists believe that rationalism had to be replaced. In the event, certain thinkers who feel the strength of the objections made by the pragmatists immediately accept the solutions they propose. The two problems, however, and this is very important, need to be separated very carefully. To do that, it is also important first of all to examine the way in which the pragmatists have imagined this rationalist – or, more generally, dogmatist[26] – conception of truth.

The dogmatic conception of truth

James sees this conception as based on a very simple principle, namely, that *the true idea is the idea which conforms to things*. It is an image, a *copy* of objects, the mental representation of the thing. An idea is true when this mental representation corresponds accurately to the object represented. This conception, moreover, is not peculiar to rationalism: it is also a feature of empiricism. For John Stuart Mill, for example, the mind simply copies external reality. Ideas are dependent on facts, for they merely express sensations. They refer to sensory images and, consequently, thought can only translate sensations which come to us from the external world.

Despite appearances to the contrary, the same is true of rationalism, which also sees an external reality which the mind must translate if it is to be in the truth. In rationalism, however, this reality does not consist of objects perceivable by the senses, but is an organized system of ideas with their own existence, a system which the mind must reproduce. One can recognize Plato's doctrine here; and it is in fact Plato whom Schiller likes most to attack.[27] For others, ideas are the thoughts of God. '"God geometrizes", it used to be said; and it was believed that Euclid's elements literally reproduced his geometrizing. There is an eternal and unchangeable "reason"; and its voice was supposed to reverberate in *Barbara* and *Celarent*.'[28] For Hegel, whom James bitterly attacks,[29] the absolute Idea is identified with Reason, which envelopes everything and is 'the absolute all of alls', in which all contradictions are reconciled. In all these cases, however, reason is thought of as existing outside us: there is a Reason which dominates all individual reasons, and which the latter have merely to copy.

Both forms of dogmatism therefore consist in admitting that truth is given, either in the sensory world (empiricism) or in an intelligible world, in absolute thought or Reason (rationalism). Hamelin's idealism, for example, in which things are merely concepts, would provide a third solution. This really amounts to the same thing, since ideal states exist in things themselves, and the system of truth and reality (which here are one and the same thing) is still pre-existent and external to us.

Thus truth, in all dogmatic conceptions, can be no more than the transcription of an *external* reality. Since this truth exists outside individual minds, it is *impersonal*. It does not express man, and is not attached to him. Consequently, it is *ready-made*. It 'holds or obtains', says James,[30] it *imposes itself* on us absolutely. The human mind does not have to construct it: to copy is not to bring into being. The mind has no active part to play. The opposite is the case: its task is to efface itself as much as possible and seek, as it were, a *duplicate* of reality. For, if it had its own activity, if it imposed its own style on truth, it would distort the truth. It would express itself instead of expressing truth. Everything contributed by the mind would be a source of error. Finally, according to dogmatism, truth is not only external and impersonal but also a completed system – a complete whole independent of time and becoming. 'I have never doubted', says an Oxford Hegelian whom James quotes,[31] 'that truth is universal and single and timeless, a single content or significance, one and whole and complete'.

A few words of discussion. At first sight it is rather surprising to think that Leibnitz and Kant are included in this definition of rationalism and dogmatism. The pragmatists, it is true, are not too concerned with such fine detail. They show a certain carelessness with regard to doctrine which they see as being of no major importance.

The objection will immediately be raised that in the opinion of Leibnitz, the mind draws all its thought from itself. The *monad* is without relationship to the universe, and all its ideas come to it from within, not from without. However, if we look at it more closely, we can see that the pragmatist criticism applies to Leibnitz as well as to other rationalists. The monad works on a model which it has not created, but which is contributed by God and given to it. The world is as God made it, and not as the monad wants it to be. The plan that the monad progressively carries out as it rises to clear thought is imposed on it. The monad is not its creator.

In Kant, it is certainly the mind which creates truth, but only when it is a question of *phenomenal* truth. But phenomenal truth is simply appearance and, in one sense, in relation to the noumenon, it is error, or at least only an effect of noumena, the intelligible world, on the phenomenal plane. (The noumenon itself is a datum: we do not create it.) The only way of reaching it is that which the *moral law* opens up for us. It is the moral law which tells us that there is something other than the phenomenal world. What, then, are the characteristics of the moral law? They are *fixity* and *impersonality*. In one sense, we do discover the moral law within ourselves: but we do not invent it, we simply find it. We have not made it, nor has our mind given birth to it. It is thus, once again, a reality outside us which imposes itself on us. Thus it can be accepted that the dogmatist or rationalist conception – the ordinary conception, we might say – of truth is indeed the one which pragmatism describes for us.

Criticism of dogmatism

What are the objections which pragmatism makes to this conception? First of all, it raises the question of the purpose of truth, if truth is merely a transcription of reality. If it is that, then it is a useless redundancy.[32] Why do things need translating? Why should they not be sufficient unto themselves? Representation of that kind adds nothing to what exists. James indeed sees truth as 'not a copying, but an enrichment'. He invites us to imagine[33] an individual who for a moment is in himself the whole reality of the universe, and who then learns that another being who will know the whole of this unity is about to be created. How could he hope to benefit from this knowledge? Of what use would that replica of himself in the mind of the newcomer be to him? How would his universe be enriched? Nothing is useful apart from what our mind *adds* to things. What is important for man is less that substance of things than their secondary qualities: light, colour, warmth and so on. What counts is the use to which we put reality. If the mind only 'saw' reality, of what use would that be?

Let us suppose that a perfect system of objective truths,[34] like the world of Plato's 'Ideas', really existed. What would be the interest in the 'light of intelligence' being reflected in the multitude of individual minds which could only reproduce it very imperfectly? That is a *fall*, which also features in the theological hypothesis. Why did God, the sovereign truth, not remain alone in his perfection? What did he add to himself? For if the world comes from him, it expresses him, but in a very incomplete and deficient way!

But, it is said, we benefit from knowing the truth as it is, with, specifically, a view to action itself. This truth must therefore be as exact a copy as possible of reality. But to enable us to act we should still have to establish that our thought does copy reality. Thus we come to make truth a good in itself, which imposes itself through itself, and which the mind seeks simply for the joy of contemplating it. Truth would be established for the sole purpose of being thought. It becomes a god to which one raises altars.

There is no doubt that when we contemplate an idealism such as that of Leibnitz, we may wonder what is the function of truth. Each monad copies the whole range of other monads (that is, the universe), and all copy the same universe. Why is there such a waste of intellectual energy, if one does not posit the notion that knowledge is a good in itself?

Truth and human knowledge*

May I repeat that I do not intend to give a history or even a complete account of pragmatism? What I am chiefly trying to do is to identify the general tendency that is common to its various representatives, and to discover what has led them to this way of thinking. To do this, we must to some degree become pragmatists ourselves, setting aside the objections that spring to mind. When we have done this and understood where the strength of pragmatism lies, we shall be able to take up our own stance again and move on to discussion.

In this respect, the fundamental element in pragmatism is its criticism of traditional rationalism, or rather dogmatism. In order to understand this criticism, we have tried to see what the pragmatists' idea of dogmatism is. According to them, dogmatism regards the true idea as the *copy* of an external reality, whether this reality consists of material objects on the one hand, or on the other of the ideas, concepts or thoughts of the absolute mind. If the latter is the case, then truth is objective, transcendent and impersonal. We have already encountered one of the objections that pragmatism makes to this conception. If truth does nothing but duplicate reality, of what use is it? It seems *useless*. Here, however, another difficulty arises. If the reality of which the idea is a copy is external and transcendent, *how can we know it?* If it is outside us, immanent in the world or transcending it, a part of the world or a totality in itself, how can we grasp it? Let us remind ourselves of the Platonic hypothesis. Ideas, by definition, are above the world of experience. How can we raise ourselves to this ideal world which is the only reality? There is an abyss between it and us: how is it possible to bridge it? Or how, on the other hand, can these ideal realities descend at all into our world? 'It is impossible to explain', says Schiller,[1] 'how man can rise to the contemplation of eternal truth, or why the Idea should descend, and distort itself in human thoughts.' Plato may well attribute special powers to the mind: this does not eliminate the difficulty.

*Notes to the Third Lecture, of 23 December 1913, are on pp. 117–18.

15

According to Aristotle, too, the divine cannot know the human without degenerating. Inversely, however, one cannot imagine how man would be able to picture the divine. How could something finite like the human mind succeed in thinking of the absolute spirit? We should have to admit that there is no separation, and that the two worlds are only one.

In more general terms, if thought is a copy of things, we do not see how it can grasp them; for there is an abyss between mind and its object. James says, in *The Meaning of Truth*, that thought would have to accomplish a *'salto mortale* across an "epistemological chasm"' (p. 114). We can grasp the object only by thinking of it. If it is thought of, it is interior to us. Thus it is impossible to verify the truth of the idea, that is, to verify its conformity with the object, as is required by the hypothesis: thought cannot go beyond itself. 'In whatever form this "copy" theory be stated, the question inevitably arises as to how we can compare our ideas with reality and thus know their truth. On this theory, what we possess is ever the copy; the reality is beyond. In other words, such a theory logically carried out leads to the breakdown of knowledge' (Dewey).[2]

Such is the conception that Schiller, James and Dewey have of rationalism. Traditional rationalism separates thought from existence. Thought is in the mind; existence is outside it. Hence the two forms of reality can no longer meet. If by a hypothesis one places thought outside existence, the abyss that separates them can no longer be crossed. The only way to solve the difficulty would be to refuse to admit the existence of this gap between existence and thought. If thought is an element of reality, if it is a part of existence and of life, there is no longer any 'epistemological abyss' or 'perilous leap'. We have only to see how these two realities can participate in each other. *Linking thought and existence to life – this is the fundamental idea of pragmatism.*[3]

EXTRA-HUMAN TRUTH AND PURE INTELLECT

There is another difficulty in the dogmatic conception. If truth is impersonal, it is *foreign to man*, it is *extra-human*. How, then, can it act on the human mind, attracting and fascinating it? It corresponds to nothing in our nature. It is often said that truth lays an obligation on us, that to obey true ideas is a *duty*, that to seek the truth and to flee from error is a 'categorical imperative'. But how can we understand this if truth is not something human? What force would ever be able to make us go spontaneously to something that is foreign to us and constrain us to obey it? This is the objection that is often levelled at the 'moral law' as

16

Kant presents it. In reality, however, the pragmatists say, the question never arises in this way. The exigencies of truth, like all others, are always 'exigencies that are subordinated to certain conditions'. In real life, when a question concerning truth arises, we ask ourselves, when must I adhere to one such truth and when to another? Should my adherence be expressed or remain tacit? And supposing that at some times it should be tacit and at other times expressed, in which of these two cases do I find myself at this very moment? Of course, we have an obligation to accept the truth. However, this obligation depends on the circumstances; for it is never a question of truth with a capital T, of single truth, of abstract truth; it is always a matter of 'concrete truths' that are more or less expedient depending on the case.[4] If we suppose, on the contrary, that truth is purely objective, it will leave man completely indifferent. To attribute to truth an 'independence' with respect to human ends, an 'absolute character' that separates it from life, is to 'dehumanize' knowledge (Schiller, *Studies in Humanism*, p. 69).

If one conceives of this idea of a purely objective and impersonal truth, one admits the presence of a very special faculty in man – that is, *pure intellect*, which has its function, precisely, to go to truth in a spontaneous and almost mechanical movement, to think truth solely for the sake of thinking and contemplating it. In order to explain how truth, in itself extra-human, can be related to man, we assume in him an extra-human faculty for conceiving it, one foreign to all the other factors of life. The pragmatists say, however: 'We deny that properly speaking such a thing as pure or mere intellection can occur. What is loosely so called is really also purposive thought pursuing what seems to it a desirable end.'[5] There is no impersonal reason in us, there is an intellect that is a living function and is in close relation to all other living functions that make up our thought. Far from being impersonal, it shares in all the particularity of consciousness. When we seek the truth, it is always *with a goal in mind*. Truth can be determined only by means of selection and choice; and it is human interest that determines this choice. According to Schiller, 'the development of a mind is a thoroughly personal affair. Potential knowledge becomes actual, because of the purposive activity of a Knower who brings it to bear on his interests, and uses it to realize his ends' (*Studies in Humanism*, p. 186).

One can object, however, that the pure intellect is in itself a source of pleasure. Just as there is, as Kant admits, a sort of rational sensitivity, a joy that we feel in submitting ourselves to law, so is there a particular pleasure in seeking, discovering and contemplating truth. This *contem-*

plative conception of truth is characteristic of all dogmatism. The pragmatists claim[6] that the idea that the intellect serves only to procure this pleasure is an absurd conception, unless one sees it in a simple game to amuse those who possess it. Our intellectual activity cannot, of course, always be in a state of tension. It must relax; there must be moments when the intellect amuses itself in order to rest from the fatigue caused by the assiduous search for truth. This is the pleasure of dreams, of imagination, of disinterested meditation. This play must have only a limited place in our life, however, for it is as susceptible to excess as any other game. It cannot be the principal and constant goal of the intellect, 'which is intended for serious work'. Its role is best seen in its practical function (in the broadest sense of the term), in its relations with reality. All pragmatists are in agreement on this point: truth is human; the intellect cannot be isolated from life, nor *logic* from *psychology*. James, like Schiller, and even Dewey (although Dewey admits the necessity of a certain check on the personal element) refuse to separate these two sciences.[7] According to them, all fundamental logical notions, notions of necessity, evidence, etc. start from psychological processes. Thus truth must be attached to our 'interests' as men: truth is made for the life of man.

IDEAL TRUTH AND CONCRETE TRUTHS

There is a new difficulty. If truth is impersonal, if it consists of a system of ideals such as Plato's 'Ideas', it must be *the same* for all men; it must be immutable and unique. One cannot perceive it; but once one attains it, one can see it only as it is: *one, identical, and invariable.* Concerning such a truth, the pragmatists observe that it contrasts singularly with the truths which men actually attain. Human truths are fugitive, temporary and perpetually in the process of transformation. Today's truth is tomorrow's error. Can one say that in the course of time truths tend to become fixed? Almost the opposite is true. Before the sciences were established, the acknowledged truths were almost unchanging for centuries. Religious truths did not change, at least for the faithful. It is with the growth of science that we see the emergence of diversity and change. Not so long ago, of course, it was still believed that there existed, at least in science, only one truth; it was even believed that science brings us the total and definitive truth. But today we know that this is not so:

The enormously rapid multiplication of theories in these latter days has well-nigh upset the notion of any one of them being a more literally objective kind of thing than another. There are so many geometries, so many logics, so many physical and chemical hypotheses, so many classifications, each one of them good for so much and yet not good for everything, that the notion that even the truest formula may be a human device and not a literal transcript has dawned upon us.[8]

Truth is thus a living thing, that changes ceaselessly; and the more we advance, the clearer this life of truth becomes. A truth that ceased to be flexible and malleable would be no more than 'the dead heart of the living tree' (*Pragmatism*, p. 65).

What a difference there is between the ideal, immutable truth of dogmatism and the real, concrete truths that we experience! Their characters are diametrically opposed. The former can only discredit the latter, since the ideal truth is sufficient in itself. But ideal truth is inaccessible to us. Thus we tend to lose interest in real truths, since they seem to be of little importance when compared to ideal truth. Intransigent rationalism risks finishing as *scepticism*,[9] since it places its ideal too high, at a level where we cannot attain it.

But let us see whether the very nature of reality permits us to attribute this unity and fixity to truth. Reality includes both *mind* and *things*. And by what are minds[10] characterized if not by their extreme diversity? A single understanding, common to all, does not exist; what exists are understandings that differ greatly from each other. Hence if truth is one, the diversity of minds can only prevent men from discovering this truth that is always one and identical with itself. On the other hand, why are minds so diverse? We have just seen that this diversity is an obstacle to the perfect communion of all men in one truth. Why does it exist if the ideal is an essentially impersonal truth? It is the source of 'logical sin', as well as of moral sin, and it remains totally inexplicable (in Leibnitz's doctrine, in particular, where the plurality of monads raises an insoluble problem).

Is it not simpler and more logical to say that the diversity of minds corresponds to a diversity in truth and in reality itself? 'What right have we', asks Schiller, 'to assume that even ultimate "truth" must be one and the same for all? ... Why should not the "truth", too ... adjust itself to the differences of individual experience ... ?' (Schiller, *Studies in Humanism*, p. 360.) Why not admit that what is true for one is not necessarily true for another and, thus, that truth is something much more complex than current rationalism admits? Here, the pragmatists give us some examples that, to be honest, do not always prove their point, like the one that Schiller offers us.[11] The judgement, 'this is a chair', can be true for me and not for another; if I am looking for something in which to sit, the chair is true for me in its function as a seat; but this may not be true, or may be true in a different way, for somebody else – an antique dealer or collector for instance – who sees in it 'a piece of antique, ornamental furniture'.

According to the pragmatists, the final difficulty presented by the dogmatic conception is that when one accepts that there is a single truth, when one does not understand that there is a reason for the diversity of judgement and opinions, one runs the risk of ending up in *intolerance*. The truly tolerant man not only admits that among thoughts there are differences that must be respected and that one does not have the right to do violence to the consciences of people, but also understands that the diversity of opinions and beliefs corresponds to a necessity, to the demands of emotional and intellectual life. In short, if these divergencies exist, *it is good* that they do.

Thus pragmatism is very keenly aware of the diversity of minds and the living character of truth. But it fails to explain them. It runs headlong into a problem of general philosophy which goes far beyond it: why are there individuals? What is the reason for the existence of the diversity of minds?

Criticism of dogmatism*

THE STATIC CONCEPTION OF REALITY

Let us sum up what we have said so far. (1) If truth is impersonal, it becomes foreign to man, dehumanized and located outside our lives. (2) If truth is the same for all men, it is impossible to understand the reason for the existence of the diversity of minds, which, nevertheless, must have a function in general life. (3) If truth is identical for all, conformity becomes the rule, dissidence is an evil, and 'logical evil' can be explained no better than moral evil.

Let us add that if one sees truth as the rationalists do, that is, as something that is static, immutable in time and space, and the expression of reality, then reality, too, must be conceived of as eternally remaining in a stationary state. If, on the contrary, reality is something alive that continuously changes and engenders something new, truth must follow it in its transformations, and must also change and live.

But, it can be asked, why does reality change? Where does this change come from? If the universe is tending toward something, it is because it lacks something. The universe is not yet completely reality. Perhaps this change is only illusory, and novelty is only appearance. It is easy to reply that what is referred to in this way as 'illusory' is precisely everything that gives life its interest. To deny or to diminish the reality of change is to remove everything that attaches us to things, and to depreciate both their value and the way they affect us. Yet this static conception of reality is so current that we find it even in the writings of those who, it seems to us, should be taking a different direction – an evolutionist like Herbert Spencer, for example. Although Spencer starts from a principle that should have led him to recognise universal change, he bases his argument on such notions as the indestructibility of matter and the conservation of energy, notions which are fundamentally incapable of justifying the conception of real progress or real change in the true

*Notes to the Fourth Lecture, of 6 January 1914, are on p. 118.

21

meaning of the world.[1] As a result, in his system change is only apparent; the basis of things always remain the same; and underlying everything is the homogeneity of the universe. Spencer allows for a kind of cosmic 'diastole' consisting of a process of differentiation, but which has as its counterpart a 'systole' which brings everything back to homogeneity, so that in the last analysis the universe finds itself restored to its former state, 'neither richer nor poorer, neither better nor worse'.

It is very difficult to limit oneself to a conception which, if pushed to its logical consequences, leads us back to the notion of a reality that is always the same, a notion that can only end in an attitude of detachment from existence. It has been said that the conclusion that one might draw from this notion is that we ourselves are only illusions and transitory appearances and that this is the reason why we attach so much value to something which is merely illusory and passing. But does this not amount to recognizing, in a sense, the reality of what is called illusory? Does it not give a meaning to these so-called appearances?[2]

Our inclination to visualize everything under the aspect of immutability is actually only an expediency. It is a means of giving the mind a sort of intellectual security. There are intellects that feel the need to base themselves on something fixed, to have a ready-drawn line of conduct that admits neither hesitation nor doubt, to tell themselves that there are no two ways of acting and thus no necessity to find out which of them is better. Such intellects need a ready-made discipline, a pre-established truth and code of laws. Otherwise they feel disoriented. All change, risk and attempts at exploration cause them disquiet and uneasiness. Hence the very natural tendency to believe in immutable truth and immutable realities. According to the pragmatists, this is the attitude that is characteristic of the rationalist mind: it represents a need for stability and assurance, ultimately, for repose.

But at what price, say the pragmatists, is this assurance acquired! It calms us, but it removes the reality of life, it impoverishes life by simplifying it, and the means by which it is obtained is purely illusory. For that matter, what difference does it make whether there is a code of laws written in advance, a predetermined truth? We should still have to discover these laws, and in this sense too they would still be of our making. We must discover them with our human faculties, and we must use them with our human forces. For this we can count on no one but ourselves. We are abandoned to ourselves on the 'raft of our experience', and even if there were 'absolute sailing-directions', the only assurance we have of our being able to follow them lies 'in our human equipment'. Human caprice and, along with it, human error are always possible: 'All the sanctions of a law of truth lie in the very texture of experience. Absolute or no absolute, the concrete truth for us will always be that way of thinking in which our various experiences most profitably combine' (*The Meaning of Truth* [pp. 71, 72 and] p. 73).

The sense that dominates pragmatism is thus the very opposite of that which inspires dogmatism. It is the sense of everything that is variable and plastic in things. For it, the universe is something unfinished, something never completely realized; there is a gap between what is and what will be, just as between what is and what was. The world is rich in boundless possibilities, which can be heightened as circumstances permit. 'For rationalism (James says) reality is ready-made and completed from all eternity, while for pragmatism it is still in the making, and waits part of its completion from the future. On the one side, the universe is absolutely secure, on the other it is still pursuing its adventures' (*Pragmatism*, p. 257). And the novelties that can be produced in this way not only affect superficial details, but may also draw in the essential.

The principal factor of novelty in the world is *consciousness*. As soon as consciousness appears, it introduces something new. Take, for instance, the constellation of the Great Bear.[3] Who made out seven stars in it and counted them? Who noticed its very vague resemblance to the form of an animal? Incontestably, it was man. Of course, we can say that before he did these things, there were the seven stars arranged in this way. But their number and their arrangement were only implicit or virtual. One condition was missing, and that condition was 'the act of the counting and comparing mind'. Man seems to be limited to translating, to *discovering*. But, in a sense, he also adds and creates: he creates the number seven; he creates the resemblance.

His thought is not a *copy* of the real: it is a true *creation*. This novelty that the mind contributes is still more apparent where the future is concerned. In this case, our judgements become generators of acts that change the character of *future reality*. This is particularly true of the representations that precede important acts, namely, beliefs.[4] Belief creates reality itself: belief in success is the best condition for succeeding; belief that one is in good health is a condition for feeling well. Here, thought is not an expression of what is; it is a factor in the reality that is to come. Consequently, reality itself is not something fixed and decreed, something enclosed within unsurmountable boundaries. Reality advances ceaselessly with human experience. As that experience extends, it encroaches on the void and is itself enriched. From this arises an essential idea on which all pragmatism rests: *thought, linked to action, in a sense creates reality itself.*

This idea is important. The physical world doubtless seems to have reached a sort of equilibrium. We no longer witness the genesis of new species of living beings. Such creations are always taking place in the moral realm, however.[5] All human societies, far from remaining always identical with themselves, are forces that develop. More complex societies in which new forces arise are appearing. We see these forces at work in the present, although we can no longer visualize them in the past except statically. Be this as it may, there is a whole domain of reality that has manifestly been created by thought: social reality. And this example is certainly the most significant that can be cited.

Thus it is understandable that, since reality is not something completed, truth cannot be something immutable. Truth is not a ready-made system: it is formed, de-formed and re-formed in a thousand ways; it varies and evolves like all things human. In order to make this idea understood, James compares truth to law or justice, to language or grammar. Magistrates and professors sometimes seem to believe that there is only one justice, one code of laws, one truth: the Truth. In reality, according to James, 'Truth, law and language fairly boil away from them at the least touch of novel fact ... Our rights, wrongs, prohibitions, penalties, words, forms, idioms, beliefs, are so many new creations that add themselves as fast as history proceeds' (*Pragmatism* p. 242). But 'these things *make themselves*', they are not ready-made; and it is the same with truth as with other things: truth is an uninterrupted process of changes.

Some remarks are necessary here. The pragmatists certainly show us how truth is enriched and becomes more complex. But does it necessarily follow that truth changes, properly speaking? If, for example, new species develop, are the laws of life changed thereby? In the same way, it is certain that new social species have appeared; but does this give us the right to conclude from this that the laws of life in society are no longer the same? Let us not confuse the enrichment of truth (or of reality) with the fugitive nature of truth. Pragmatism is keenly aware of the fact that what is true for one time may not be true for another. But how inconclusive its proofs are. We said before that its representatives have never felt compelled to give a systematic exposition. Very similar arguments that seem to come to the same conclusion are expounded separately, and the same example is couched sometimes in one form, sometimes in another. Nevertheless, it is the feeling that animates pragmatism, more than its modes of argument, that is of particular interest to us. Pragmatism has always had an intense feeling for the diversity of minds and the variability of thought in time. Hence the diversity of names by which it has designated itself: pragmatism, humanism, pluralism and so on.

Criticism of dogmatism

The implication of this last point is quite clear. What has preceded shows us how the debate between pragmatism and rationalism comes to involve, according to James,[6] not only the theory of knowledge but also the manner in which 'the structure of the universe itself' is conceived. The same antithesis that exists between the static truth of the rationalists, and the fugitive truth that is dear to the pragmatists, also exists between the *monist* and *pluralist* conceptions of the universe. If the universe is actually one in the sense that it forms a closely linked system, all the elements of which imply each other, a system where the whole commands the existence of the parts and where individuals are only appearances that in sum constitute one being, then change is impossible. For the place of each element is determined by the whole and the whole, in its turn, is determined by the elements. This is the monist point of view.

Why, James asks, is there this superstition, this religion of the number 'one'? (*Pragmatism*, p. 132.) In what way is 'one' 'superior' to 'forty-three', for example? Moreover, there are many ways of conceiving of this unity. There is no doubt that in one sense, the world is one. But why would it not be one, as it is from the *pluralist* point of view, in the sense that it is made up of parts which are linked to each other by certain relationships, but which, nevertheless, remain distinct and retain a certain independence, a certain autonomy, so that there is room for change, diversity and contingency?

Let us take up in the pragmatist position and consult facts and experience.[7] To begin with, we see that the world is one in the sense that it is the object of a representation: for thought and discourse it is one. But this in no way leads us to monism; for, in this sense, 'chaos', once it is named, has as much unity as 'cosmos'. The world is also one in the sense that all of its parts are continuous[8] in space and time, but this unity is completely external: for pragmatism, space and time are only 'vehicles of continuity'. A more profound unity results from the internal actions and reactions, from the influences that each part of the world exercises on the other parts. The propagation of heat, electricity and light are examples of these influences that unite everything in the physical world. Thus there is an infinity of networks that are made up of various 'lines of influence', networks that are little worlds that serve as a basis for our action. Many things, however, fall outside these lines of influence. In addition, we must choose suitable intermediaries. If, for example, we insert a substance that is a poor conductor into an electrical circuit, the current either does not pass or must make a detour, leaving the substance outside its path. James says that such networks also exist in the moral world. Men are enmeshed in vast networks of social relations. Suppose that A knows B, B knows C and C knows D: it is then possible to get a message from A to D. But here, too, we are stopped short when we make a bad choice in one of our intermediaries. If by chance B does not know C, the message does not arrive at its destination. There are also lines of sympathy that spread and develop and are organized in different groups. The more a society evolves, the more these lines of sympathy organize themselves and the more they multiply. Thus, in every society there are systems that link individuals to each other – religious systems, professional groups and so on – and these links cause moral forces to communicate themselves to all members of the group.[9] Sometimes, as in economic relations, this communication is more capricious. But each group is foreign to the others, so that a society that is one in appearance is, in reality, composed of a multitude of small groups or small social worlds which, although they sometimes come into conjunction, live their own lives and remain basically external to one another.

From this we see in what unity and plurality consist for the pragmatists. There is a unity for them, but it is not that of the monists. The world is made up of an incalculable number of networks that unite things and beings with each other. These networks are formed of complicated and relatively independent links. The elements that they connect are not fixed, and the very form of the network is subject to change. Made up of a plurality of small systems, each of which is endowed with an autonomous life, it is ceaselessly formed, de-formed and trans-formed.

The pluralism of the pragmatists is thus opposed to the monism of the rationalists. For the former, multiplicity is as real as unity: there is both union and disjunction. The 'all-form' exists, according to James,[10] but 'the *each* form', the particular form of each element, 'is logically as acceptable and empirically as probable'. Indeed, there is an 'all', but in this 'all', there is a certain free play. The world is a federal republic that leaves a large degree of autonomy to each of its parts; it is not a monarchical society. For example, we can visualize the physical universe as a world in which all things are inert; with, above it, a world in which there is only mechanical manifestations, a world of forces, and so on. In the same way, we can conceive of conscious beings doing completely without each other, or of men loving or hating reciprocally; finally, we can imagine all minds entering into communication, intermixing completely. The unity becomes more complete, and yet it always remains partial, relative and progressive. The world is not, James indicates,[11] anything rigid, formal and bureaucratic; it does not have the beautiful order that the rationalists perceive in it – the rationalists for whom the pragmatists' world is a 'strung-along' universe.

In spite of the interest of this argument, one is right to wonder whether it reaches what is essential in rationalism. Rationalism admits that the function of truth is to translate reality. Pragmatism tries to show that reality is neither immutable nor the same for all persons, and it concludes that truth cannot be a copy of reality. But why should the copy not evolve like the model? In order to prove that it does not, it would have to be demonstrated that thought cannot be a copy, not only of an immutable reality, but of any reality whatever. It would have to be proved, in other words, that there is a radical heterogeneity between reality and thought. The pragmatists have not demonstrated this.[12]

In the last years of his life, however, James gleaned such a demonstration from the works of Bergson. In Bergson, whom he considered the destroyer of intellectualism, James believed that he found his best arguments.

The criticism of conceptual thought*

Pragmatist criticism, as I have said, does not seem to have reached the basic principle of rationalism. This criticism mainly attacks the notion of the copy theory of truth. But why, we have asked, should true thought not be the variable copy of a variable model? And, in addition, is it quite so evident that a copy, as a duplicate of reality, is useless? It is not a question of knowing whether it is useful, but of knowing whether it is true. At the end of the last lecture, I said that in order to establish the pragmatist thesis, it would be necessary to prove that thought and reality are essentially heterogeneous. James attempted this demonstration in chapter VI of *A Pluralistic Universe*, basing it on Bergson's arguments. This chapter is entitled 'Bergson and his critique of intellectualism'.

Let us examine these arguments as he presents them. According to James, truth presupposes judgements, and judgements presuppose concepts. Thus it is apparently conceptual thought, and it alone, that can be the generator of truth. But in order for this to be the case, there would have to be a natural affinity between the concept and the things. For James, on the contrary, as for Bergson, the real and the concept have opposite characteristics.

1.   The concept[1] is something *definite* and distinct; it is the very opposite of such vague, shifting and confused representations as images. Cut out from the stream of our experience, the concept is circumscribed within very narrow limits. Whereas impressions mutually interpenetrate each other in the sensory flux of images, concepts are isolated from each other. There is no contact or confusion among them, such as that which takes place among images.

2.   Each concept expresses one aspect of things and only that aspect. Doubtless there are concepts that express things or groups of things, but these are compound concepts. The true and pure concept is *simple*. It is analogous to what in Descartes is the object of intuition; one moves toward it but never reaches it. In everyday life, of course, we use

*Notes to the Fifth Lecture, of 13 January 1914, are on pp. 118–19.

28

complex, loosely contoured concepts, because they have not been systematically defined. But the concept, properly speaking, requires definition and limitation, so that when we use it we think it alone and nothing else. The characteristic feature of the concept is to be an *isolated* representation, because it must express only one thing or one aspect of the thing, one condition, one element.

3.   Because concepts have this character, the principle of identity or non-contradiction dominates all of conceptual life: 'For conceptual logic, the same is nothing but the same, and all sames with a third thing are the same with each other.'[2] The concept is what it is and cannot be anything else. Consequently, in order for conceptual thought to be a copy of reality, reality would have to be constituted according to the same model; that is to say, it must be made up of stable elements that are entirely distinct from each other and have no reciprocal communication; and things themselves must have the same discontinuous, finite and separate character. But, says James, nature presents diametrically opposed characteristics: reality is continuous and ceaselessly in formation. 'What really exists, is not things made but things in the making. Once made, they are dead; and an infinite number of alternative conceptual decompositions can be used in defining them.'[3] If we admit even for an instant that reality consists of stable and distinct elements, how can we tell the number of these elements? In order to be consistent, the rationalists must recognize that this number is infinite and, consequently, that the number of concepts necessary to translate these elements, too, is infinite. But since an infinite number cannot be an actual, real thing, no movement can ever be completed or finished. If a moving object must traverse an infinite number of points, it will never reach the end, since the end always remains outside the series. (This is the old argument of Achilles and the tortoise which was developed by Zeno.) Thus the universe is condemned to immobility.

Yet movement and change do occur. 'This paradox ... gives trouble then', says James, 'only if the succession of steps of change can be infinitely divisible.' But change does not take place in this fashion, by an infinity of infinitesimal modifications; it is rather accomplished by units of a certain size, of a certain extent, that is, by finite quantities. If, when we empty a bottle, it were necessary for its contents to undergo 'an infinite number of successive decrements', the operation would never end. The bottle is emptied by a finite number of diminutions, each of a finite quantity. 'Either a whole drop emerges or nothing emerges from the spout.' It is thus, 'by discrete pulses', that change takes place in the world; and every time one of these 'pulsations' takes place, we say, 'here is something more' or 'here is something less'. The discontinuity is still more evident when something new appears or something old disappears. 'Fechner's term of the "threshold", which has played such a part in the psychology of perception, is only one way of naming the quantitative discreteness in the change of all our sensible experiences.'[4]

Does James's argument really meet intellectualism? We may well doubt it. The greatest contemporary rationalist, Charles Renouvier, who has demonstrated the impossibility of an actual infinity of parts, takes up Zeno's arguments.[5] Thus to insist on this impossibility is not necessarily to ruin intellectualism. Moreover, the question is secondary. It is much less important to know whether the number of parts making up the world is finite or infinite than it is to know whether these parts are, or are not, distinct.

What are James's arguments on this point? According to him, concepts are something *stable*. In order to express movement and change, each concept would have to express one of the states through which the movement passes. But to resolve the movement into *states* is to make of it something fixed. The concept can therefore express movement only by stopping it at a given instant, by immobilizing it.[6] The only way of making concepts coincide with changes is to stipulate arbitrarily the points at which the change stops, since it is these stopping-points that our concepts can express. But all we obtain in this way is a discontinuous series of positions and dates, with which it is impossible to reconstitute movement and change. In the first place, a series of concepts that expresses pauses or stops cannot translate what moves. This is the old argument of the Eleatic school: the arrow in flight is motionless because if we consider a position of the arrow at any given moment in its course, this position is necessarily a state of rest. In the second place, if concepts were to be capable of expressing change, change would have to be divided up and fragmented into discontinuous elements. But how can we make the discontinuous into the continuous? How can we reconstitute the unity of change once this unity is broken? A void, however small it may be, separates concepts that express a position or state of something changing from other concepts, and this void is impossible to fill. In this way we obtain only 'a retrospective patchwork, a postmortem dissection'.[7]

This is all the more serious because what changes is the very soul of things, the essential. This is precisely what the concept is unable to express. Concepts can give us a 'synoptic picture' of phenomena; but the metaphysician who is trying to grasp reality in depth, whose curiosity bears on the intimate nature of things and on that which moves them, will have to 'turn his back on ... concepts'. Thus conceptual thought 'touches only the outer surface' of things; it is incapable of 'penetrating' reality.[8]

Here is another way of expressing the same idea: what makes up the reality of things is the network of *influences* they exert on each other. My thought *acts* on my body; it animates it. A movement of my body exteriorizes this thought, and by means of this intermediary my thought communicates with that of others. James writes that things must be able to combine, to 'compenetrate and telescope'.[9] But, he says, 'Intellectualism denies ... that finite things can act on one another, for all things, once translated into concepts, remain shut up to themselves'.[10] Concepts 'make the whole notion of a causal influence between finite things incomprehensible'.[11] From the point of view of conceptual logic, all distinctions are 'isolators'. Contagion of concepts would be confusion, and confusion is the major logical sin.

A fortiori, life itself cannot be converted into concepts, since 'the essence of life is its continuously changing character'.[12] A living being is a being who not only is, at a given moment, different from what he was before, but also one who is, at the same instant, himself and different from himself. The Achilles who is pursuing the tortoise is not only the being who, at a given moment, coincides with a certain determined space; he is also the being who is dashing, and this dash is a concrete fact in which the moments of time and the divisions of space are indivisibly involved: 'End and beginning come for him in the one onrush.'[13]

But it is just the same from a *static* point of view. It is not life alone that is made up of a network of actions and relationships. Let us consider any being whatever: it is constituted of a group of traits, among all of which and in the whole of which there is solidarity: any one of them can be isolated only artificially. Neither can its present be isolated from its past and future. The same is true for things. There is no one single concept of a thing. Each thing includes a plurality of elements, and each element, a plurality of elements.

What is the result of all this? Conceptual thought lives by distinctions, while the world is continuous, and the continuous is vague and confused. This antithesis explains the great *prestige* that has been given to concepts. Conceptual thought longs for fixity and hence for precision and clarity; it is very aloof to all that is fleeting. 'The ruling tradition in philosophy has always been the platonic and aristotelian belief that fixity is a nobler and worthier thing than change. Reality must be one and unalterable. Concepts, being themselves fixities, agree best with this fixed nature of truth ...'[14] When it had succeeded in establishing a

31

system of these immobile concepts, philosophic thought experienced great self-admiration and believed that what it had created was truth itself. It was Plato's illusion to believe that above this changing and fleeting world there exists a world of fixed and immutable essences. He was taking fiction for reality. Inevitably, James says, 'Logic being the lesser thing ... must succumb to reality' (*A Pluralistic Universe*, p. 207). We must bow before the facts; reality must be seen as greater than reason. And the result of this chain of reasoning, too, is that the principle of identity and the law of non-contradiction do not apply to reality.[15]

DEFICIENCIES OF THIS CRITICISM

The gravity of this consequence helps us to perceive a deficiency no less grave in James's thought. He does not explain to us how it happens that logical thought, based on the principle of identity, can serve to guide us in the midst of things to which, according to him, the principle of identity does not apply. Actually, none of the pragmatists really thinks that conceptual thought is useless, even though it is not a copy of reality. James says that it is largely inspired by 'the interests of practice'.[16] But how can conceptual thought play this role if it has no common measure with reality? Moreover, James himself recognizes that these concepts, 'cut out from the sensible flux of the past ... give us knowledge' and have 'some theoretic value'.[17] It is, in fact, very difficult to escape from concepts and logical principles. When James tells us that one cannot make something continuous from something discontinuous, is he not using a logical principle? Is he not affirming with the aid of conceptual thought something that touches on reality itself?[18]

To a very great extent, James's whole argument closely follows developments in Bergson. The positive conclusions at which the two men arrive are not identical, but their attitude toward classic rationalism is the same. Both have the same hypersensitivity to everything that is mobile in things, the same tendency to present reality in its obscure and fugitive aspect, the same inclination to subordinate clear and distinct thought to the troubled aspect of things. But the main thing that James has borrowed from Bergson is the form of argumentation that directly challenges conceptual thought. His fundamental ideas had already been in his thought for a long time, as is shown by his earlier *Principles of Psychology*, where he insisted, for example, on the perfect continuity of the 'stream' of consciousness.[19]

+++

The secondary aspects of pragmatism*

Let us recapitulate. What pragmatists chiefly object to is the view that the true idea is a copy of reality. The arguments we have described are not peculiar to James, but are found in all other pragmatists, even if they do not always express their thought in such a well-defined form. They have clearly felt, furthermore, that there is a contrast between the confused complexities of reality and the characteristics of logical thought, and are at one in refusing to grant to such thought the pride of place which it has always enjoyed in rationalism. This is the common feature of their philosophy and that of M. Bergson.

But pragmatism is not wholly contained within these basic theses. It has secondary aspects which are, in fact, no less important. Pragmatism is really a metaphor of its own way of seeing the world and, like that image of the world, it is polymorphous and takes on appearances which are so varied that it is difficult to grasp them precisely. We have so far considered it mainly as a form of *continuism*. It can also, however, be seen as a form of *radical empiricism* and of *pluralism*.

Pragmatism and radical empiricism

'Radical empiricism', as defined by James, is that doctrine which acknowledges nothing outside of experience. 'Experience as a whole is self-containing and deems on nothing' (*The Meaning of Truth*, p. 124). For that to be so, experience must be explained in its own terms, and the world must contain within itself all the principles necessary for its own explanation. What does 'explaining' mean, in fact? For pragmatists, as for us, it means establishing relationships between things. There are, however, two mutually exclusive possibilities. Either one admits that reality is composed of distinct parts, with the relationships which unite them necessarily external to such parts. To say that things are discontinuous is to say that their elements are separate and distinct, and

*Notes to the Sixth Lecture, of 20 January 1914, are on pp. 119–20.

consequently that they do not contain within themselves the principle which unifies them. This principle must therefore be outside the things themselves, in *thought*, which creates these relationships and imposes them from without, whether such thought be that of a man or that of an absolute spirit, as in the system of Thomas Hill Green.[1] But once one posits in this way an absolute which is external to reality, one is compelled to go beyond experience and to abandon empiricism.

On the other hand – and this second hypothesis is that adopted by James – the world is continuous and everything in the universe is linked. One cannot say of any given part of it that it 'extends to such and such a point and no further', for each part compenetrates every other, and they 'support each other'. In this sense, 'relations of every sort, of time, space, difference, likeness, change, rate, cause, or what not are just as integral members of the sensational flux as terms are', this being true of both conjunctive and disjunctive relationships.[2] These relationships can be experienced, and are therefore as real as the terms which they unite; and change also, which is itself a fact of experience, is one among these conjunctive relationships.[3] To experience things means to move continuously from one term to another, trying and testing the links between them.

This, for James, is what constitutes *radical empiricism*. But why is it described as radical? The intention, James himself tells us,[4] is to distinguish it 'from the doctrine of mental atoms which the word "empiricism" so often suggests' – and in particular from the empiricism of Hume, which believes that it restricts itself to reality by refusing to admit any links at all between things. In Hume's view, experience consists of heterogeneous, and consequently unrelated, elements, and is pure discontinuity and chaos. It involves 'no manner of connection'; each act of perception is a distinct 'existence', and 'the mind never perceives any real connection among distinct existences'.[5] Empiricism of this kind, however, which sees such discontinuous experience as necessarily self-sufficient, must remain an incomplete explanation. It means that for the mind there is still one way of escaping from experience, a way that Kant was to use when, moving from Hume's concept of the 'rhapsody of perceptions', he re-established the idea of a reality which both anticipated and lay beyond experience, in the world of *choses en soi*, or 'things-in-themselves'.[6]

There is, however, one discontinuist doctrine which James does not mention, that of *radical idealism* as described by Hamelin in his *Essay on the Main Elements of Representation*.[7] In this, reality is indeed considered as being formed of discontinuous elements, namely con-

cepts, which are defined, marked out and distinct from each other. And yet in this view the real world certainly does not owe its unity to an external source. The innumerable concepts of which reality is composed attract each other, reach out to each other and are related to each other. In his book, Hamelin tries to reconstitute and construct categories: there are links between them, and here too one can say that the elements which make up reality have no existence outside of the relationships which unite them. Reality has an immanent unity. Neither James nor Dewey took that solution into account; and they did not see that radical idealism enables one to conceptualize reality as made up of a system of elements, but without requiring that one goes beyond the system of thought itself. This way of seeing things was nevertheless worth examining. In one sense it is perhaps only another way of expressing the continuist hypothesis of radical empiricism. Its author, of course, would never have admitted such an interpretation, but there is certainly a great affinity between the two concepts.

What characterizes radical empiricism is its emphasis upon the absolute uniformity of existence. It refuses to admit the idea that there are two worlds, that of experience and that of reality. One of James's most frequent objections to Spinoza[8] concerns the latter's distinction between nature as a creator and nature as created. He sees this distinction as inadmissible. For him, things do not possess this double aspect. They all exist at the same level, on the same plane, and thought too moves on just one plane. In this way radical empiricism differs from simple empiricism, which takes the opposite view and insists on the separateness of mind and things. James criticizes simple empiricism for not seeing the wood for the trees, and for not perceiving that the whole of reality and the whole of thought are on the same plane and are part of the same process.

Pragmatism as pluralism

We can now see what comprises the other aspect of pragmatism, namely, its 'pluralism'. This idea does not imply absence of unity, but rather a certain kind of unity; what has been called an 'untidy' unity[9] or, in other words, a unity of a very supple and totally flexible kind. In the continuous mass of things, each one is closely related to others. This unity, however, does not imply immutability, as each thing can separate itself from its surroundings and enter into other relationships; and thus each object, when it changes its context, also changes its nature. What makes it so easy for one and same thing to assume such a diversity of forms is the fact that, just as the whole of reality is multiple, so each element of that reality itself contains a certain complexity, a multitude of different characteristics. It is easy to imagine that a thing which has a relationship with other things through one or other of its characteristics can dissolve that relationship when circumstances induce it to combine with others, and that a host of possible combinations exists. Nothing real is simple, and each relationship is only one of the variable aspects of the characteristics or actions of things.

The true meaning of pluralism can thus be seen. The implication is not that the world consists of a plurality of elements which are alien to each other. The expression should not be understood literally. It could even be said that in one sense, pragmatism is *monistic*, and that to a far greater degree than metaphysical monism itself. Pragmatism affirms the unity of the world, but it is a unity which is supple, flexible, polymorphous and consisting of a mass of phenomena which is undivided but ever-changing, like a lake in which the water, blown about by the wind, looks different at every moment, as it separates and comes together again, moving and changing in a thousand different ways. The appearance of the lake changes, but the water is the same. The idea of a unity that is at once variable and lasting is one consequence of the continuist hypothesis.

All these different aspects of pragmatism are interlinked, and pragmatism itself is a doctrine which is both unitary and varied.

THE POSITIVE THESES OF PRAGMATISM

This concludes our examination of the *negative* aspects of pragmatism, which basically amounts to a criticism of rationalism. We must now examine the *positive* doctrine it claims to put in the place of that rationalism. Increasingly, our difficulty will be the lack of agreement about the theses of pragmatism. Each writer presents the doctrine in his own way. Just as was the case with its negative aspects, no complete overall treatment is available. Despite several divergencies, there is nevertheless a general line of thought which is followed by all those who share these views. The fact that no co-ordination has yet been achieved can only make the work all the more interesting.

The various arguments which pragmatists use against rationalism are doubtless not all equally valid. It is, however, certain that rationalism must come to terms with these criticisms and, to some extent, modify its own position. The best way of assessing the value of the objections to rationalism is to consider the theoretical consequences to which pragmatism is led by them. Basing itself upon these objections, pragmatism claims to have abolished rationalism. We must try to find out how solid the 'edifice' is, bearing in mind that our task is not to reconstitute a doctrine from mere curiosity, but rather to draw potentially instructive conclusions from it.

The central problem of pragmatism is the *problem of truth*. Its doctrine can be summarized for the time being in the following three basic theses:

1 Truth is human
2 It is varied and variable
3 It cannot be a copy of a given reality.

Thought and reality

We will first consider the third thesis, and have indeed already commented on it to some extent. To say that truth is not a copy implies an admission that the value of an idea is not seen by its relationship with a present, given reality. Put another way, the criterion of the truth of an idea is not to be sought *behind* it but *before* it. It is not its relationship with something already in existence that needs to be considered, but its relationship with something which is to be brought into existence. Thus, any idea is in a close relationship with action, and it is through its relationship with the action to which it gives rise that its character as truth must be appreciated (Dewey, *Essays In Logic*, Chap. I; Moore, *Pragmatism and its Critics*).[10]

Let us imagine an organism which finds everything that it needs in the milieu in which it lives. It will function mechanically. Consciousness will not appear, as there will be no need for it. That is precisely what happens in the case of beings who only act within a limited sphere. What is true of consciousness is even more true of *reflection*, of *thought* in its real sense, which Dewey distinguishes very carefully from what he calls 'constitutive' thought.[11] To the extent that its sensations meet its needs, there is no problem; the animal senses whether an object is or is not what it wants, and moves away from it or towards it according to that sensation. That is what constitutes simple consciousness.

As soon as there is tension or conflict, however, the situation changes. If the animal does not find what it needs, the sensation alone is no longer enough, and it has to seek the new something which contains what it needs, it has to 'reflect', to wonder where it will find it. Reflection therefore only occurs when a choice is necessary, and it is then that thought, in the proper sense of the word, lying neither in instinct, routine nor habit, comes into existence.[12] Reflective thought, or 'knowledge', appears in very special conditions, at a cross-roads situation in which the being is faced with a whole range of possible solutions. And, in such a situation, what are our feelings? Uncertainty, tension, anxiety.[13] We try to bring the situation to an end and to re-establish the lost equilibrium. The aim of thought is therefore not to contemplate what is. The very opposite is the case. That which is finished, fully achieved, serves to anaesthetize consciousness. The function of thought, far from being to express what is clearly defined or established, is to bring into being what does not yet exist, to procure what is missing and to fill a vacuum. It is not directed towards the past or even the present, but completely turned towards the future, looking *forwards*. Its function is not *speculative*, but primarily *practical*: it is an initial awareness of the act, an initial stimulus to accomplish it, as the action begins to take shape in the mind and the whole being. Thought thus comes into existence not in order to *copy* reality, but to *change* it.

The rationalist objection here will be that thought merely adds itself to reality without transforming it, claiming that it is an exaggeration to maintain that the mere appearance of an idea involves a change in reality itself.

To this the pragmatist would reply that in fact reality is changed as soon as an idea appears. Moore[14] suggests the following example: I have toothache, and the mere idea that it *is* toothache, that the pain must come from such and such a tooth and so on, modifies the situation. The idea is not there in order to express pain. It is rather an instrument, a cause of the cessation of pain, perhaps a tiny cause of the reversal of the existing state of affairs, but nonetheless a cause.

Once that is granted, the place and the role of thought in the world appear in a quite different light. For rationalists, the mind is separated from reality by a kind of gulf, with mind on one edge and reality on the other, both belonging to different worlds. Pragmatists see things quite differently. In their view, thought and reality are part of *one and the same process*. The series sensation, idea and action is perfectly continuous. The datum gives rise to a sensation of tension, which gives rise to an idea, which in turn gives rise to action. This perfect continuum is the process of life itself, and thought cannot be separated from it, as it is one of a range of ways in which life functions. It is not outside of, or opposite to things, but belongs amongst them. There is thus a very close kinship between reality and thought. Both are instruments which co-operate in life, hence the term *instrumentalism* by which the Chicago School designates its own interpretation of pragmatism. Hume's empiricism saw two different levels for reality and the mind; but here the whole of reality is on the same level, with the mind in things and things in mind, with no discontinuity between them.

This idea is in no way peculiar to Dewey. We find it in James in perhaps an even clearer form, in particular in his famous article of 1904 entitled 'Does consciousness exist?'[15] in which he criticizes the generally held view of a division between consciousness and things, and from there goes on to see, as a result of the idea of *pure experience*, consciousness itself as an inseparable part of reality.[16]

Thought and reality*

Whereas most theorists see thought as a mirror which receives and reflects the image of things, for pragmatists, the opposite is the case: thought becomes a part of things. It is a vital organ, and its purpose is to re-establish equilibrium in a living organism whose functioning has been disturbed. In James, much more than in other pragmatists, thought is not only a part of the single continuous process which starts from reality in the form of a feeling of unease created by this disturbance, and then returns to reality and acts upon it. There is also, between things and thought, simply a difference of aspect and point of view. Reality is integrated into the active process of consciousness.

By his *Principles of Psychology*,[1] James saw the current notion of the subject on the one hand and the object on the other, with a radical difference between them, as untenable. If it were so, he maintained, knowledge would be impossible. First, let us suppose that we were to remove from consciousness everything that comes to it from outside. What would be left? Nothing but a faculty, a mere potentiality with no content, rather like Leibnitz's monad, which consists of 'perceptions', that is, of representations of the world, and which would be nothing if it were emptied of those representations. Secondly, there exists a whole series of attributes which are neither exclusively objective nor exclusively subjective and we apply these sometimes to thought, to states of awareness and sometimes to things. Thoughts, like things, can be complex or simple. They can be compared, added, subtracted, arranged in different series. They can be natural and easy, or laborious. We describe them as 'happy, intense, interesting, wise, idiotic, focal, marginal, insipid, confused, vague, precise, rational, casual, general [or] particular'.[2] The qualities which we appreciate are attributed by us to things; but, 'for example, does the beauty reside in the statue, in the sonata, or in our minds? . . . We speak of a terrible storm, a hateful man or an unworthy action, and we believe that we are speaking objectively,

*Notes to the Seventh Lecture, of 27 January 1914, are on pp. 120–1.

40

and that these terms only convey an account of our own emotional sensibilities.'[3] How could we apply these epithets indiscriminately to our subjective states and to external objects if both were not to some degree akin?

Since Descartes, it has been normal to define thought as something absolutely non-spatial, and to see body and soul as opposites in the same way as the extended and the unextended. But, James objects,[4] is it certain that consciousness has no spatial aspects? 'What possible meaning has it to say that, when we think of a foot-rule or a square yard, extension is not attributable to our thought? In every extended object the *adequate* mental picture must have all the extension of the object itself.' The only difference between objective and subjective space lies in the relation to a context. Subjective space is more flexible and elastic. Each of its parts is not linked to each of the others in a rigid relationship, whereas in the physical world they are linked to each other in a stable way.

In James, there is a very ancient idea, which can be seen as early as his *Principles of Psychology.* This is the idea that our sensations, of whatever nature, all have, to a more or less heightened degree, a spatial character. Our mental picture of a triangle has something of the triangle and hence something spatial. Even hearing, taste and internal sensations have an element of this kind.[5] The dialectical reason which led James to this conclusion is that if space were not already in our subjective representations, we should never have been able to construct the idea of it. The idea can be given a more general application: in the sensation of warmth, there is something which corresponds to warmth itself; a very forceful image can produce a sensation, which means that the image contains something of the same nature as the sensation. As we have already seen, the homogeneity is even greater if we consider properties which are *appreciated*: the perception of something beautiful is a 'beautiful' perception. Thus, there are in thought properties which in some way resemble the properties of objects. If object and thought were different, their respective contributions should be discernible, and these similarities would not be explicable. Subject and object are therefore a single and identical reality which, in different circumstances, have different contexts. 'In the final analysis, things and thoughts are in no wise completely heterogeneous: they are made of the same stuff, a stuff which cannot be defined as such, but only put to the test of experience, and which can be called, if one wishes to give it a name, the stuff of experience in general.'[6] This conclusion explains the paradox in James's title 'Does consciousness exist?'

41

Let us review, with James, the different types of knowledge. In *sensory perception*, the object perceived and our representation of it are the same: '*La réalité est l'aperception même*'.[7] Things are what we picture them as being. When I say 'the walls of this room', the words mean simply 'the fresh and sonorous whiteness around us in which there are these windows and which are framed by these lines and these angles'. Thus 'here the physical has just the same content as the psychic. Subject and object merge.' Things do not have an 'inner life' which is different from their appearance. If we restrict ourselves to their 'public life', which we know through our common sense, we shall see that they are homogeneous with thought.

Yet in one sense there is a certain duality. But where exactly is the difference? Duality can only become something verifiable and concrete if it is made 'an affair of relations'.[8]

A point is common to two lines if it lies at their intersection. In the same way, an object can be at two different points in reality at the same time. It is, to some extent, at the intersection of two processes which link it to two different groups of relationships; it is part of two contexts, two associative systems which overlap and cover some common ground.[9] On the one hand, as thought and representation, the object is an element of my personal biography, the end point of a series of sensations, feelings, memories, acts of the will, and the starting-point for a similar series of 'internal' operations extending into the future. On the other hand, as a 'thing', the object is part of another history, that of the physical operations which produce it.

The room one is in, for example, is a part of the history of the house. It owes its existence to the fact that architectural work, bricklaying, joinery, painting, furnishing and so on have been carried out, and it is also linked to other parts of the building. All that constitutes a group of facts and relationships quite different from those involved in my biography. That difference has a *practical* importance; for as a 'thing', the room can be destroyed by fire, for example, whereas as a 'representation' there is no risk of that. If I want to cancel it, I need only close my eyes. Thus, the properties *subject* and *object*, *represented* and *representation*, *thing* and *thought*, signify a practical distinction, which is of extreme importance, but which is of a FUNCTIONAL kind only, and in no way ontological as it has been represented in classical dualism.[10] Only one reality is perceived from the viewpoint of two distinct experiences.

What has been said of sensory perception can also be said of *images*, although we normally see our images as the opposites of objects. In our imagination, in dreams or when we daydream, the physical and the psychic are intermingled. If I dream of a mountain of gold, that mountain, in my dream, is of a perfectly physical nature.[11]

The same conclusion can be extended to *concepts*, for these are fragments of experience, and form an area co-ordinate with that of perceptions. Thus, like perceptions, they belong both to the context of objects and to that of our mental states and our 'inner history'.[12]

In short, in all our modes of knowledge, 'subjectivity and objectivity are functional attributes solely, realised only when the experience is "taken"',[13] but their unity remains radical as long as the two aspects of that experience are not divided up in terms of the two different contexts. There is a problem here: that of knowing what the context of the initial experience consists of, and what the prime stuff of the seats of subjectivity might be. According to James, these primary seats consist of *internal sensations*, muscular and respiratory sensations and so on. In them, there is nowadays an even more blurred distinction between the internal and the external than in any other. In our first sensations of movement, however, 'the whole world was moving with us'; and this is still found in certain illusions of movement or in states of vertigo.[14]

The unity of knowledge and existence

These developments are of importance because they show the extent to which the pragmatists insist on *the unity of the level of existence and that of knowledge*. Once more, the pragmatist 'pluralism' ultimately leads to what is really *monism*: subject and object are made of the same substance. The prime datum is neither the mind nor things, but 'pure experience'. Hence, what for pragmatists is the major stumbling-block in classical philosophy, the gap between thought and reality, disappears.

But what then becomes of knowledge? It is no longer the *salto mortale* needed to project the mind into the world of things. In order to reach that world, thought need only take the intermediate steps which lead imperceptibly to reality. Thus (1) The whole doctrine rests on the basic notion of that continuity; (2) we have already also noted that conception precedes, particularly in James's case, *the pragmatist theses*, and had already been formulated in *The Principles of Psychology*; (3) if knowledge is to be possible, it seems that there must be a certain kinship between reality and thought. For the idealists, thought is essentially the concept, and it is that concept which is at the basis of reality. For James, it is rather the opposite which is the case: reality is at the basis of the concept. These are no more than two forms of the same way of seeing things.

This position of pragmatism calls for a comment. It is rather strange to find pragmatism, which had originally posited the concept as different from reality, finally adopt such a solution.[15] This, moreover, is not the only contradiction to be found within the doctrine, indicating the possible scope for critical review that there is in it. The objection is even greater if we consider knowledge as primarily *an instrument of action*. This is precisely the thesis of pragmatism.

Pragmatism maintains that knowledge cannot be considered from any other point of view. If the world were to be suddenly paralysed, reduced to inaction, how could the true idea, which facilitates action, be distinguished from the false idea, which hampers or hinders it? It is *failure* which characterizes error, and is indeed the *penalty* for it. 'All the *sanctions* of a law of truth lie in the very texture of experience. Absolute or no absolute, the concrete truth *for us* will always be that way of thinking in which our various experiences most profitably combine.'[16] Every action has as its end something which is important in human terms. Consequently, a true idea has the same end. Thus truth is embodied in other vital human interests. The term *truth* is only, as Schiller says, a 'laudatory label'[17] which is applied decoratively to our experience to indicate its value.

The unity of truth and value

We should assess the consequences of these theses. Moral good, like the truth, serves our 'interests', our values. Hence, there is no longer any distinction between the true and the moral. The contrast between the true and the real instituted by Kantian thought disappears. The true and the good are simply two different aspects of the useful, the advantageous. 'The "true", to put it very briefly, is only the expedient in the way of our thinking, just as "the right" is only the expedient in the way of our behaving.'[18] Thus, 'truth is one species of good, and not, as is usually supposed, a category distinct from good, and coordinate with it'.[19] The only difference left between the two orders of values is one of degree, not of kind. We can see here the same tendency of pragmatism never to accept any solution of continuity. The useful and the good are values and, consequently, in that system of thought, all judgements, including judgements of truth as well as others, are value judgements. Logical value is not a separate value. There is only one value, *utility*, which merely assumes varying forms in particular cases.

44

Knowledge as an instrument of action*

Let us recall some of the ideas mentioned earlier. Once we have posited consciousness, with its own role, how can an object be both within me and outside me at the same time? It is inside me, the pragmatists reply, through its extension. Its extension, however, is still part of it. Hence there is certainly something of the object inside me.

We have seen this in the case of *sensation*. In a certain sense, the object radiates inside me. The effects which it produces are there at the same time and within the same space. Objects, moreover, are no more than our representations of them. Consequently, in the case of sensation, the object and its extension within us are indistinguishable.

With regard to the *image*, the difference between the object and the internal state seems greater for, although the image of the object is inside us, the external object is no longer present. No doubt, say the pragmatists: but between them there is a series of images which re-establishes continuity, and the link between the interior and the exterior, the subjective and the objective, is not broken, for it consists of imperceptible gradations. This explains why James can say that external objects are indistinguishable from our representations of them.

This will help us to understand other aspects of pragmatist doctrine. In that doctrine, the sole function of ideas is to guide our action. How, one might ask, can they do that if they are in no way a copy of reality? In the case of *sensation*, the question hardly arises. For all pragmatists, it should be repeated, sensation is indistinguishable from the object. For them, it is this *fusion* of subject and object which forms the basis for real knowledge. According to James: 'The maximal conceivable truth in an idea would seem to be that it should lead to an actual merging of ourselves with the object, to an utter mutual confluence and identification ... *Total conflux of the mind with the reality* would be the absolute limit of truth.'[1] One might even wonder whether, for the pragmatists, there is properly speaking such a thing as 'truth'. We should rather speak

*Notes to the Eighth Lecture, of 3 February 1914, are on pp. 121–2.

of an *identity* between subject and object, and that identity is so complete that there no longer seems any place for error.

With regard to the *image*, the same fusion is not possible, as there is then a distance between the two terms. As we have seen, however, that distance is not a void. When the image is a true one, it produces a series of connected images related to it, and if we follow the chain of these images, we come back to the object. There, in its simplest form, is the beginning of the area of truth.

Its real area, however, is the *concept*. James says that the concept is different from the object, and distorts things. How then can it play a practical, useful role? According to James, concepts are general ideas. This postulate is debatable; for if every general idea is a concept, it does not necessarily follow that it is the *whole concept*.[2] Let us accept it, however. Each concept represents a special kind of thing: there is a likeness between things, and things seem once for all to have been created in kinds.[3] We should note in passing that what James supposes here is rather surprising: for if, as he maintains, concepts are incapable of expressing reality adequately, how is it possible to find in reality something corresponding to the categories which they represent?

CONCEPTS AND ACTION

However that may be, they are general, and they are connected, with determined relationships between them. The concepts which express them are therefore also connected, and integrated into a system of relationships. The process which assures us of the truth of the concept is thus the same as the one which assures us of the truth of images, and we verify the concept in the same way as we verify the image, by attaching it to a whole: 'Truth here is a relation, not of our ideas to non-human realities, but of conceptual parts of our experience to sensational parts.'[4] But there is a difference, as follows. On the one hand, sensations and images are particular, and include only quite a small part of reality. On the other hand, a sensation does not allow us to proceed quickly, for it also expresses the multiplicity of all kinds of qualities proper to the object to which it relates. Thus it slows down our thought and our action: it does not enable us to distinguish between the relevant and the irrelevant in a particular case. Concepts have quite different characters. Since they are universal, each concept includes a digest, so to speak, of a multitude of individual cases. Thus the geometrician, concerned for the moment with a specific figure, is perfectly aware that his arguments can be applied to innumerable other figures of the same kind.[5] Concepts are also 'short cuts' which 'yield inconceivably rapid transitions', and: 'owing to the "universal character" which they frequently possess, and to their capacity for association with one another in great systems, they outstrip the tardy consecutions of the things themselves, and sweep us on towards our ultimate termini in a far more labour-saving way than following the trains of sensible perceptions ever could'.[6] In order to play this role, James says, concepts do not need to be a *copy* of objects. The word which designates them is enough to set in motion the necessary process and thus to guide our action, since it has relationships and dynamic or at least potential connections. This interpretation is reminiscent of Bergson's *schéma dynamique*.[7]

To sum up: the task of knowledge is to bring those objects which are necessary for us into our grasp more quickly. The virtue of the concept is that it cuts down the number of actions we have to take to maintain our existence. Ideas have value in that they enable us, as James says, to 'ambulate' through the relations between things: 'I say that we know an object by means of an idea, whenever we ambulate towards the object under the impulse which the idea communicates.' And James often contrasts the *ambulatory* nature of thought with the *saltatory* nature implied in the discontinuist conception of the universe.[8]

Nor does the conceptual faculty thus understood seem to James in any way something to be despised. Quite the opposite: it is a veritable miracle which enables us to control time and space: 'But with our facility of abstracting and fixing concepts we are there in a second, almost as if we controlled a fourth dimension, skipping the intermediaries as by a divine winged power, and getting at the exact point we require without entanglement with any context.'[9] Thus both sensation and concepts have their different parts to play. Sensation is limited, and in addition does not allow us to meet the demands of life, which force us to act quickly. Concepts, which have a primarily practical[10] role, fill both these gaps. But sensation gives us in depth what it cannot provide in breadth.[11]

There is still the problem, however, of knowing how concepts, if they represent a move away from reality, can, as James maintains, enable us to adapt to it. Does that not perhaps represent a partial return to rationalism? For the pragmatists, a concept is certainly the idea of a reality, of something which really exists, and James frequently insists on this point.[12] The world of abstract ideas, just as the world of sensory facts, is real. Each concept, in its own measure, represents a part of past experience and hence a well-founded experience, and thus the conceptual process brings us back to a *datum*.

This could however only be seen as a return to rationalism if pragmatism accepted that, once in the presence of one of these series, thought truly made us grasp something in reality. But for pragmatism, the initial state to which knowledge brings us back is much less the representation of a thing, a reality, than a plan of action, the representation of an *act* to be performed. At the origin of the process of knowledge, the idea to be checked is the idea of something *to be done*, and the final stage of this process is not the contemplation of the object which has been finally encountered (as is the case with rationalism), but always an *action*. Verification consists of discovering whether the action *will be successful*, whether it will produce the expected effects. The function of the true idea is much less to bring us closer to the object as such than to *put us into a relationship with it*, to dispose us suitably towards it: 'The ideas is thus, when functionally considered, an instrument for enabling us the better to *have to do* with the object and to act about it.'[13] 'Knowing ... may be only one way of getting into fruitful relations with reality, whether copying be one of the relations or not.'[14]

SATISFACTION

But how can we know that the final act to which the idea leads us is indeed the correct one? *By means of the satisfaction which we receive from it*, James replies. This satisfaction is the sign of truth: 'At each and every concrete moment, truth for each man is what that man "troweth" at that moment with the maximum of satisfaction to himself.'[15] Thus there is a double criterion for the true idea: 'First ... the ideas must point to or lead towards *that* reality and no other, and then that the pointings and leadings must yield satisfaction as their result.[16]

One objection spontaneously arises here. If 'satisfaction' is made one of the criteria of truth, does this not imply a lapse into subjectivism? Any satisfaction is in itself merely a subjective condition. The pragmatist must therefore conclude that truth does not exist outside the subject, and that consequently the subject can shape it as he wishes.[17] This has meant that a pragmatist like Dewey[18] has had to part company with James here, and has vigorously refused to accept that a satisfaction, of whatever kind, created by ideas, could be a sufficient criterion of truth. James's reply was to say that the satisfaction in question, which, moreover, is only *one* of the criteria of truth, is not simply *any* satisfaction.[19] The result must be not only that which corresponds to our existing idea of it but, most importantly, that which 'fits' the situation.

Nevertheless, it should be noted that such a criterion is to a high degree uncertain. The initial idea may be false, and yet satisfaction nevertheless be obtained. Let us suppose, for example, that a sane man has been persuaded that the physical distress he is afflicted with is due to the fact that evil spirits have entered into his body (a case which is common in certain primitive societies). He is given an unpleasant substance which, he is assured, will drive away the spirits which are tormenting him. He believes this, and is cured. The result is certainly the one expected, and is even the 'suitable' one. Nevertheless, the idea was false.

••

The pragmatist criteria of truth*

Let us first recall the pragmatist principles. The result by which truth is defined is not any kind of result: it must be a *useful* truth. We know what must be understood by that: each process of knowledge has its origin in a sense of *unease* experienced by an organism, and that unease must be ended and a *balance* re-established, and thus suffering is calmed, pain ended and so on. What matters here is not so much to learn whether the equilibrium obtained is the one we had in mind, as to be certain that it is the one which *is suitable* for us. But what means have we of ascertaining this? The sign is a feeling of satisfaction, which for pragmatists is so indispensable that Dewey himself who, as we have seen, refused to accept it as the criterion of truth properly speaking, nevertheless felt himself obliged to grant to it a certain value. Indeed, given pragmatist principles, it is impossible not to take the principle of satisfaction into account. Basically, it is the essential need amongst all needs that the idea must satisfy. The true idea, said James, is the one which 'helps us to *deal*, whether practically or intellectually, with either the reality or its belongings, that doesn't entangle our progress in frustrations, that *fits*, in fact, and adapts our life to the reality's whole setting'.[1]

THE SATISFACTION OF INTELLECTUAL NEEDS

James endeavoured to find a place for needs other than purely 'practical' ones, in the ordinary sense of the term, and particularly for those needs of a *speculative* order. He clearly found it disagreeable that rationalism should have the advantage over pragmatism of being the only system capable of explaining certain needs of the human mind, and he set himself the task of showing that pragmatism too accounted for these. Of course, he said, we need to be 'in agreement' with things. But our mind is real too. It can be compared to a living organism, and has the same needs as any other organism. If it is not functioning properly, we are ill. That

*Notes to the Ninth Lecture, of 10 February 1914, are on p. 123.

50

is why we also need to be *in agreement with ourselves*: 'we find *consistency* satisfactory, consistency between the present idea and the entire rest of our mental equipment, including the whole order of our sensations, and that of our intuitions of likeness and difference, and our whole stock of previously acquired truths'.[2] When a new idea is born in our mind, when a new fact occurs and impresses it, if they are not in agreement with what is already there, they break the harmony of the mental organism. Thus, it is not sufficient for the new idea to be in 'agreement' with things; it must also be in harmony with the other already existing representations which are a part of our mental life. Ideas already in our mind correspond to modes of reaction which are habitual. If they are habitual, it is because they are indeed those which were suitable; and the ideas which trigger them have established themselves in our minds as strongly as the reactions themselves. The new idea is thus obliged to conform to ideas already present in the mind. It is only fully *true* if it is reconciled with them. Agreement with external things is therefore not the only condition of truth: internal repercussions must also be considered.

VERIFICATION AND VERIFIABILITY

In both cases, moreover, the 'agreement' in question is a *practical* one. What *verifies* ideas is 'the acts which they cause us to engage in'. It is as a result of these acts, and of 'the other ideas which they instigate', that these ideas: 'lead us ... into or up to, or towards, other parts of experience with which we feel all the while – such feeling being among our potentialities – that the original ideas remain in agreement. The connections and transitions come to us from point to point as being progressive, harmonious, satisfactory.'[3]

Thus *the pragmatist conception of truth* becomes increasingly clear. Truth is never a lifeless copy of reality. It is rather something living, and its function is to increase and enrich our being. The true idea enables us to move easily among things, and since it is easier, action is more certain. Thus the true idea brings us both interior and exterior peace – a state comparable to health, wealth or happiness.

It is, however, we ourselves who make wealth, happiness and health: and it is the same with regard to truth. Truth, says James,[4] is something that is made true, it is something that is there to help us to live, to make thought and action easier for us, and its becoming is achieved as our life develops. In one sense, it is *we ourselves who make it*; for, far from being a character that is essentially immanent in the idea, it needs our co-operation. The idea only is true and only *becomes* true when we have used it, tried and tested it, and when it has enabled us to reconcile old truths and new truths. Truth thus '*happens* to an idea' and is the result of an *effort* which has made it true. The word 'truth' is simply a designation of that function which consists in 'marrying previous parts of experience with newer parts'.[5]

Truth and *verification* are therefore synonymous. 'Truth for us is simply a collective name for verification processes, just as health, wealth, strength, etc., are names for other processes connected with life.'[6] We can distinguish at best only an abstract or logical sense in which truth is no longer these processes themselves but the *product* of these verifications.

James sees a possible objection here. Are there then no true ideas apart from those which we verify? Yet we believe that there is a country called Japan, although we have never been there. That is a true idea, and yet we have never verified it. James replies that such ideas, although they have not at the moment been verified, are nevertheless *verifiable*: 'Truth in these cases . . . [means] nothing but eventual verification.'[7] The pragmatist, he says, is the first to recognize the practical utility of the process which consists of substituting *verifiability* for verification, for the former is 'potential'truth.[8] Furthermore, there are ideas which we deem trustworthy because we have faith in the experience of other people: 'Truth lives, in fact, for the most part on a credit system . . . you accept my verification of one thing, I yours of another. We trade on each other's truth. But beliefs verified concretely by *somebody* are the posts of the whole superstructure.'[9]

James maintains that truth implies a certain agreement with reality. The only difference between his thought and rationalism in this respect is that for the latter this agreement is purely theoretical, whilst for pragmatism it is essentially practical. However, unless we suppose that such an agreement is fortuitous and inexplicable, or the mysterious work of a transcendental providence, reality must be plastic if it is to be capable of satisfying our needs, in order to be able to adapt to them. Hence the notion of a reality which also *makes itself*, and which is partly our creation, as we have already seen.[10]

NECESSITY AND FREEDOM

There is, in short, a double notion in the world of pragmatism – a notion of necessity, of determination, and a current of freedom, of non-determination. The necessity is due to (1) the internal *and* external order of sensations and perceptions; (2) the mass of already acquired truths. Our mind, caught between these two boundaries, cannot think what it wants; and James stresses the idea that our abstractions are as inescapable as our sensations: 'We can no more play fast and loose with these abstract relations than we can do so with our sense experiences. They coerce us; we must treat them consistently, whether or not we like the results.'[11] Parallel to this idea of determination, however, there is one of non-determination, which for pragmatists is no less important. What tempers the double necessity which we have seen, and means that finally we are more free than we believe, is the fact that reality, like truth, is largely *a human product.*[12] The world is a 'chaos' from which the human mind 'cuts out' objects which it has arranged, put in place and organized in categories. Space, time, causality: all these categories come from us. We have created them to meet the needs of practical life.[13] Thus the world, as it is, is as we have constructed it. Pure sensation does not exist: it only takes shape by virtue of the form that we give it.

Basically, there is an original *substratum,* an original 'chaos', which we could reach if we stripped the universe of all the successive additions made to it by our thought, if we could imagine a world without man. We can, however, only move towards that knowledge without ever reaching it. Such a substratum, stripped of all those qualities and categories which are human in origin, would be a pure ὕλη, original matter without form,[14] whereas for pragmatists the opposite is the case. The first .character of the real universe is its *plasticity,*[15] its ability, in other words, to assume all the forms conferred on it by human thought and human action. Here we encounter once more the pluralist conception of a *malleable universe* which presents itself to us not in a single guise but under forms which differ according to the way in which we wish to act on it.

Constructing reality and constructing truth*

For pragmatism, reality is something that we make. We are, Schiller says, 'genuine makers of reality',[1] not in the sense that we are 'creators' in the absolute sense of the term, producing reality from nothingness, but as beings who 'co-operate' in creating it. Moreover, we 'remake' the world by our actions, and our institutions in particular modify the future shape of the world. We construct or 'make' the world for our own purposes, just as truth too is a human product which also has practical ends. Constructing truth and constructing reality are one and the same process. 'What we judge to be "true", we take to be "real", and accept as "just" ... It is in this cognitive elaboration of experience that both reality and truth grow up *pari passu*.'[2] In creating truths, we also create realities. In James's words, 'In our cognitive as well as our active life we are creative.'[3] However, seeing the *logical* process (i.e. that of thought) as identical with the *active* process (i.e. that which 'creates' reality) raises a serious problem for pragmatism. The world, reality, it says, is constructed by human thought. That may be so, but in order to be able to say that the two processes are identical, we have to be able to say that this construction of reality is true simply because it exists. A statement of that kind is of course meaningless: the construction is fact, it *is*. Saying that it is *true* raises quite a different problem. Perceiving or constructing reality does not necessarily imply that that perception or that construction is not illusory. In other words, it is one thing to organize our sensations but quite another thing to reflect on the *logical value* of that organization, and it is our duty to pose that problem. Pragmatism merely tells us that constructing reality and constructing truth both operate with a practical aim in view. It does not seem, however, to have succeeded in separating the two questions.

DEWEY'S INTERPRETATION

Dewey, however, saw the difficulty, and tried to avoid confusing these

*Notes to the Tenth Lecture, of 17 February 1914, are on pp. 123–4.

two problems. In his view, the only work which is important for us is that which is described and given values by man. We give it the values which it has for us. We highlight what interests us and ignore the rest. The world is made up of a system of value which *we* have given to things, which thus become the directing factors of our conduct and our thought. Since we are caught up in a given environment, we take things in a given sense. But, Dewey goes on to say, this constituting of *qualities* and *values* is not at all a conscious or voluntary act. It is *pure experience* that tells us, before any *reflection* occurs, that objects are divided up into certain groups and have certain qualities. It is consciousness that gives us the immediate value of objects, and there are 'empirical values of unreflective life'.[4] The opposite is the case: truth is the product of reflective thought which, as is known,[5] only occurs when the system of values is disturbed. At this level, it is no longer the very nature of the world which dictates our conduct, but reflective thought.

However ingenious it may be, this attempt to maintain the distinction between the two orders of the real and the true is nevertheless not a very defensible one. In the first place, Dewey postulates that there is only knowledge properly speaking, and hence *truth*, when there has been an earlier *loss of equilibrium* and consequently the arrival of *doubt*. Without that doubt, there can be no truth. It is difficult, however, to accept such a postulate for two reasons: (1) there are propositions which for us are truths, even though we have never cast doubt upon them or have not doubted them for a long time, such as $2+2 = 4$; (2) the difference between instinctive consciousness and reflective consciousness, at least as understood by pragmatism,[6] is not great enough to justify the difference which Dewey establishes between the apperception of reality and the construction of truth. Both no doubt help us to live better, but whilst one arranges and organizes reality, the other *reorganizes* it on new bases. The difference here may seem slight, but it is crucial. Even instinctive consciousness is not unaware of this process of rearrangement and reorganization; when equilibrium has been lost, the animal itself seeks, gropes towards, tries out other movements appropriate to the situation. Doubt and uncertainty are thus not exclusive to reflective thought. Consequently, they are not sufficient to differentiate our construction of reality from our examination of the logical value of that construction.

It would perhaps be better to examine things from the point of view of the element of *satisfaction* to which pragmatism allots such a major role. To the extent that it stresses this element, however, pragmatism changes its name and is called *humanism*, a designation given to it, as we know, by Schiller. Humanism consists in maintaining that the individual factor is an essential element in the construction of truth: 'No judgement could come into being, even in the world of thought, if some individual mind were not impelled by its total physical contents and history to affirm it upon some suitable occasion, and to stake its fortunes on this personal affirmation ... The judgement, therefore, essentially pre-supposes a mind, a motive, and a purpose.'[7] In seeking for truth, we try to find ideas which satisfy our needs for action and for thought. Every act and every movement is *personal* and, since the idea is the instrument of the action, it too is something personal and at the same time to some degree a function of a milieu. This is so because when the loss of equilibrium, which is the basis of the act of knowing, occurs, it varies according to the milieu and the person it affects. All pragmatists unanimously reject the distinction normally made between *real* or *personal* thought and *logical* or *impersonal* thought.[8] The personal factor probably never acts in isolation, but its role is nevertheless important and even decisive.

FROM INDIVIDUAL TO IMPERSONAL TRUTH

Here, a question arises. If the personal and affective factor plays such a major role, should we not conclude that truth is essentially individual and consequently incommunicable and untranslatable, since translating it means expressing it in concepts and thus impersonally? Moreover, if judgements are affected by this weighting of subjectivity, the result is that they are of unequal value. Some are preferable to others.

We are told that a quite spontaneous choice is established, and that as a result of experience those of least worth are eliminated, whilst the others emerge, come closer to each other and come to form the common treasure of humanity. One might, however, ask for whom the value of these judgements is unequal. There are judgements which for me are good and therefore true, but bad and therefore untrue for others. 'Satisfaction', for different people, depends on different things.[9] Amongst all these, which will constitute such a 'treasure of humanity'? Pragmatists tell us that they are those which are worth most for the general run of men and correspond to the similarities between them. 'Truth' thus appears to be a residue of particular beliefs.

Does a truth of this kind deserve to be called impersonal? Pragmatists tell us that we could no doubt have an idea of an objective, impersonal and, in this sense, absolute truth, containing no differences or changes. But it would, they say, only be possible to see it as an *ideal* towards which we would be moving, closely linked to the progress of human knowledge, and only indicating an orientation of thought.[10] Here, the danger of error would be to take this tendency for an already established reality. However that may be, we can see here how it would be possible to explain from the pragmatist point of view that truth, although individual in origin, never remains rigorously so.

But what will bring about and strengthen mental agreement more than anything else is the action of society. Once this[11] 'consensus of opinion' has been established, once this 'great stage of equilibrium in the human mind's development' which James calls 'the stage of *common sense*'[12] has been reached, society exerts pressure towards imposing a certain intellectual conformism.[13] There is a yardstick for measuring truth which gradually takes shape, and which society tends to sanction and guarantee; for if truths remained individual, they would clash with each other[14] and be ineffective. We can thus see that in order to explain that there is an impersonal truth (although this in its view is a secondary attribute) pragmatism is obliged to propose interpretations of a sociological nature.

Let us now consider the GENERAL CONCEPTION OF TRUTH which follows from this analysis.

Usually, the *determining, necessitating* character of truth is proclaimed. We assume that once it is known, truth will impose itself on our minds with the necessity of a divine decree, and that the procedures by which we reach it will present the same character. As seen by the pragmatists, however, truth is certainly good, useful and 'satisfying', but has no character of logical necessity. We create it and create it thus for our needs. We are therefore completely *free* in the work of constructing it. James tells us too that modern epistemology shows us this clearly. In place of the absolute principles of bygone times, it shows us axioms or postulates which are more or less conventional and, in place of rigorous laws, mere approximations: 'Thus human arbitrariness has driven divine necessity from scientific logic.'[15]

The consequence of this conception with regard to *method* must be considered. It can no longer be a question of setting up a *single* method or a defined rule of conduct. There is no system of verification with absolutely fixed methods. Our attitude towards the universe can no longer be the doctrinaire and authoritarian attitude of rationalism. The attitude of pragmatism is a 'happy-go-lucky' one.[16] We must abandon both scientific and moral Pharisaism, since from now on it is no longer possible to claim that we can weigh on some kind of scales the value of proofs. The only way in which we can recognize truth is the way in which it increases our vitality.

It is thus logic itself which is called into question. Is a more or less definite method possible, enabling men to find truth and to follow one way in preference to another? If logical thought is a lower form of thought, we shall have to find another form capable of fulfilling its task.

Pragmatism as a method [lost text]*

An intermediate lecture, replying to the question posed at the end of the Tenth Lecture, on the *method* pragmatism intends to substitute for the logical methods generally adopted, seems to be missing here in both versions of the text. Such a lecture would also fill a further gap. In the Second Lecture (p. 11), Durkheim described pragmatism as being at the same time a method, a theory of truth and a theory of the universe; but only the last two have been discussed. We have reason to believe that Durkheim took up here the indications given by James in *Pragmatism*, pp. 45–54, on the 'pragmatic method'. The basic ideas are (1) the 'attitude' represented by pragmatism is often related to that of empiricism, but a *renewed* empiricism. (2) Pragmatism takes up a position against abstract thought and, more generally, against rationalism and intellectualism. (3) It is hostile to all metaphysical dogmas, all 'closed systems' and all definitive solutions which bar the way to further investigation. (4) Pragmatism sees as solely important not first *principles*, but practical *consequences*, so that we must 'bring out of each word its practical cash-value'. In other words, one must draw out from each idea 'an indication of the ways in which existing realities may be changed' [p. 53].

*Almost certainly that of 24 February 1914.

Pragmatism and religion*

We have looked at the theses and general methods of pragmatism and can now look at the way in which it is applied to special determined problems. It must be said that examples of such applications are infrequent in the accounts which pragmatists give of their thought. There are none from the knowledge of the physical world. There ought to be some from the field of human affairs, but they too are rare. One might nevertheless expect pragmatism to be applicable to moral problems, but there is *no such thing as a pragmatist morality*. There are many articles by Dewey on moral questions,[1] but when he deals with such matters, his writings have nothing of a pragmatist character: his moral theories seem quite independent of his theory of truth. Only in Moore does one find one or two vague moves in this direction.[2]

The only question to which the pragmatist method has been consistently applied is that of *religion*. In particular, James's book *The Varieties of Religious Experience*[3] deals with this matter.

How does he deal with this problem? James asks himself what the *value* of religion is. In order to solve this problem, an inventory of all those facts presenting a religious character must be drawn up. Where are they to be found? Only, replies James, in 'personal religion', in the personal experience of the individual consciousness. 'Personal religion', he writes, 'will prove itself more fundamental than either theology or ecclesiasticism.'[4] He thus neglects the whole dimension of institutions, churches, hallowed practices. In his view, religious life is religious life only when it is not fixed; for like all kinds of life it is a *course*. He therefore sees it as necessary to remove the rigid forms of religion, and go to its source before these forms have been assumed. This means, ultimately, going back to the individual consciousness, for 'the axes of reality runs solely through the egoistic places'.[5]

What facts then does a study of individual consciousness show us at the roots of religious life? James here distinguishes five kinds.[6] These

*Notes to the Twelfth Lecture, of 3 March 1914, are on pp. 124–6.

are: *the reality of the unseen*; religious *optimism* (trust, belief in happiness); religious *pessimism* ('sick souls', the need for redemption); spiritual states in which *the soul is divided between doubt and faith*; and *conversion*. This choice seems to me quite arbitrary, but I do not intend to discuss it here.[7] I shall simply note that there are religions in which these individual senses do not, so to speak, occur.

Moreover, according to James, the value of religion does not depend to any great extent on these analyses. It depends neither on organic nor on psychological states. The science of religions must judge the *truth* of religion not by any dogmatic method[8] but on its *results*: '[I believe] the pragmatic way of taking religion to be the deeper way'.[9] If we want to know the value of a tree, we do not consider its roots, but rather the fruit it yields. We should therefore ask what the *products* of religious life are, and these should be considered at the point at which religious life is at its most intense, even if we wish to know what it can produce in average cases. In other words, we should study it in the *saints*.

Sanctity

What is sanctity? To answer that question, should we have to make a choice between various theologies, establish the existence of God and posit 'a limited number of theological and moral conceptions and definitions' concerning his nature and the nature of man? There is no point in asking such questions, says James.[10] It would achieve no purpose for, whether we accept or deny the existence of God, we do so not for speculative reasons, but because of aspirations and needs to use one conception rather than another. The only guides we have in such matters are 'our general philosophic prejudices, our instincts, and our common sense'.[11] *They* are our criteria. These 'prejudices' (in the etymological sense of the word), these instincts and this common sense, and along with them our religious conceptions, are ceaselessly evolving. Thus, according to whether or not the saint fits in with the feelings that such developments produce in us, we shall accept him as a model or question him. James admits that 'the reproach of vagueness and subjectivity and "on the whole-ness"' can be addressed to this empirical method, but it is 'after all a reproach to which the entire life of man in dealing with these matters is obnoxious'.[12]

The great virtues of the saint are devotion, charity, spiritual strength (resignation, contempt of danger), purity of life (a horror of everything bogus or deceitful), asceticism (which can even include a love of suffering) and obedience and poverty.[13] These virtues are usually the opposite of those of the man of action. What value have they respectively? It is true that 'saintly conduct would be the most perfect conduct conceivable in an environment where all were saints already; but ... in an environment where few are saints ... it must be ill-adapted'.[14] In imperfect societies, such as those we have at present, charity and non-resistance to evil often seem scarcely appropriate, and the virtues of the man of action seem preferable. But, since a perfect society would be precisely a society of saints, it would, in spite of everything, be the ideal state. In addition, James continues,[15] even in our present societies it is not without point that certain men meet hardness with goodness, offence with forgiveness and so on. The saints are 'authors ... of goodness', and their mission is to revive the instincts of goodness that we carry within us. Consequently their fervour plays 'a vital and essential' function in social evolution.[16]

Mysticism and the 'subliminal self'

So far, the question has simply been that of the *practical fertility* of religion. But, says James, some people will object that it is impossible to judge religion by its fruits in the physical world: 'It is its *truth*, not its utility ... upon which our verdict ought to depend.'[17] Is religion true? In attempting to answer that question, James disdainfully rejects the arguments of the philosophers and the theologians.[18] On the other hand, he lays great value on mystical intuition.[19] The basis of mystical experience is a direct communication with reality, something analogous to sensation, in so far as sensation is the apprehension of the *thing* itself, rather than knowledge *about* the thing.[20] Only those who have experienced that sort of sensation have felt the power of the divine.

The only theoretical justification of religious belief in James's book is to be found in the final chapters.[21] James tries to prove, not that God exists, but that belief in the divine can be reconciled with 'the results of natural science', that there is still 'a residuum of conceptions that at least are possible'.[22] He sees as the basis of the religious life the idea that there is something GREATER than ourselves.[23] This idea is of course closely akin to the concept of the *subconscious*, of the *subliminal self* which, says James, plays a large part in the interpretations suggested by contemporary psychologists. 'Our normal working consciousness ... is but one special type of consciousness, whilst all about it, parted from it by the filmiest of screens, there lie potential forms of consciousness entirely different.'[24] Outside the field of that normal consciousness, there are other kinds of consciousness focussed on psychic realities of a different kind, and it is here that inspiration and sudden illuminations have their origin. The study of mystical states, conversion and prayer shows the major role played in religious life by these incursions of the sub-conscious. The way in which these forces act on our spiritual life indicates their superiority. We must therefore admit that there is something apart from bodies and the material world, and even apart from consciousness as it appears to us. Thus, 'whatever it may be on its *farther* side, the "more" with which in religious experience we feel ourselves connected is on its *hither* side the subconscious continuation of our conscious life'.[25] The 'science of religions', in other words philosophy, can be based on 'a recognised psychological fact' 'and at the same time justify the theologian's affirmation that man, in his religious experience, suffers the action of a force which goes beyond him. The divine takes its place in the world of experience; and God becomes one of those experimental forces whose existence is indicated by empirically observable effects.' 'God is real since he produces real effects.'[26]

Polytheism

Must one even speak of 'God' in the singular? The sole 'truth' demanded by religious experience is that 'we can experience union with *something* larger than ourselves and in that union find our greatest peace'. From this 'something greater', both 'philosophy with its passion for unity, and mysticism with its monodeistic bent' make a unique and absolute God. But to meet man's 'practical needs' and the data of religious experience, it is sufficient to accept that 'for each individual' there exists a higher power with which he can become one and which is favourable towards him. This higher power need not be single and infinite. It can even be seen as 'only a larger and more god-like self. Of which the present self would then be but the mutilated expression, and the universe might conceivably be a collection of such selves, of different degrees of inclusiveness, with no absolute unity realised in it at all.'[27] In this way coming back again to the idea of pluralism, we finally arrive at the kind of polytheism which has, moreover, James adds, always been 'the real religion of common people'. There are around us spirits endowed with strength and action, consciousness similar to our own, but distinct from it and superior to it, which are nevertheless 'in a fashion continuous with' it and can enrich and strengthen our life.[28] Such experiences are what constitutes religion.

The facts which James alleges could certainly be explained differ-ently. The facts of subliminal consciousness could, as many writers have thought,[29] be connected with the facts of the splitting or disintegration of the personality. But what explains and supports James's arguments is his declaration[30] that he has expressed here his own feelings, his own aspirations or in his own words, his 'overbeliefs'. Everyone's feelings and aspirations have their value,[31] since they suppose earlier experiences, but with the limitation that they should not be transformed, as James's are, into a source of insight. It is for the same reason that James sees *satisfaction* as the most important element. What he is saying, in short, is that one must take the path of least resistance.

CONCLUSION OF THE ACCOUNT: THE GENERAL SPIRIT OF PRAGMATISM

We can now attempt, as a general conclusion to this account, to define *the general spirit of pragmatism*.

It has been said that pragmatism is above all an attempt to *liberate the will*. If the world is to solicit our activity, we must be able to change it; and for that to occur, it must be malleable. Things are not chiefly important for what they are, but for what they are worth. The basis of our action is a hierarchy of values which we ourselves have established. Our action is therefore only worthwhile if that system of values can be realized, made incarnate, in our world. Pragmatism thus gives a meaning to action.

Nevertheless, this preoccupation with action, which has been seen as the defining characteristic of pragmatism, is not, in my view, its major feature. Man's burning desire to transform things is apparent in the thought of all the idealists. When we have an ideal, we see the world as something obliged to conform to it. Pragmatism, however, is not a form of idealism, but a radical empiricism. What is there in it which could justify such a desire to transform things? We have seen that for pragmatism there are not two planes of existence, but only one, and consequently it is impossible to see where the ideal could be located. As has just been shown, God himself is an object of experience in pragmatist doctrine.

We can therefore conclude that pragmatism is much less of an undertaking to encourage action than an attack on *pure speculation and theoretical thought*. What is really characteristic of it is an impatience with any rigorous intellectual discipline. It aspires to 'liberate' thought much more than it does action. Its ambition, as James says, is to 'make the truth more supple'. We shall see later what reasons it adduces to support its view that truth must not remain 'rigid'.

....

General criticism of pragmatism*

We can now move on to the general discussion of pragmatist doctrines.

They can, first of all, be criticized for certain gaps in them. As I have already pointed out,[1] the pragmatists often take too many liberties with historical doctrines. They interpret them as they wish, and often rather inexactly.

Above all, however, we must indicate the *abstract nature* of their argument, since it clashes with the general orientation, which they claim is empirical, of their doctrine. Most of the time, their proofs have a *dialectical* character; everything is reduced to a purely logical construction. This provides one contradiction.

But their thought presents other flagrant contradictions. Here is an example: on the one hand, we are told that consciousness as such does *not exist*, that it is nothing original, that it is neither a factor *sui generis* nor a true reality, but is only a simple echo, a 'vain noise' left behind by the 'soul' that has vanished from the heaven of philosophy.[2] This, as we know, is the theme of the famous article, 'Does consciousness exist?', a theme which James took up again in the form of a communication in French to the Congress of 1905.[3] On the other hand, however, the pragmatists maintain that reality is a *construction* of thought, that reality is apperception itself.[4] In so doing they attribute to thought the same power and the same qualities as the idealists ascribe to it. They urge both epiphenomenalism and idealism, two incompatible theses. Pragmatism therefore lacks those basic characteristics which one has the right to expect of a philosophical doctrine.

Here we must ask ourselves a question. How does it happen that, with such defects, pragmatism has imposed itself on so many minds? It must be based on something in the human consciousness and have a strength that we have yet to discover.

*Notes to the Thirteenth Lecture [presumably that of 10 March 1914] are on p. 126.

THE FUNDAMENTAL MOTIVATION OF THE PRAGMATIST ATTITUDE

Let us ask ourselves, then, what feeling animates the doctrine, what motivation is its essential factor. I have said already that it is not a practical need, a need to extend the field of human action. There is, to be sure, particularly in James, a liking for risk, a need for adventure; he prefers an uncertain, 'malleable' world to a fixed and immobile world, because it is a world in which there is something to do. This is certainly the ideal of the strong man who wishes to expand the field of his activity. But how, then, can the same philosopher show us as an ideal the ascetic who renounces the world and turns away from it?

Actually, pragmatism has not been concerned with picturing a particular ideal for us. Its dominant trait is the need to 'soften the truth', to make it 'less rigid', as James says – to free it, in short, from the discipline of logical thought. This appears very clearly in James's *The Will to Believe*.[5] Once this is posited, everything becomes clear. If thought had as its object simply to 'reproduce' reality, it would be the slave of things, and chained to reality. It would simply have to slavishly 'copy' the reality before it. If thought is to be freed, it must become the creator of its own object, and the only way to attain this goal is to give it a reality to make or construct. Therefore, *thought has as its aim not the reproduction of a datum, but the construction of a future reality.* It follows that the value of ideas can no longer be assessed by reference to objects but must be determined by their degree of utility, their more or less 'advantageous' character.

We can thus see the scope of the pragmatist theses. If, in classical rationalism, thought has this character of 'rigidity', for which pragmatism criticizes it, it is because in rationalism truth is conceived of as a simple thing, a thing quasi-divine, that draws its whole value from itself. Since it is seen as sufficient unto itself, it is necessarily placed above human life. It cannot conform to the demands of circumstances and differing temperaments. It is valid by itself and is good with an absolute goodness. It does not exist for our sake, but for its own. Its role is to let itself be contemplated. It is so to speak deified; it becomes the object of a real cult. This is still Plato's conception. It extends to the faculty by means of which we attain truth, that is, reason. Reason serves to explain things to us, but, in this conception, itself remains unexplained; it is placed outside scientific analysis.

'To soften' the truth is to take from it this absolute and as it were sacrosanct character. It is to tear it away from this state of immobility that removes it from all becoming, from all change and, consequently, from all explanation. Imagine that instead of being thus confined in a separate world, it is itself part of reality and life, not by a kind of fall or degradation that would disfigure and corrupt it, but because it is *naturally* part of reality and life.[6] It is placed in the series of facts, at the very heart of things having antecedents and consequences. It poses problems: we are authorized to ask ourselves where it comes from, what good it is and so on. It becomes itself an object of knowledge. Herein lies the interest of the pragmatist enterprise: we can see it as an effort to *understand* truth and reason themselves, to restore to them their human interest, to make of them human things that derive from temporal causes and give rise to temporal consequences. To 'soften' truth is to make it into something that can be analysed and explained.

It is here that we can establish a PARALLEL BETWEEN PRAGMATISM AND SOCIOLOGY. By applying the *historical* point of view to the order of things human, sociology is led to set itself the same problem. Man is a product of history and hence of becoming; there is nothing in him that is either given or defined in advance. History begins nowhere and it ends nowhere. Everything in man has been made by mankind in the course of time. Consequently, if truth is human, it too is a human product. Sociology applies the same conception to reason. All that constitutes reason, its principles and categories, has been made in the course of history.

Everything is a product of certain causes. Phenomena must not be represented in closed series: things have a 'circular' character, and analysis can be prolonged to infinity. This is why I can accept neither the statement of the idealists, that *in the beginning there is thought*, nor that of the pragmatists, that *in the beginning there is action*.

But if sociology poses the problem in the same way as does pragmatism, it is in a better position to solve it. The latter, in fact, claims to explain truth psychologically and subjectively. However, the nature of the individual is too limited to explain alone all things human. Therefore, if we envisage individual elements alone, we are led to diminish unduly the amplitude of the effects that we have to account for. How could reason, in particular, have arisen in the course of the experiences undergone by a single individual? Sociology provides us with broader explanations. For it, truth, reason and morality are the results of a becoming that includes the entire unfolding of human history.

Thus we see the advantage of the sociological over the pragmatist point of view. For the pragmatist philosophers, as we have already said several times, experience can take place *on one level only*. Reason is placed on the same plane as sensitivity; truth, on the same plane as sensations and instincts. But men have always recognized in truth something that in certain respects imposes itself on us, something that is independent of the facts of sensitivity and individual impulse. Such a universally held conception of truth must correspond to something real. It is one thing to cast doubt on the correspondence between symbols and reality; but it is quite another to reject the thing symbolized along with the symbol.[7] This pressure that truth is seen as exercising on minds is itself a symbol that must be interpreted, even if we refuse to make of truth something absolute and extra-human.

Pragmatism, which levels everything, deprives itself of the means of making this interpretation by failing to recognize the *duality* that exists between the mentality which results from individual experiences and that which results from collective experiences. Sociology, however, reminds us that what is *social* always possesses a higher dignity than what is individual. It can be assumed that truth, like reason and morality, will always retain this character of being a higher value. This in no way prevents us from trying to explain it. The sociological point of view has the advantage of enabling us to analyse even that august thing, truth.

Until now there has been no particularly urgent need to choose between the points of view of sociology and pragmatism. In contrast to rationalism, pragmatism sees clearly that error does not lie on one side and truth on the other, but that in reality truths and errors are mixed, the latter having often been moments in the evolution of truth. In the history of creations, there are unforeseeable novelties. How, then, could truth be conceived of as something fixed and definitive?

But *the reasons that pragmatism adduces* to support this idea are susceptible to a great many objections. Moreover, the fact that things change does not necessarily mean that truth changes at the same time. Truth, one could say, *is enriched*; but it does not really *change*. It has certainly been enlarged and increased in the course of the development of history; but saying that truth grows is quite different from saying that it varies in its very nature.

The variations of truth*

Let us return to the reasons that pragmatism gives in order to prove that truth is subject to change. There are really two: (1) truth cannot be immutable because reality itself is not immutable; hence truth changes in time. (2) Truth cannot be one because this oneness would be incompatible with the diversity of minds; hence truth changes in space.

1   In order to be able to say that truth has varied in time, one would have to show that a proposition can legitimately be considered true at a given moment and in particular circumstances, and that this same proposition at another moment and in other circumstances cannot be held to be true, even though it relates to the same object. This has not been shown. Pragmatism alleges that reality has changed; but does this mean that old truths become false? Reality can evolve without truth thereby ceasing to be truth. The laws of the physical world, for example, have remained what they were when life first appeared, and as the biological world has taken form.

2   The pragmatists base their case on the diversity of individual minds. But does progress perhaps not consist precisely in the removal of individual differences? Will the pragmatist then maintain that truth belongs only to the individual? This is a paradox that pragmatism itself has not dared to attempt to resolve.[1] Nor do the pragmatists explain what relationship there is between the diversity of minds and the diversity of truth. From the fact that in penetrating individual minds, truth takes on diverse forms, it does not follow that truth in itself is multiple. In short, pragmatism offers no proof of the thesis that it advances, the thesis that *truth is amorphous*.

Yet this thesis is not without some foundation, for it rests on certain facts. However, these facts, which the pragmatists sense only vaguely, must be restored to their true meaning. Let us see what explanation of them is offered by sociology.

Sociology introduces a *relativism* that rests on the relation between

*Notes to the Fourteenth Lecture, of 17 March 1914, are on pp. 126–7.

69

the physical environment on the one hand and man on the other. The physical environment presents a relative fixity. It undergoes evolution, of course; but reality never ceases to be what it was in order to give way to a reality of a new kind, or to one consisting of new elements. The original world survives under successive additions that enrich it. New realities were, in a sense, already present in the old ones.[2] The organic world does not abolish the physical world and the social world has not been formed in contradistinction to the organic world, but together with it.

The laws that ruled the movements of the primitive nebulae are conserved in the stabilized universe of today. It seems that in the organic world the era of great transformations closed with the appearance of the human species. Can this be true of man and the social milieux in which he lives? Social milieux are the products of different elements, combined and fused together. Our present-day French society is made up of Gallic, Germanic, Roman and other elements; but these elements can no longer be discerned in an isolated state in our present civilization, which is something new and original, a synthesis which is the product of a true creation.[3] Social environments are thus different from each other, since each of them presents something new. Therefore, the institutions of which they are composed must also be different. Nevertheless, these institutions fulfil the same functions as those that preceded them. Thus it is that the family has evolved in the course of history, but it has always remained the family and has continued to fulfil the same functions. Each of the various forms has been adapted to these functions. Similarly, we see that the same ideal political regime cannot be suitable for all types of societies. And yet the city regime was proper for the ancient cities, just as our present political regime is suitable for us. In the same way, there is no single morality, and we cannot condemn as immoral the moral systems that preceded ours, for the ideal that they represent was valid for the society in which they were established. The same can be said for religion. In sum, there is not one religion, one morality and one political regime, but different types of religion, types of morality and types of political organization. In the practical order, diversity may be considered as established.

Why should things not be the same in the theoretical order, in thought itself? If the value of a particular act has changed, it means that speculative thought has changed, and if speculative thought has changed, why should the content of truth not change too?

Action cannot be separated from thought. It is impossible for us to say that the generations which preceded us were capable of living in total error, in complete aberration. For false thoughts produce erroneous acts. Thus if men had been completely mistaken about the nature of things, their actions would not have been the right ones; and their failures would have produced suffering which would have led them to seek something else. Nothing authorizes us to think that the affective capacities of men of former times were radically different from our own.

Speculative and theoretical thought vary as practice varies. Aesthetic speculation itself shows variations, each people has its own aesthetic. Hence we tend to believe that speculation and its value are variable and that consequently, truth, too, is variable.

These variations occur not only in time but also in space, that is to say, not only from one type of historical society to another but also among the individuals of the same society. In fact, an excess of homogeneity within a society would be its death. No social group can live or – more particularly – progress in absolute homogeneity.[4] Both intellectual and practical life, both thought and action, need diversity, which is, consequently, a condition of truth. We have moved beyond the intellectual excommunication of all those who do not think as we do. We respect the truths of others. We 'tolerate' them, and this tolerance is no longer the sort that preceded the development of our modern civilization. It is not the kind of tolerance that has its source in weariness (as happened at the end of the wars of religion), nor is it the kind that is born of a feeling of charity. Rather it is the tolerance of the intellectual, of the scientist, who knows that truth is a complex thing and understands that it is very likely that no one of us will see the whole of all its aspects. Such tolerance mistrusts all orthodoxy, but it does not prevent the investigator from expressing the truth as he feels it.

It is in this way that the thesis enunciated by pragmatism is justified from the sociological point of view. Considerations of an abstract or metaphysical order cannot provide us with a satisfactory explanation. It is provided instead by its heightened sense of human reality, the feeling for the extreme variability of everything human. We can no longer accept a single, invariable system of categories or intellectual frameworks. The frameworks that had a reason to exist in past civilisations do not have it today. It goes without saying that this removes none of the value that they had for their own eras. Variability in time and variability in space are, moreover, closely connected. If the conditions of life in society are complex, it is naturally to be expected that this complexity and with it many variations are to be found in the individuals who make up the social groups.

HOW THESE VARIATIONS CAN BE EXPLAINED

Given this variability of truth in time and space, let us see what explanation of it pragmatism offers. (So far, of course, we have seen this dual variability posited, but not explained.)

Pragmatism gives us the 'why' of these variations very briefly: *it is the useful that is true*. However, it finds the attempt to demonstrate this proposition a far from easy undertaking. In our view, the proper way to do this would very probably be to take all the propositions recognized as true and determine whether or not they are useful and, if so, how. But such a procedure would be contrary to the method of pragmatism. If, as pragmatism maintains, there is no true idea but that constructed, there can be no given or established idea of truth that can be verified.

Pragmatism attempts to show that its own *theory* of truth is useful. For it, the important thing is not so much what truth really *is* but what it must be, even if it is recognized by no one. What the pragmatists are trying to determine is the *ideal* notion of truth. But how can we know that the notion thus constructed is really the ideal one? Pragmatism can call anything it pleases 'ideal truth'. Therefore, its method is arbitrary and leads to a purely verbal definition with no objective validity. It is analogous to the method used by the classical moralists when they try to determine the ideal notion of morality,[5] a notion which may well be unrelated to morality as it is actually practised. But just as it is better to begin by studying moral facts, the best method of establishing an ideal notion of truth seems to consist in observing the characteristics of recognized truths.

That is only a question of method, however. Much more important is the pragmatist thesis itself. We shall see that the proposition that *the useful is the true* is a formula that brings us back to utilitarianism. The pragmatist theory of truth is a *logical utilitarianism*.

••

Truth and utility*

Before examining the value of pragmatism as a form of logical utilitarianism, let us look first at the characteristics of truth. We see at once that it is linked to:

1   a *moral obligation*. Truth cannot be separated from a certain moral character. In every age, men have felt that they *were obliged* to seek truth. In truth, there is something which commands respect, and a moral power to which the mind feels properly *bound* to assent;

2   a *de facto necessitating power*. There is a more or less physical impossibility of not admitting the truth. When our mind perceives a true representation, we feel that we cannot not accept it as true. The true idea *imposes itself* on us. It is this character that is expressed in the old theory of the *evident* nature of truth; there emanates from truth an irresistible light.

PRAGMATISM AS A FORM OF LOGICAL UTILITARIANISM

Is pragmatism, as a form of logical utilitarianism, capable of explaining these two characters? It can explain *neither* of them.

1   Seeking the useful is following nature, not mastering it or taming it. There is no place here for the *moral constraint* implied in the idea of obligation. Pragmatism indeed cannot entail a hierarchy of values, since everything in it is placed on the same level. The true and the good are both on our level, that of the useful, and no effort is needed to lift ourselves to it. For James, the truth is what is 'expedient',[1] and it is because it is advantageous that it is good and has value. Clearly this means that truth has its demands, its loyalties,[2] and can give rise to enthusiasm, but at the level of the useful, this enthusiasm is only related to what is capable of pleasing us, that which is in conformity with our *interests*.

2   Nor is it possible to see how pragmatists could explain the necessitat-

*Notes to the Fifteenth Lecture, of 24 March 1914, are on pp. 127–8.

ing character of truth. Pragmatists believe that it is we who construct both the world and the representations which express it. We 'make' truth in conformity with our needs. How then could it resist us? Pragmatism no doubt accepts that beneath those intellectual constructions which make up truth there is nevertheless a prime matter which we have not created.[3] For pragmatism, however, this prime matter is only an ideal limit which we never reach, although we always tend towards it. It is wiser, says Schiller,[4] to ignore it, since absolute truth could 'give us no aid', and is rather an obstacle to a more adequate knowledge of realities which are in effect accessible to us. Besides that prime matter, there is of course the whole system of mental organization, acquired truths and 'previous truths'.[5] But that is 'a much less obdurately resisting factor' which 'often ends by giving way': ideas are soft things, which we can twist as we like when there is no objective reality (provided by sensations) which prevents us from doing so.

In short, when pragmatists speak of truth as something good, desirable and attractive, one wonders whether a whole aspect of it has not escaped them. Truth is often painful, and may well disorganize thought and trouble the serenity of the mind. When man perceives it, he is sometimes obliged to change his whole way of thinking. This can cause a crisis which leaves him disconcerted and disabled. If, for example, when he is an adult, he suddenly realizes that all his religious beliefs have no solid basis, he experiences a moral collapse and his intellectual and affective life is in a sense paralyzed. This sense of confusion has been expressed by Jouffroy in his famous article *Comment les dogmes finissent*.[6] Thus the truth is not always attractive and appealing. Very often it resists us, is opposed to our desires and has a certain quality of hardness.

3   Truth has a third character, and one which is undeniable: imperso-nality. The pragmatists themselves have indicated this.[7] But how can this character be reconciled with their definition of truth? It has been said, with some justice, that moral utilitarianism implies moral subjec-tivism. Is the same not true of logical utilitarianism?

The notion of the useful is, moreover, a very obscure one. Everything is useful in relation to certain ends, and even the worst things are useful from a certain point of view. Inversely, even the best, such as knowledge, have their disadvantages and can cause suffering: those ages in which knowledge has increased must have been the most anguished. Any phenomenon has infinite repercussions in the universe, some of them good and others bad. How could we weigh advantages against draw-backs? It would probably be possible to trace all effects back to a cause and consequently to a criterion which would both be single and determining. One could, for example, accept the existence of an impersonal and universal moral end which all men are obliged to seek. But pragmatism excludes any determination of this kind. The truth, says James, is what is 'expedient in almost any fashion; and expedient in the long run and on the whole of course; for what meets expediently all the experience in sight won't necessarily meet all further experiences equally satisfactorily'.[8] And yet not everything can be true. A choice has to be made, but on what basis? Only on that of personal experience.[9] If something causes us more *satisfaction* than discomfort, we can say that yes, it *is* useful. But the experience of other people can be different. Although pragmatism does not totally accept this consequence, truth can be totally subjective in such conditions. It is a question of temperament:[10] the temperament of the ascetic, for example, and that of the man of action; both have their reason for being, and thus correspond to two different modes of action.

But here a problem arises. If truth thus has a personal character, how can *impersonal truth* be possible? Pragmatists see it as the ideal final stage towards which all individual opinions would ultimately converge.[11] What then are the causes which would determine such a convergence? Two are mentioned by the pragmatists. (1) Just as experience varies with individuals, so does its *extent*. The person who posesses the widest and best-organized experience is in a better position to see what is really useful. Gradually, his authority here imposes itself and attracts the commendation of others. But is that a decisive argument? Since all experience and all judgements are essentially personal matters, the experience of others is valid for them, but not for me. (2) There are also *social* considerations. 'Every recognition of a judgement by others is a social problem', says Schiller.[12] Everyone, in fact, has an interest in acting in concert with his fellow men, since if he does he feels himself to be stronger and consequently more efficient and more 'useful'. But the usefulness of joint action implies shared views, judgements and ideas. The pragmatists have not disregarded this entirely. The difficulty is that we do not in fact picture things as we desire them to be, and that the pragmatist theses run the risk of making us not see this gap, and consequently of making us see as true that which conforms to our desires. In order to overcome this difficulty, we should have to agree to see the general opinion, not as something artificial, but as an authority capable of silencing the differences between individuals and of countering the particularism of individual points of view. If, however, public opinion is to be able to impose itself in this way it is essential that it should have an extra-individual origin. But this is not possible in pragmatist doctrine, since it holds that individual judgements are at the root of all human thought: no purely individual judgement could ever become an objective truth.

Moreover, above all these dialectics, there is one fact. If, as pragmatism maintains, the 'common' truth was the product of the gradual convergence of individual judgements, one would have to be able to observe an ever-greater divergence between the ways of thinking of individuals as one went further and further back through history. However, what happens is exactly the opposite.[13] It is in the very earliest ages that men, in every social group, all think in the same way. It is then that uniformity of thought can be found. The great differences only begin to appear with the very first Greek philosophers. The Middle Ages once again achieved the very type of the intellectual consensus. Then came the Reformation, and with it came heresies and schisms which were to continue to multiply until we eventually came to realize that everyone has the right to think as he wishes.

Let us also go back in the series of propositions of pragmatist doctrine. We see that if pragmatism defines the true as the useful, it is because it has proposed the principle that truth is simply an instrument of action. For pragmatism, truth *has no speculative function*: all that concerns it is its *practical utility*.[14] For pragmatists, this speculative function is present only in play and dreams.[15] But for centuries humanity has lived on non-practical truths, beliefs which were something quite other than 'instruments of action'. *Myths* have no essentially practical character. In primitive civilizations they are accepted for themselves, and are objects of belief. They are not merely poetic forms. They are groupings of representations aimed at explaining the world, systems of ideas whose function is essentially speculative. For a long time, myths were the means of expression of the intellectual life of human societies. If men found a speculative interest in them, it is because this need corresponded to a reality.

Speculation and practice*

The pragmatist philosophers, and Schiller[1] in particular, deny that thought has a speculative value. How valid is that opinion?

It is contradicted by the facts. According to pragmatism, knowledge is essentially a plan of action, and proposes practical ends to be attained. Yet the mythological beliefs encountered in primitive societies are cosmologies, and are directed not towards the future but towards the past and the present. What lies at the root of myths is not a practical need: it is the intellectual need to understand. Basically, therefore, a rationalist mind is present there,[2] perhaps in an unsophisticated form, but nevertheless enough to prove that the need to understand is universal and essentially human.

After mythology came philosophy, born from mythology, and it too satisfies purely intellectual needs. The belief in the existence of speculative truths has neither been a hallucination nor a view more purely appropriate to Plato. It predates him by a long time, and is affirmed in all the philosophers. It is true that from a very early age philosophy set itself practical problems, both moral and political. But even if it tried to engage in practical action (of a very general nature, be it noted) with regard to human problems, it has never claimed to have any effect with regard to action or things. Morality has never been more than the handmaiden of philosophy. In the Middle Ages, it was a secondary concern; and scholastic philosophy often paid no attention to it. The same is true of the seventeenth century. A practical concern does not therefore represent a permanent current of philosophical thought.

The same is also true of science. Speculation and practice were of course intermingled in the very early stages. Alchemy, for example, was less concerned with finding the real nature of bodies than with a method of producing gold. In this sense, it could be said that in origin the sciences are pragmatic. But as history progresses, the more scientific research loses the mixed character that it originally possessed. Science

*Notes to the Sixteenth Lecture, of 31 March 1914, are on p. 128.

has increasingly less to do with purely technical concerns. The scientist contemplates reality, and becomes less concerned with the practical consequences of his discoveries. In all research there is no doubt a point of departure, an optimistic act of faith in the utility of research; but that is a transitory stage. The essence of the scientific mind is that the scientist takes up a point of view which is sharply opposed to that of the pragmatists.

History too is no less of an embarrassment for pragmatists. Their view is that ideas exist to act on the real. But historical facts are facts from the past. How could there be any question of acting on this? James[3] and Dewey[4] reply that the past is not wholly dead, that there are 'present prolongations or effects of what the past harboured', and that an assertion relating to the past can make a present assertion true or false. But this is playing with words, for the adaptation of thought to historical reality is entirely an intellectual process and satisfies purely speculative needs, not practical ones.

Moore says that historical knowledge can be useful in directing our individual conduct in circumstances similar to those of the past. Although the eventuality of using history for practical and individual ends is perhaps not impossible, it has nothing to do with historical studies and the establishment of historical truth as such. When the historian asks whether Caesar really crossed the Rubicon, as is related in his *Commentaries* on the Civil War, he does so solely to know and to make known. Fustel de Coulanges said that history serves no purpose, and that that was its greatness. That aphorism is perhaps rather too absolute; but we must admit that the practical benefits of history are singularly slim. Times change, circumstances change, and the events of history cannot recur in precisely the same way, because the conditions are different.

There is of course one science which is close to history and which can extract practical consequences from historical facts. This science is *sociology*. It is however a recent one, and still in its very early stages. Even if it were more advanced than it actually is, it would still be separate from history. For example, it is no pressing concern of sociology to know whether Madame de Montespan played a political role in the events of her time or not, but history certainly does not neglect problems of this kind.

Thus, the search for truth for truth's sake is neither an isolated case, nor a pathological fact, nor a deflection of thought. Indeed, even if we suppose that it is an aberration, and that men were driven by illusion to seek for a truth which could not be grasped, we should still have to explain that illusion.

DEWEY'S ARGUMENT FOR SUBORDINATING THOUGHT TO ACTION

Let us now examine those arguments which pragmatism has used in claiming to have established that knowledge exists only for the sake of action.

Dewey in particular thought that he could cite a number of facts which he saw as conclusive. These are: (1) consciousness and reflection[5] most often come into being in such conditions that they seem to have been called into existence by the very necessity of practice. When balance is disturbed in a living organism, consciousness awakes: it begins to question itself, the subject becomes aware of problems. Consequently, it can be said that the appearance of consciousness is a response to practical ends, for it comes into being to re-establish the disturbed equilibrium. (2) The same applies to habits of all kinds:[6] consciousness disappears when it no longer serves a purpose. It only awakes when habit is disrupted, when a process on non-adaption occurs. (3) This is also true of human society.[7] When a political or social regime is functioning smoothly, it is accepted passively and men do not reflect on it. It is when it does not function smoothly that we seek remedies and think of getting to the causes of the trouble.

These facts are clearly undeniable. What provokes argument, however, is the way in which they are interpreted. From them, it is concluded that since consciousness appears only for the sake of action, it is simply a substitute for it. In this view, an idea is no more than a representation of an end to be achieved, the movement itself being this representation expressed as an act. But there are facts which contradict this assertion of the pragmatists, and which show that there can be *antagonism* between thought and action. (*a*) In some cases, consciousness can hinder action instead of facilitating it. For example, a pianist who can play a given piece perfectly will make mistakes if he thinks about what he is doing. Similarly, someone who searches for words instead of speaking naturally will stutter. In both cases, consciousness slows down, overloads or paralyzes action. (*b*) Inversely, action can paralyze thought, and this is constantly happening. The psychology of attention indicates it. Attention is a concentrated form of awareness: consciousness sharpened in this way is what enables us to understand better what the constitutive characters of consciousness are. Attention implies a tension in organic

79

functions, a suspension of movement, and that suspension of movement is even, as Ribot has shown,[8] an essential condition for it. That is why it has been said that in order to think deeply it is necessary to abstain from all movement: 'To think is to refrain from . . . acting.' It is impossible to think intensely while walking, playing and so on.

Hence it is a fact that the two very different human types, the man of action and the intellectual, are so diametrically opposed. What is dominant in the man of action is overall sensations, which are synthetic and confused, but sharp and strong. With his representations are associated motor mechanisms which he combines appropriately and adapts almost unthinkingly to circumstances. If you want his advice, do not ask his reasons for giving it, for more often than not he does not know what they are, and thinking about them would disturb him and make him hesitant. On the other hand, the intellectual, the thinker, always tends to put off the decisions he has to take. He hesitates because he never finds satisfactory reasons for acting. For him, the time for reflection is unlimited; and when he finally decides to act, he violates his intellectual temperament. We never of course encounter these two types in as absolute or clear-cut a form as that which I have just described, but it is quite true that there are in fact two contrasting casts of mind.

Why is there this sharp contrast? Because the *conditions* of thought and those of action are different. (1) First, thought is a *hyperconcentration* of consciousness, and the greater the concentration, the smaller the circle of reflection. Action, on the other hand, is a sudden release. Acting means *externalizing oneself*, and spreading out beyond oneself. Man cannot at one and the same time be both entirely *within* himself and entirely *outside* himself. (2) Secondly, thought, the reflecting consciousness, demands *time*. The faster a representation passes through consciousness, the greater the proportion of the unknown it contains. We can only truly know a representation in successive stages, part by part. To know it, we must analyse it, and to analyse it we must fix it, hold it in our consciousness; that is to say, keep it motionless for a certain time. Action does not call for that kind of fixity. What it wants is the exact opposite. Movement flows, and to the extent that it is also flux and movement consciousness does the same. But if it is to exist truly, to manifest itself, it must stop, and this also supposes a halt, a suspension of action. By way of contrast, when there is an equilibrium between our dispositions and the surrounding environment, our vital movements occur automatically, and pass so quickly that we have no time to know them, since they merely skim over consciousness. Consciousness does not therefore move off-stage like an actor whose part is over. It disappears because the conditions for its existence have not been met. And in the same way, if the movement is stopped and consciousness appears, it is not only because something must fill the gap which movement no longer occupies, but also because the suspension of movement has made consciousness possible.

We can conclude that, contrary to the pragmatist thesis, thought and action are not akin in nature. It is therefore very surprising to see the pragmatists maintain that knowledge has only practical ends, since the opposite is the case: it has demands radically different from practice.

The role of truth*

The antithesis noted in the last lecture between truth and action is all the more marked when one considers higher forms of thought. Knowledge ascends in a series of stages.

Sensation is the lowest. It provides us with merely fleeting knowledge, and is barely sufficient to set off the necessary reactions. This is apparent in the working of instinct.

Images, like sensations, are closely connected with tendencies to action. We cannot imagine something called desire without movements making themselves felt to some degree. These movements remain, however, in a state of potentiality and are, as it were, unfinished sketches. Nevertheless, representations at this stage begin to take on an appearance of having a life of their own.

Concepts have a very low motive power.[1] If we are to think in concepts, we have to put aside the emotions which cause us to act, and reject feelings which would prevent us isolating the intellectual element. Concepts are isolated from acts, and they are posited for their own sake.

THE TRUE ROLE OF CONSCIOUSNESS

The error of the pragmatists is precisely that of denying the specific nature of knowledge and consequently of thought and even of consciousness. The role of consciousness is not to direct the behaviour of a being with no need of knowledge: it is *to constitute a being who would not exist without it*. This seems to me to be proved by the role played in psychic life by 'coenaesthetic' sensations, which emanate from all parts of our body and are, so to speak, the kernel of our personal consciousness.[2] This is what caused Spinoza to say that the soul is the idea of the body.[3] Consciousness is therefore not a function with the role of directing the movements of the body, but the *organism knowing itself*,

*Notes to the Seventeenth Lecture, of 21 April 1914, are on p. 129.

and solely by virtue of the fact that the organism knows itself, we can say that something new occurs.

For consciousness to come into being, there must be gaps or spaces in action; and it is through these that the being becomes aware of himself. A being who knows himself is one who stops movement and then starts it again. Consciousness, far from having only the role of directing the movements of beings, exists in order to produce beings.

Pragmatism tends to deny this function of consciousness, which it sees as part of the external world, simply a moment in the series of movements which make up this world, and is lost in them.[4] And yet pragmatism claims to be a *spiritualist* doctrine. It is a strange kind of spiritualism which claims to deny the specific nature of consciousness!

It is no doubt quite natural that when the unthinking play of movements is disturbed thought should intervene to stimulate those which are deficient. This practical role of thought is not unimportant; but it is neither the only nor perhaps the chief one. Indeed, a conscious being, a being which knows itself, cannot act completely like a being which has no knowledge of itself. Its activity will rather be of a new kind. It will of course still consist of movements; but these movements will now be directed by ideas. In other words, there will be *psychological* activity.

Reducing the conscious being to nothing but his actions means taking from him the very thing which makes him what he is. Moreover, consciousness finds such a role distasteful, for it forms only schematic plans and can never take immediate command over real behaviour. Intelligence can only provide very general and hypothetical plans of action, whereas movement needs to be categorical and precise. Only the experience of action itself can tell us whether a given act is really the appropriate one in given circumstances. We have to act in order to know how we should act.

What really shows us that consciousness is in some measure obliged to do violence to itself, when it attempts to direct attention, is the fact that once it is freed from this task or escapes from it, movements gradually become established in the organism and consciousness itself disappears. This is what occurs in the formation of habit.

The initial error of pragmatism is thus to deny the proper nature of consciousness and subsequently of knowledge. It does, however, have the merit of causing us to reflect on the question of *how the notion of truth should be constructed.*

As I have already said, the reply to that question is that one must look at truths which are recognized as such, and examine why it is that they are accepted. A representation is considered to be a true one when it is thought to express reality. I am not concerned here with whether that is a correct view. We may hold it erroneously. It may be that ideas are held to be true for other reasons. That is of little consequence for the moment. Let us simply say that when we *believe* an idea to be true, it is because we see it as adequately conveying reality.

The problem is not to know by what right we can say that a given proposition is true or false. What is accepted as true today may quite well be held to be false tomorrow. What is important is to know what has made men believe that a representation conforms to reality. Representations which have been accepted as true in the course of history are of the same interest for us: there are no privileged ones. If we wish to escape from all that is too narrow in traditional rationalism, we shall have to broaden our horizons by freeing ourselves from ourselves, from our own point of view.

Generally nowadays, when we speak of 'truth', we have in mind particularly scientific truth. But truth existed before science; and to answer the question properly, we must also consider pre-scientific and non-scientific truths such as *mythologies*. What were mythologies? They were bodies of truths which were considered to express reality (the universe), and which imposed themselves on men with an obligatory character which was just as marked and as powerful as moral truths.

What, then, caused men to consider these mythological propositions or beliefs as true? Was it because they had tested them against a given reality, against spirits, for example, or against divinities of which they had had real experience? Not at all. The world of mythical beings is not a real world, and yet men believed in it. Mythological ideas were not considered as true because they were based on an objective reality. The very opposite is the case: it is our ideas and beliefs which give the objects of thought their vitality. Thus, an idea is true, not because it conforms to reality, but by virtue of its creative power.

COLLECTIVE REPRESENTATIONS

These ideas, however, do not originate with individuals. They are *collective representations*, made up of all the mental states of a people or a social group which thinks together. In these collectivities, of course, there are individuals who do have some role to play; but this very role is only possible as a result of the action of the collectivity. In the life of the human race, it is the collectivity which maintains ideas and representations, and all collective representations are by virtue of their origin invested with a prestige which means that they have the power to *impose* themselves. They have a greater psychological energy than representations emanating from the individual. This is why they settle with such force in our consciousness. That is where the very strength of truth lies.

Thus, we come back to the double thesis of pragmatism, but this time transposed onto a different level: (1) the model and the copy are one; (2) we are the co-authors of reality. However, one can now see the differences. Pragmatism said that *we* make reality. But in this case, 'we' means the individual. But individuals are different beings who cannot all make the world in the same way; and the pragmatists have had great difficulty in solving the problem of knowing how several different minds can know the same world at once.[5] If, however, one admits that representation is a collective achievement, it recovers a unity which pragmatism denies to it. This is what explains the impression of resistance, the sense of something greater than the individual, which we experience in the presence of truth, and which provides the indispensable basis of objectivity.

In the last analysis, it is thought which creates reality; and the major role of the collective representations is to 'make' that higher reality which is *society* itself. This is perhaps an unexpected role for truth, but one which indicates it does not exist simply in order to direct practical affairs.

The different types of truth*

In the history of human thought there are two kinds of mutually contrasting truths, namely, *mythological* and *scientific* truths.

MYTHOLOGICAL TRUTHS

In the first type, all truth is a body of propositions which are accepted without verification, as against scientific truths, which are always subjected to testing or demonstration. If they are unproven, from where do they acquire the character of truth attributed to them? It is representations which create the character of objectivity which mythologies have, and it is their collective character which confers on them the creative power that enables them to impose themselves on the mind. Collective representations carry with them their objects, and entail their existence. Mythological truths have been, for those societies that have believed in them, the conditions necessary for their existence. Communal life in fact presupposes common ideas and intellectual unanimity. By the very fact that the collectivity accepts them, mythological ideas are no longer subject to individual contingencies. Hence their objective and necessitating character.

But are peoples completely free to create truth as they will? Can society transform reality just as it wishes? If this were the case, we should be able to adopt a more or less attenuated version of pragmatism, giving it a more or less sociological slant. But a correction of that kind would not be enough. Ideas and representations cannot become collective if they do not correspond to something real. Nor can they remain divorced from the conduct of individuals; for experiencing failure, disappointment and suffering tells us that our action corresponds to an inadequate representation, and we immediately detach ourselves from both of these. Indeed, it is untrue to say, as the pragmatists do, that an idea which brings us 'satisfaction' is a true one by the very fact that it

*Notes to the Eighteenth Lecture, of 28 April 1914, are on p. 129.

does so. But, although it is false to think that any idea which satisfies us is a true one, the reciprocal idea that an idea cannot be true without bringing us some satisfaction is not false.

It is the same with truth as with moral rules. Moral rules are not made *with the purpose* of being useful to the individual. However, we could not do what we ought to do if duty contained no attraction for individuals or if they found nothing satisfying in it.[1] Truth is similar to moral rules, in having an impersonal and a necessitating character; but if that were the sum of its characteristics we should constantly tend to reject or ignore it. In order to become really a part of ourselves, it must serve us and be useful to us. At the practical level, any collective representation must serve individuals, in the sense that it must give rise to acts which are adjusted to things, to the realities to which the representation corresponds. Hence, if it is to be able to give rise to such acts, the representation itself must be adapted to these realities.

Mythological creations therefore have some connection with reality. There must be a reality of which these representations are the expression. That reality is none other than society.[2] The forces that religions and myths believe that they recognize in mythological creations are not mere illusions, but forces which are collective in origin. What religion expresses in its representations, its beliefs and myths, is social realities and the way in which they act upon individuals. Monotheism, for example, is the expression of the social group's tendency towards greater concentration, as a result of which particularist groups increasingly disappear.[3] Just as 'coenaesthetic' sensations are the central core of consciousness for the individual, collective truths are the basis of the common consciousness for society.

Society cannot become aware of itself in the absence of any relationship with things. Social life demands agreement between individual consciousnesses. In order to notice it, each one must express what it experiences. It can only do so, however, by means of things taken as symbols. It is because society expresses itself through things that it has managed to transform and transfigure reality. That is why, in representations in the form of a myth, plants, for example, become beings capable of expressing human feelings. Such representations are false with respect to things, but true with respect to the subjects who think them.

It is for this reason that truth has varied historically. We have seen that the pragmatists have been well aware of that idea; but they express it by talking of the truth as neither fixed nor definite, as being constantly formed. This formulation is not satisfactory; for although there are new truths, that does not mean that old ones change or are abolished. All the cosmologies immanent in mythological systems are different from each other, but can nevertheless be said to be equally true, because they have fulfilled the same function for all the peoples who have believed in them, and because they performed the same social role.

Nowadays we see *scientific truths* as being the very type of truth. At first glance, scientific representations seem very different from mythological ones. The latter express ideas which society has about itself, the former express the world as it is. The social sciences, in particular, express what society is in itself, and not what it is subjectively to the person thinking about it. Nevertheless, scientific representations are also collective representations.

It will be objected that scientific representations are impersonal; but perhaps so too are collective representations? We can answer in the affirmative, for they express something which is outside and above individuals.

Scientific ideas have all the characteristics necessary to become collective representations. Scientific truth helps to strengthen social consciousness, as does mythological thought, though by different means. One might ask how individual minds can communicate. In two possible ways: either by uniting to form a single collective mind, or by communicating in one object which is the same for all, with each however retaining his own personality; like Leibnitz's monads, each expressing the entirety of the universe while keeping its individuality.[4] The first way is that of mythological thought, the second that of scientific thought.

Nor has science taken on this task fortuitously or, as it were, unconsciously, for it is its very *raison d'être*. When pragmatists wonder why science exists, and what its function is, they should turn to history for a reply. History shows us that it came into existence in Greece, and nowhere else, to meet certain needs. For both Plato and Socrates, the role of science is to unify individual judgements. The proof is that the method used to construct it is 'dialectics', or the art of comparing contradictory human judgements with a view to finding those in which there is agreement. If dialectics is the first among scientific methods, and its aim is to eliminate contradictions, it is because the role of science is to turn minds towards impersonal truths and to eliminate contradictions and particularisms.

Science and the collective consciousness*

We have seen that the great thinkers of Greece tried to ensure intellectual unity and understanding among men. The means they used was to take *objective reality* as their object, since it must necessarily be the same for all men, given its independence from the observing subject. This aim will therefore be achieved if one can attain a representation of things in the manner in which an impersonal understanding would represent them.

But the object of science as we see it today is precisely to represent things as if they were seen by a purely impersonal understanding. August Comte understood that perfectly, and saw the role of 'positive philosophy' as that of ending the intellectual anarchy paramount since the Revolution, but having much earlier real origins. From the 'metaphysical age', that is, from the birth of the critical mind,[1] there could no longer be a common consciousness. Comte's view was that it was science that could provide the mental equipment to reconstitute that common consciousness. Individual sciences, however, are not up to that task, since they are too specialized. A discipline capable of including all specialisms and synthesizing individual sciences was needed, and that discipline was philosophy.[2] It is possible to see Comte as mistaken here, as he did not see that philosophy can never be anything but personal.

Yet the collective consciousness can, even if not necessarily by means of a philosophical approach, take possession of scientific truths and fashion them into a co-ordinated whole. That is how a *popular philosophy*, made by and for all, can be created. Such a philosophy will not have as its concern solely physical things, but also, and indeed chiefly, man and society. Hence the important part that history must play. As Comte said, philosophy looks not so much towards the future (which is what the pragmatists believe) as towards the past; and it is through philosophy that society becomes aware of itself. There is also a science which, with the help of history, is called to play the most important role in this area. That science is sociology.[3]

*Notes to the Nineteenth Lecture, of 5 May 1914, are on pp. 129–30.

Pragmatism and sociology

It is not, however, necessary that philosophy should investigate all the forms of scientific knowledge, for they are recorded and retained in the collective consciousness. Philosophy can only provide general orientations; it cannot be coercive. Comte exaggerated not only the role of philosophy, but also that of science. He believed that once mankind reached the positive age, there would be an end to mythological ideas. Men, he thought, would no longer have views on questions not elucidated by science. Our lives would be based on positive scientific truths, which would be considered established, and the rest would be the domain of intellectual doubt. I accept that this is so with regard to knowledge about the physical world, but it cannot be the case as far as the human and social world is concerned. In these areas, science is still in a rudimentary state. Its methods of investigation are difficult, since direct experiment is impossible. Under such conditions it is not hard to understand why ideas expressing social matters in a really objective way are still rather rare.

If Comte could believe that sociology would one day be able to provide guidelines for the public consciousness, it was because he had simplistic ideas about social development, or rather an essentially philosophical concept of it. His sociology was really a philosophy of history. He was fascinated by the 'law of the three stages' and thought that in enunciating it he had established the whole of sociology. This was, of course, far from being the case. Sociology, as he himself recognized, has a more complex object than other sciences. It can only express fragmentary hypotheses, and so far these have had scarcely any effect on popular consciousness.

What action should we take in these circumstances? Should we take refuge in doubt? That would certainly be a kind of wisdom, at least with regard to the physical world. But, as we have said, it is difficult to extend that attitude to the social and human world. In that world, we have to act and live; and in order to live we need something other than doubt. Society cannot wait for its problems to be solved scientifically. It has to make decisions about what action to take, and in order to make these decisions it has to have an idea of what it is.

Where can we find that representation of it, which is indispensable for its action and its life? There is only one solution. If there is no objective knowledge, society can only know itself from within, attempt to express this sense of itself, and to use that as its guide. In other words, it must conduct itself with reference to a representation of the same kind as those which constitute mythological truths.

What characterizes such mythological representations is the fact that they express a unanimous conception, and this is what gives them a force and authority which enables them to impose themselves without their being subject to verification or doubt. That is why there are formulae in our societies which we imagine are not religious, but which nevertheless do have the character of dogma, and are not questioned. Of this kind are ideas such as 'democracy', 'progress', 'the class struggle' and so on. Thus, we can see that scientific thought cannot rule alone. There is, and there always will be, room in social life for a form of truth which will perhaps be expressed in a very secular way, but will nevertheless have a mythological and religious basis. For a long time to come, there will be two tendencies in any society: a tendency towards objective scientific truth and a tendency towards subjectively perceived truth, towards mythological truth. This is also one of the great obstacles which obstruct the development of sociology.

IMPERSONAL TRUTH AND INDIVIDUAL DIVERSITIES

We are now faced with a further problem. So far we have seen truth as characterized by its impersonal nature. But should we not keep a place within it for *individual diversity*? As long as mythological truth holds sway, conformity is the rule. Once scientific thought becomes paramount, however, intellectual individualism appears. Indeed, it is this very individualism which has made scientific truth necessary, since social unanimity can no longer centre on mythological beliefs.[4] The impersonal truth developed by science can leave room for everyone's individuality. The fact is that the diversity of objects found in the world encourages the differentiation of minds; for individual minds are not all equally suited to studying the same things, and thus tend to parcel out amongst themselves the questions to be investigated.

But this is not all, and not even the real question, which is whether, with a *given problem*, there is room for a plurality of mental attitudes all of which in a sense are justified. Each object is, of course, extremely complex and includes a multitude of elements which intermingle. We cannot exhaust reality either as a whole or in any of its constituent parts. Therefore every object of knowledge offers an opportunity for an infinity of possible points of view, such as the point of view of life, of purely mechanical movement, of stasis and dynamics,[5] of contingency and determination,[6] of physics and biology and so on. Individual minds, however, are finite, and none can work from all points of view at once. If each of these aspects is to be given the attention it merits, the whole mind must be devoted to it. Consequently, each mind is free to choose the point of view from which it feels itself most competent to view things.[7]

This means that for every object of knowledge there are differing but equally justified ways of examining it. These are probably partial truths, but all these partial truths come together in the collective consciousness and find their limits and their necessary complements. Thus intellectual individualism, far from making for anarchy, as would be the case during the period of the domination of mythological truth, becomes a necessary factor in the establishment of scientific truth, so that the diversity of intellectual temperaments can serve the cause of impersonal truth.

Furthermore, intellectual individualism does not necessarily imply, as James seems to think, that everyone may arbitrarily believe what he wishes to believe. It simply means that there are separate tasks within the joint enterprise, and that everyone may choose his own in accordance with his temperament.

Thus, on the one hand, scientific truth is not incompatible with the diversity of minds; and on the other, as social groups become increasingly complex, it is impossible that society should have a single sense of itself. Hence there are various social currents. Here, society will be seen as a static phenomenon; there as a dynamic one. Now it will be seen as subject to determinism; now chiefly sensed as an essentially contingent entity, and so on. Basically, all these ideas are reasonable, for they each correspond to various needs which express the different ways in which society senses and experiences itself.

A further consequence of this transformation is that *tolerance* must henceforth be based on this idea of the complexity and richness of reality, and then on the diversity of opinions, which is both necessary and effective. Everyone must be able to admit that someone else has perceived an aspect of reality, which he himself had not grasped, but which is as real and as true as those to which he had gone from preference.

We can also see at the same time that the task of speculative truth is to provide nourishment for the collective consciousness. This means that we can answer the pragmatists' objection, which says that if the sole function of truth is to express reality, it is merely redundant; it must *add* something to truth, and if it does, it is no longer a faithful copy. The fact is that truth, the 'copy' of reality, is not merely redundant or pleonastic. It certainly 'adds' a new world to reality,[8] a world which is more complex than any other. That world is the human and social one. Truth is the means by which a new order of things becomes possible, and that new order is nothing less than *civilization*.

Are thought and reality heterogeneous?*

We must now examine pragmatism as a doctrine which claims that thought and reality are heterogeneous. At the same time, we shall have to examine the arguments which the pragmatists borrow from Bergson to support that thesis.

We recall that the pragmatists' line of argument is as follows: truth implies the existence of distinctions between elements; reality consists of a lack of distinction; therefore truth cannot express reality without presenting as distinct something which is not distinct; without, in short, distorting reality. Reality, like a mass, forms a unity where everything holds together without any radical separation. What emanates from one part has repercussions within the whole. Thus it is only *in abstracto* that we separate one part from the whole. Concepts, on the other hand, are limited, determined and clearly circumscribed; and the world of concepts is discontinuous and distinct. The conceptual and the real are thus heterogeneous.

This heterogeneity is heightened when we try to express, not the universe as a whole, but change, movement and, above all, life. In order to express change, we have to break it down into its components, split it up into its elements, and each of these elements necessarily becomes something fixed. A series of fixed elements, however, will never restore the mobility of change, just as from inert matter one can never create life. Concepts express only the coagulated, the ready-made, and never what is being made or is becoming. But in reality everything is continuous, complex and moving. There is nothing simple about the world. Everything can be broken down infinitely; and it is pluralism, as a negation of simplicity and an affirmation of diversity, which is an affirmation of the true.

That is the pragmatist line of argument. But, because reality is continuous and undivided, does it necessarily follow that what is distinct is simply a product of thought and that alone? Because there are

*Notes to the Twentieth Lecture, of 12 May 1914, are on pp. 130–1.

no absolute distinctions, does it follow that there is a lack of distinction and absolute confusion? There is nothing absolute in the universe, and absolute confusion is as impossible as absolute separation. In things there is already a relative discrimination. If the real were in fact totally indistinct, if confusion were paramount in it, we should have to admit that the principle of contradiction could not apply there. In order to be able to say that A is A, it is necessary that A should be determined, must be what it is and not something else. Pragmatism itself rests on reasoning which involves concepts,[1] and which is based on the principle of contradiction. Denying this principle would mean denying the possibility of any intellectual relationship. We cannot make a judgement or understand anything at all if we do not first agree that it is this object and not another that is at issue. Similarly, in discussion, we first have to agree that we are talking about this object, and not another.

But it may be objected, with Bergson, that the natural state of life is precisely one of undividedness. Life is a unity, a concentration, in which nothing is properly speaking outside the other parts.

Our answer is that reality, whatever it is, is far from resistant to any form of distinction, and to some degree tends of itself towards it. When Spencer says that the universe moves from 'the homogeneous to the heterogeneous', the expression is inexact. What exists originally is also heterogeneous in nature; but it is the heterogeneity entailed by a state of confusion. The initial state is a multiplicity of germs, of ways and means, and of different activities which are not only intermingled, but, as it were, lost in each other, so that it is extremely difficult to separate them. They are *indistinct* from each other. Thus, in the cell of monocellular organisms, all the vital functions are so to speak included. They are all there, but not separately, and the functions of nutrition and of sensitivity seem confused, and it seems difficult to distinguish them. The same is true of the embryo: in the human foetus, all the functions of the human organism are already present. The child who is born carries within him all his hereditary tendencies, although it is not possible to see them clearly at that stage, and it is not until later that they will really separate.

In social life, that primitive undivided state is even more striking. *Religious life*, for example, contains a rich abundance of forms of thought and activities of all kinds. In the field of thought, these include myths and religious beliefs, an embryonic science[2] and a certain poetry. In the sphere of action we find rites, a morality and a form of law[3] and arts (aesthetic elements, songs and music in particular). All these elements are gathered up into a whole and it seems extremely difficult to separate them. Science and art, myth and poetry, morality, law and religion are all confused or, rather, fused. The same observations could be made about the early family, which is at one and the same time, for example, a social, religious, political and legal unit.[4]

Thus the primitive form of any reality is a concentration of all kinds of energies, undivided in the sense that they are only various aspects of one and the same thing. Evolution consists of a gradual separation of all these various functions which were originally indistinct. Secular and scientific thought has moved away from religious thought; art has moved away from religious ceremonies; morality and law have moved away from ritual. The social group has been divided into the family group, the political group, the economic group and so on.

We are thus brought round to the view that *what we are told is the major form of reality*, that is, the non-separation and interpenetration of all its elements, *is really its most rudimentary* form. Confusion is the original state.

DISTINCT THOUGHT AND THE 'LIFE FORCE'

But here once again we encounter Bergson's objection. Life is seen as essentially an undivided force; and this 'life force', struggling with rigid, fixed, inert matter, is obliged to diffract and sub-divide.[5] Matter itself is also seen as a slackening, an intermission and an inversion, of this rising force.[6]

We do not see, however, if matter is still life in a slowed-down and so to speak condensed form, how both can engage in a struggle or why they should be opposed to each other. The hypothesis of life and matter as two mutually hostile forces is inadmissible. Life does not break up and sub-divide *in spite of itself*. It does so spontaneously to achieve its potential more fully and to emancipate itself. In the beginning, all forms of activity and all functions were gathered together, and were, in a manner of speaking, each other's prisoners. Consequently they were obstacles for each other, each preventing the other from achieving its nature fully. That is why, if science is to come into being, it must differentiate itself from religion and myths. If the link which originally united them slackens and weakens, it is not a fall or a collapse, but progress.

The need for distinction and separation thus lies in *things themselves*, and is not simply a mental need. Things are rich in potentially diverse elements, separable parts and varied aspects. Consequently, there are discernible elements, since they tend of themselves to separate, although they never manage to free themselves of each other completely.

In social life, individuation is simply one of the forms of that movement towards distinction.

Such a distinction probably cannot be a mere abstraction, as we know that every element that we isolate keeps its relationship with all the rest. Nevertheless, the isolation of one element from everything to which it is connected is a legitimate action. We have the right to say that A is A, provided we are aware that we are doing so *in abstracto* and conditionally. In so far as we are considering A, not as absolutely distinct from B and C, but in itself, we are making a concept of it. Isolating this real aspect of things is not doing violence to the nature of things. All we are doing is to follow the natural articulations of each thing. Using concepts to think about things means establishing a quite relative distinction. The concept certainly expresses a reality and, if it is distinct, it is because it expresses distinctions which are in no way purely mental ones. Thought and reality are thus not at all heterogeneous.

There remains the objection which sees concepts as unable to express change and life. Becoming, we are told, is something which 'occurs', not a series of ready-made states. Concepts are unable to express the transition from one stage to another. There is however a contradiction in that idea of life. Life cannot be defined by mobility alone. Reality has a static aspect. That aspect, in the view of the doctrine we are discussing, is that of matter. If matter is spoilt, or fixed by life, there must be something in life which is inclined towards that process of becoming fixed. Even in change itself there must be a static aspect.

The fact is that nothing changes except to achieve a result. What right have we to postulate that these results have no fixity? Life has a perfect right to rest on its laurels occasionally! Movement and change can surely be seen as means of achieving results. If becoming were a kind of frantic, incessant and restless flight, with never a fixed point, it would simply be sound and fury. By fixing consecutive *states*, we are therefore expressing real elements of becoming, and they are indeed its most important ones.

Nor can we represent something changing without representing 'something'; and that something is necessarily something already constituted. We make the new from what we have, and the new is new and meaningful only in relation to what we already have.

It is true that we still have to think out the link between the two. One might ask how it is possible to think about what is 'making itself'. Things in that state do not yet exist, they are indeterminate in nature, and therefore not susceptible to thought. We can only represent what is, because it 'is' in a certain way, and this offers some purchase for thought.

The tendency to be can only be thought about in terms of elements already acquired.

But is it really true that we cannot think of movement and the transition from one stage to another? When thought is applied to change, it always contains three terms: the idea of an achieved state, the idea of a state thought about in rudimentary terms because it still does not exist and the idea of a *relationship* between these two notions. That last idea can certainly be represented by a concept.

The difficulty lies chiefly in understanding how a participatory relationship can be expressed. Concepts are never really isolated by us. We can loosen the context which constrains them, but we have *judgement* and *reason* which enable us to re-establish mutual relationships. That is how we learn that two things are in communication.

Distinction is thus a need of conceptual thought, but it already exists in things as it does in the mind. Similarly, continuity and communication exist in the mind, as they do in things.

CONCLUSION

Rationalists were accused of seeing truth as a sort of luxury of reality, something given, achieved, created simply to be contemplated. But that contemplation, it was also said, is a sterile, selfish intellectual's joy, of no use from the human point of view.

The expression of reality, however, does have a truly useful function, for it is what makes societies, although it could equally well be said that it also derives from them.[7] It is true that when we imagine truth as something ready-made, we are obliged to see it as a transcendence. But although truth is a *social thing*, it is also a human one at the same time, and thus comes closer to us, rather than moves away and disappears in the distant realms of an intelligible world or a divine understanding. It is no doubt still superior to individual consciousness; but even the collective element in it exists only through the consciousness of individuals, and truth is only ever achieved by individuals.[8]

We should also add that truth, at the same time as being a social and human thing, is also something *living*. It mingles with life because it is a product of that higher form of life, social life, as well as being the condition for its existence. It is diverse, because that form of life presents itself in multiple and diverse forms. This 'diversification', and the 'carving out' of concepts of which pragmatism speaks, are by no means arbitrary. They are modelled on realities, and in particular on the realities of social life.

There is also one final characteristic of truth on which I have already insisted,[9] but which I would like to recapitulate in conclusion: that is its *obligatory* nature. We have seen that pragmatism, that logical utilitarianism, cannot offer an adequate explanation of the *authority* of truth, an authority which is easy to conceive of, however, if one sees a social aspect of truth. That is why *truth is a norm for thought in the same way that the moral ideal is a norm for conduct.*

••

Certainty[1]*

Certainty is generally defined as the state in which the subject finds himself when he believes that he is in possession of the truth. This is not really a definition, however, as it is not an objective one. It merely offers a completely subjective assessment. Furthermore, the subject himself does not know when he is in possession of the truth. He is mistaken about his own belief; he may think that he is certain when he is not; and he may think that he is hesitating when in fact his mind is already made up.

We must therefore seek precise and objective criteria for certainty. We must determine whether the state of certainty has *external* effects which enable us to define it.

If the subject is not certain, he hesitates when the time comes for him to express this certainty in action. On the other hand, if he is certain, he acts in conformity with the idea which he accepts as true. A faith which draws back from action is not a genuine faith.

This *disposition to act* consists of several degrees. It may necessarily entail action, as is most often the case with religious and moral faith. It may be that the act seems only conditionally indispensable. There is, however, always a disposition to act.

This definition indicates that certainty is not an absolute and has all sorts of gradations. It is the ability of the subject to transform the idea into action.

But certainty contains another element: it is a disposition to act *in conformity with a representation*. What is that representation? We distinguish between three major kinds of representation: sensation, images and concepts.

Sensation is often seen as the very type of the state of certainty. It is said that we feel with certainty: but we cannot but have such a sensation. It is the certainty of fact.

In reality, sensation is outside or below certainty. Animals have only sensations, but no certainty. Certainty is a human fact.

*Notes to Appendix I are on pp. 131–2.

When we suffer it is of course a fact that we are suffering. But, for there to be real certainty, we must make a judgement, name our impressions, subsume them in a concept. We must say and think that we are suffering, and that we are certain that we are suffering. It is the concept of suffering which intervenes to subsume the impression and classify it. Without that concept, there is no certainty. It very often happens that, properly speaking, we do not know whether we are suffering because we do not know *how* we are suffering.[2] To be certain we must affirm something; and to affirm something we have to extract it from the becoming of sensation and classify it. Thus, in pure sensation, there is no true certainty.

Images are constantly intermingled with sensation. If we consider only free images, the proper world of the imagination, we see at once that in this area there is no room for certainty. The world of art is not felt as completely real.

There remain *concepts*. It is only in the world of concepts that there is certainty. There is certainty when we are sure that a concept applies to reality. That conceptual certainty is different from so-called sensitive certainty. Of course, the process of action that they govern is comparable. Concepts, like sensations, govern movements. Concepts, however, express reality and govern movement *in a different way* from sensation. Sensation is living and passionate; concepts are abstract and cold, and do not in themselves have the qualities necessary to motivate action. Sensations immediately give the impression of reality and possess their own force of action. The opposite is the case with concepts. They are indirect expressions of reality, and in themselves have no force of action.

There are two kinds of concepts to which certainty can be attached. These are: (1) concepts which express given, achieved states, whether it is a matter of internal or external states; and (2) those which express states to be achieved, movements to be carried out and ways of acting.

Consequently, it is possible to have certainty related directly to action, in which the disposition to act immediately brings about the act. This is *religious* or *moral* certainty. There is another form of certainty which relates only to real objects, those for which, in consequence, the disposition to act is not immediate. In these cases, the act does not flow directly from the concept, since the latter is a concept of something already achieved, from which the act then only occurs as a corollary.

In short, certainty is either *practical*, and immediately results in action, or it is *theoretical*, and results in action only through a concept expressing a given thing.

What are the *causes which determine certainty*? According to a first theory, this will follow as an intrinsic characteristic of the concept. It is this character that Descartes called *évidence*.[3] It is the principle which captures the mind. No doubt the subject plays his part in this certainty, as he must place himself in an attitude of voluntary *attention*, but the character of certainty is nevertheless imposed on him.

That explanation is inadequate. Where, we may ask, does this clarity of ideas come from? And in fact there never has been any *évidence* which has not been denied at some point in history. This has been the case even with the principle of contradiction. In mythological beliefs, the whole is completely present in each of its parts. The principle of contradiction thus takes on the appearance of a postulate. Certainty varies. There is a relative quality of truth which one is compelled to recognize historically.[4] Finally, if certainty were an intrinsic characteristic of ideas, we should not be able to explain how the latter determine acts. There must be in certainty particular qualities which are nearer to action.

That was well understood by the defenders of the *voluntarist* theory of certainty, and by Renouvier in particular. In their view, certainty was not a property of ideas, but a work of man as a whole. This explains the relationship between the representation and the act, and also explains why certainty can vary, since it is individual.

But the voluntarist theory does not properly understand the necessitating character of the true idea.[5] We are not free in a state of certainty. We feel obliged to adhere to truth. We see our certainty as something that is not personal to us, and that it is to be shared by all men. Whether this is an illusion or not, we have that belief. How could that impersonality be the product of such personal factors? Whence comes that union of these two elements that we have within us, the personal and the impersonal, the free and the necessary?

In order to answer that question, let us first consider practical certainty. In the representation of a moral act to be carried out, there is something that imposes itself on us; and that something is an authority, the authority that comes from collective feelings.

But if there are ways of acting which impose themselves on us through collective authority, why should there not be ways of thinking that would impose themselves on us in the same way, through the authority of the collective consciousness? The power of opinion is as great with respect to thought as it is with respect to action. Concepts which are collective in origin (as all concepts really are) take on in our eyes, even when their object is not a real one, such a strength that it appears to be real. That is why concepts acquire the vividness and force of action of sensations. We can understand also why all our concepts vary with opinion.

Thus logical necessity would be simply another form of moral necessity, and theoretical certainty only another form of practical certainty. In this we remain firmly in the Kantian tradition.

It could well be that certainty is essentially something collective. We are only certain when we are certain that we are not *the only ones* who are certain. Even when we have worked out a personal belief, we need to communicate it, in order to be certain that we are not mistaken.

The authority of tradition and opinion is not, of course, exempt from criticism. When we criticize them, however, it is always in their own name. When, for example, we criticize popular prejudices in the name of science, we are using the authority which opinion accords to science.

APPENDIX II

Concepts*

We might be tempted to define concepts by their breadth and generality, as opposed to sensations and images which represent only particular objects.

Such a definition would, however, simply provide a generic notion, and would not specifically distinguish concepts from sensations and images. It would imply that thinking logically means simply thinking in general terms. But the general only exists as entailed by the particular. Thinking in general terms therefore means thinking in particular terms, but in a certain way.

It would be extraordinary if such a simple definition was enough to give rise to a type of thought which is as distinct from 'thought through sensations' and 'thought through images' as logical thought is. How would the particular, once it had been impoverished and simplified, come to possess those virtues which the particular in its richness and denseness does not possess? How would one, by mutilating the real, obtain a set of specially privileged representations? We must consider whether concepts are not something more.

There is no discontinuity between the individual and the genus. There are concepts for genera. Why should there not be concepts for individuals? Is the genus necessary for the existence of a concept?

There are in fact many concepts which designate only individuals. Each people and nation has a great number of heroes either legendary or historical (it matters little which). In what terms do we think about them? Not in general ideas, nor yet in images, for we have never seen them. We do have concepts of them, for we argue about them, and these concepts are the starting-points for our discussions and our reasoning.

In the same way, the concept of God is an individual concept. For believers, God is certainly an individual being, and we think of Him neither through sensations nor through images.

The idea of the native land is also a concept.

*The notes to Appendix II are on p. 132.

103

Furthermore, sensations and images are characterized by their fleeting nature and their mobility. The concept on the other hand is immutable, or at least should be. Thinking in concepts means thinking of the variable, but subsuming it *under the form of* the immutable. The fixity of vocabulary expresses the fixity of concepts, and at the same time partly causes it.

Concepts are universal or at least capable of being universal amongst men of the same civilization. They are common to all men who have the same language, or at least communicable. One cannot talk about *my* concept; although one can talk about *my* sensation. Sensations, like images, cannot be communicated to others. We can only suggest similar ones, by association. Concepts are impersonal, and above individual contingencies. That, indeed, is the feature of logical thought.

The problem is thus that of how thought has been able to fix itself in this way and, so to speak, to make itself impersonal, and not of how it has become generalized.

When the Socratics discovered that there were fixed representations, they were full of wonder; and Plato felt impelled to hypostasize, almost to make divine, these fixed thoughts.[1]

We can, however, find other explanations of the properties of concepts. If they are common to all, is it not because they are the work of the community? Classical dogmatism, which postulates the agreement of all human reasons, is a little childish.[2] There is no need to go beyond experience to seek this one, impersonal thought. A form of it, collective thought, occurs within experience. Why should concepts not be collective representations?

Everything collective tends to become fixed, and to eliminate the changing and the contingent. In addition, it is because they are collective that concepts impose themselves upon us, and are transmitted to us. Words too play a major role where concepts are concerned, and words are collective things.

Collective thought is only feebly and incompletely represented in each individual consciousness, as we have already seen in the case of moral thought.[3] The same is true intellectually. Each of our words goes beyond our individual experience, and often expresses things about which we know nothing whatsoever. If some of the objects connoted by the word are known to us, they are only examples. Concepts themselves go even futher beyond our personal experience; for they are formed by what a whole series of generations has experienced. What is superimposed on our individual experience, and 'subsumes' it by means of concepts, is thus collective experience.

104

In addition, concepts are systematized because collective thought itself is systematized. In relation to that collective thought, we stand in the same relationship as Plato's νοῦς to the world of Ideas. We never manage to see it in its entirety, or in its reality. We do not know all the concepts worked out by our own civilization; and in addition, we individualize them, and give words a particular meaning which they do not have. Hence the many differences which arise amongst individuals. Hence too lies, the lies which are said to be necessary ...

One can make an objection to this sociological theory of concepts. As we have defined them here, concepts ensure agreement between individuals. One might ask, however, where their agreement with reality comes from. We tend to think that if concepts are collective they are likely to be true; but only scientific concepts present this character. The others are worked out without method.

One can nevertheless reply that collective representations do not stand outside logical truth. The generality and fixity which they have would not be possible if they were totally inadequate with respect to truth. Verification is a reciprocal process: the experiences of all individuals are mutually critical. The concepts worked out by the masses and those worked out by scientists are not essentially different in nature.[4]

Notes

Preface to the French edition of 1955

1 *Année Sociologique* NS, vol. I, 1925, p. 10.
2 [E. Durkheim, *Moral Education: A Study in the Theory and Application of the Sociology of Education* (trans. E. K. Wilson and H. Schnurer), New York, The Free Press, 1961; *The Evolution of Educational Thought: Lectures on the Formation and Development of Secondary Education in France* (trans. P. Collins), London, Routledge & Kegan Paul, 1977. The *Leçons de sociologie* appeared in English as *Professional Ethics and Civic Morals* (trans. C. Brookfield), London, Routledge & Kegan Paul, 1957. It was originally published in Istanbul, edited by H. N. Kubali.]
3 O. Hamelin, *Le Système de Descartes* [Paris, Félix Alcan, 1911], preface, p.x.
4 In return, incidentally, Hamelin was plainly referring to Durkheim when he wrote: 'Certain sociologists profess, if we are not mistaken, that in addition to individual consciousness there is a social consciousness. This must not be assumed to exist apart from individual consciousnesses, however, and is sustained by each of them. Similarly, we recognize in every being, and especially every human being, both a consciousness of oneself and a consciousness of all else. Through this consciousness of the universe every being comes to support all the others.' (*Eléments principaux* [Paris, Félix Alcan], 1st edn [1907], p. 453; 2nd edn [1925], p. 489.)
5 Cf. *Eléments principaux*, 1st edn, p. 471: 2nd edn p. 508. 'The will does not create objects: it presupposes them ... Not having created objects, the subject only impinges upon their situation when it makes itself available, opening itself to them through awareness or, on the contrary, by closing itself off from them.'
6 D. Parodi, *La Philosophie contemporaine en France* [Paris, Félix Alcan], 3rd edn, 1925, p. 458.
7 Durkheim, *The Elementary Forms of the Religious Life* [(trans. J. W. Swain), London, George Allen & Unwin, 1915], p. 19.
8 Durkheim, *Elementary Forms*, p. 19, n. 2, see esp.: 'For example, that which is at the foundation of the category of time is the rhythm of social life; but if there is a rhythm in collective life, one may rest assured that there is another in the life of the individual, and more generally, in that of the universe.'
9 [The French text at this point reads as follows: 'C'est déjà vrai sur le plan

106

psycho-organique où la conscience coenesthésique n'est rien autre, selon Durkheim, que "l'organisme se connaissant".']

10 [The French text at this point reads as follows: 'Il est curieux de voir ainsi le réalisme sociologique de Durkheim s'achever en un idéo-realisme gnoséologique ...']

11 *Anon, Revue de Métaphysique et de Morale*, vol. 46, no. 3, July 1939, p. 545.

12 [Durkheim, *Professional Ethics and Civic Morals*, pp. xiv–xv, xxviii–xxx.]

13 [P. A. Lalande], 'Sur une fausse exigence de la raison dans la méthode des sciences morales', in *Revue de Métaphysique et de Morale*, vol. 15, January 1907, p. 18; cf. *La Raison et les normes*, [P. A. Lalande, Paris, Hachette, 1948], chap. vi.

14 Lalande, *La Raison et les normes*, p. 135.

15 Cf. E. Durkheim, *The Division of Labour in Society* [(trans. G. Simpson), New York, The Free Press, 1964], from the preface to the first edn, pp. 34–5. 'But obviously, *the supposition, man wishes to live*, a very simple speculation, immediately transforms the laws science establishes into imperative rules of conduct.'

16 E. Durkheim, *The Rules of Sociological Method* [(trans. S. A. Solovay & J. H. Mueller), New York, The Free Press, 1964], p. xxxix.

17 Durkheim, *Elementary Forms*, p. 19.

18 William James, *The Varieties of Religious Experience* [London, Longmans, Green & Co., 1912], p. 490.

19 Cf. 'Jugements de valeur et jugements de réalité', in *Revue de Métaphysique et de Morale* [vol. 19], July 1911, p. 449: 'A society cannot be constituted without creating ideals.' [This article is translated by D. F. Pocock, in E. Durkheim, *Sociology and Philosophy*, London, Cohen & West Ltd, 1953: see esp. p. 93.]

20 *Ibid.*, p. 94.

21 L. von Wiese, in *Kölner Zeitschrift für Soziologie*, vol. vi, 1954, no. 2, p. 289.

22 Morris Ginsberg, *Bulletin international des Sciences sociales* (UNESCO), vol. vi, no. 1, 1954, pp. 156–65. [Reprinted in the collection of essays by the same author, *On the Diversity of Morals*, London, Heinemann, 1956, pp. 149–62.]

23 *Professional Ethics and Civic Morals*, p. 56. [The citation in the French text is incorrect at this point.]

24 *Elementary Forms*; see also the following: 'If experience were completely separated from all that is rational, reason could not operate upon it, in the same way, if the psychic nature of the individual were absolutely opposed to the social life, society would be impossible. A complete analysis of the categories would seek these germs of rationality even in the individual consciousness' (*ibid.*, p. 16, n. 1). 'The relations which they [the categories] express could not have been learned except in and through society. If they are in a sense immanent in the life of an individual, he has neither a reason nor the means for learning them, reflecting upon them and forming them into distinct ideas' (*ibid.*, pp. 442–3).

25 [Georges Gurvitch, 'Hyper-Empirisme dialectique: ses applications en sociologie'], *Cahiers internationaux de sociologie*, vol. xv, 1953, pp. 3–33. [The anonymity of this reference in the French text is curious. The attack on

Gurvitch appears to be a part of a sustained struggle between him and Cuvillier. Gurvitch's 'dialectical' approach to sociology was opposed by the latter not only because of its resemblances to pragmatism, but because of its phenomenological foundations. Cuvillier seems to have seen himself as the champion of the Durkheimian tradition in French sociology more generally. He is singled out by Gurvitch in the article cited as 'ill-informed' and 'mediocre' (p. 5). Quite plainly in the following pages Cuvillier is indicating his belief that the approach to sociology espoused as a novelty by Gurvitch has already been exposed as inadequate by Durkheim himself in his critique of pragmatism.]

26 *Ibid.*, p. 13.

27 *Ibid.*, p. 6.

28 Hamelin, *Eléments principaux*, 1st & 2nd edns, p. 6. The phrase 'the negation of knowledge' is repeated on p. 11 (2nd edn, p. 12), in each case in connection with empiricism. Cf. E. Durkheim, *Rules of Sociological Method*, p. 33; '. . . a disguised empiricism, the negation of all science'.

29 Gurvitch, 'Hyper-Empirisme', p. 11.

30 W. James, *Pragmatism*, New York, Longmans, Green & Co., 1907, p. 259.

31 Plato, *Sophist*, 259e. [*The Dialogues of Plato*, trans. & ed., B. Jowett, Oxford, Clarendon Press, 4th edn, 1953, vol. III, p. 416.]

32 Gurvitch, 'Hyper-Empirisme', pp. 21 and 29.

33 Floyd N. House [review of G. Gurvitch, *La Vocation actuelle de la sociologie*], in *American Journal of Sociology*, vol. LX, no. 2, Sept. 1954, p. 198. [The relevance of this apparently obscure sentence becomes clear in the context of Cuvillier's general attack on Gurvitch. The phrase 'reciprocity of perspectives' is Gurvitch's description of his own sociology. The subsequent quotations are House's comment on Gurvitch.]

34 Gurvitch, 'Hyper-Empirisme', pp. 5, 6 and 9ff.

Introduction

1 There are some notable exceptions to this generalization. See D. Martindale, *The Nature and Types of Sociological Theory*, London, Routledge & Kegan Paul, 1961, pp. 297–303; Geoffrey Hawthorn, *Enlightenment and Despair: A History of Sociology*, Cambridge University Press, 1976, pp. 206–9 and 242–4. In each case, however, I believe that there is insufficient recognition of the importance of pragmatism.

Lewis Coser is one of the few historians of the discipline to give extensive coverage to the pragmatist roots of sociology. See his *Masters of Sociological Thought: Ideas in Historical and Social Context*, New York, Harcourt Brace Jovanovich, 2nd edn, 1977. An important but neglected text in this connection is C. Wright Mills's *Sociology and Pragmatism: The Higher Learning in America*, New York, Oxford University Press, 1966.

2 See Martindale, *Nature and Types*, p. 298. The quotation is from G. de Ruggiero, *Modern Philosophy*, 1st edn, New York, Macmillan & Co., 1921, p. 252.

3 See Martindale, *Nature and Types*, pp. 297ff. In Britain, at least, possibly one of the major reasons why pragmatism has been so grossly neglected has been the influence of Bertrand Russell's assessment of the movement. See Chaps. IV and V of his *Philosophical Essays*, London, George Allen & Unwin Ltd, rev. edn, 1966. (I am indebted to Mr Roger Fellows for this observation.)

4 See Martindale, *Nature and Types*, pp. 353ff.

5 This is one of the shortcomings of Coser's account, in that he tends to treat pragmatism as belonging exclusively in its American context.

6 E. Durkheim, *Pragmatisme et sociologie*, ed. A. Cuvillier, Paris, Librairie Philosophique J. Vrin, 1955.

7 Kurt H. Wolff (ed.), *Emile Durkheim: 1858–1917*, Ohio State University Press, 1960.

8 See E. Durkheim, *Sociology and Philosophy* (trans. D. F. Pocock), London, Cohen & West Ltd, 1953, chap. 1.

9 A number of commentators on Durkheim omit altogether any mention of his interest in pragmatism. See, for example, R. Aron, *Main Currents in Sociological Thought*, vol. 2, London, Weidenfeld & Nicolson, 1967; T. Parsons, *The Structure of Social Action*, New York, The Free Press, 1949: see esp. chaps. VIII to XII; Göran Therborn, *Science, Class and Society: on the Formation of Sociology and Historical Materialism*, London, New Left Books, 1976. Although Parsons may be excused here, since his study appeared well before the existence of the pragmatism lectures was widely known (the first edition of his book was published in 1937), Aron has no such claim to mitigating circumstances, and neither does Therborn.

10 For example, A Giddens (ed.), *Emile Durkheim: Selected Writings*, Cambridge University Press, 1972; and S. Lukes, *Emile Durkheim: His Life and Work*, London, Allen Lane, 1973; D. LaCapra, *Emile Durkheim: Sociologist and Philosopher*, Ithaca N.Y., Cornell University Press, 1972.

11 Terry Clark has commented on the general openness of French intellectual life to foreign ideas during this period. See his *Gabriel Tarde on Communication and Social Influence*, Chicago, University of Chicago Press (Heritage of Sociology Series), 1969, pp. 19ff. The spread of pragmatism in France is discussed in some detail in the following: H. S. Thayer, *Meaning and Action: A Critical History of Pragmatism*, Indianapolis, Bobbs-Merrill Co. Inc., 1968, pt. 3, chap. 3. See also Durkheim's own remarks at the beginning of the Second Lecture, below.

12 A useful bibliography of the French editions of James's work, up to the time of his death in 1911, is contained in the brief biography by Etienne Boutroux, *William James*, London, Longmans, Green & Co., 1912, pp. 10–11.

13 Boutroux refers to an earlier article in the *Critique* of 1870; but for a number of reasons this appears to be unlikely.

14 In addition to the volume by Boutroux already cited, bibliographical information about James has been obtained from the following sources. The principal source has been R. B. Perry, *The Thought and Character of William James*, 2 vols., Boston, Little, Brown & Co., 1936. Also of value have been:

H. James (ed.), *The Letters of William James*, 2 vols., London, Longmans, Green & Co., 1926; and the *Dictionary of American Biography*.

15 See Perry, *Thought and Character*, vol. I, p. 664. (Chaps. XLI and XLII of this volume are devoted to the relationships between James and Renouvier.)

16 *Ibid.*, pp. 670ff.

17 *Ibid.*, pp. 673ff.

18 *Ibid.*, p. 672.

19 Bergson had been initially invited to undertake this task. See Perry, *Thought and Character*, vol. II, pp. 614–15.

20 Chap. LXXXIII of vol. II of *Thought and Character* is devoted in large measure to the correspondence between James and Boutroux.

21 *Ibid.*; see also pp. 766–8.

22 James also seems to have attempted to provide for Boutroux an introduction to an American public through an article in the *Nation*.

23 Perry, *Thought and Character*, vol. II, p. 589.

24 Although attempts have been made to adduce the influence of James on Bergson, and vice versa, this is not a question that concerns us. Suffice it to quote James's biographer on the subject: 'Neither philosopher ever made any claims of priority, each rejoiced to find the other in possession of the truth, and was most extravagantly appreciative of the other's merit. The similarity of their doctrine is not complete or extraordinary – and does not disparage the originality of the other' (Perry, *Thought and Character*, vol. II, p. 600).

25 Chap. LXXXVI of *Thought and Character* is devoted to the relationship between James and Bergson. This account is largely based on that chapter.

26 This was later published as chap. VI of James's *A Pluralistic Universe* under the title, 'Bergson and his critique of intellectualism', London, Longmans, Green & Co., 1909.

27 See H. Stuart Hughes, *Consciousness and Society: The Reorientation of European Social Thought, 1890–1930*, London, McGibbon & Kee, 1967, pp. 113ff. Terry Clark suggests that Bergson's audience was not only popular among 'tourists and society ladies': 'Bergson came to symbolise for many of his followers all that the Sorbonne lacked. Georges Sorel . . . used to come up to Paris once a week from his suburban residence on Friday afternoon, stop by the office of the *Cahiers de la Quinzaine* to meet Charles Péguy, Daniel Halévy, Julian Benda, Edouard Berth and Peslouan, whence they would proceed together past the Sorbonne to the Collège de France and listen to Bergson's dramatic weekly lecture.' See his 'Emile Durkheim and the institutionalisation of sociology in the French university system', in *Archives Européennes de Sociologie*, vol. IX, no. 1, 1968, p. 65. There is an interesting parallel between James and Bergson, which is worth noting here; that is, they were both ardent popularizers of philosophy. One consequence of this stance was that both of them suffered a great deal of hostility from professional philosophers, not only for what they said, but for the ways in which they said it.

28 Bibliographical information relating to the translation of Dewey's work into

French is compiled from the following sources: Milton H. Thomas, *John Dewey: A Centennial Bibliography*, Chicago, University of Chicago Press, 1962; Emmanuel Leroux, *Le Pragmatisme américain et anglais*, Paris, Félix Alcan, 1923; Paul A. Schlipp (ed.), *The Philosophy of John Dewey*, New York, Tudor Pub. Co., 2nd edn, 1951; W. W. Brickman, 'John Dewey's foreign reputation as an educator', *School and Society*, vol. LXXX, 22 Oct. 1949, pp. 257–65.

29 The question of the existence or non-existence of close personal relations between Dewey and French philosophers is not readily answered in view of the absence of any good biography, or any collection of his correspondence. I have relied principally upon the following sources: John Dewey, 'From absolutism to experimentalism' (a brief autobiographical sketch), in G. P. Adams and W. P. Montague (eds.), *Contemporary American Philosophy*, London, Allen & Unwin Ltd, 1930, vol. II, pp. 13–27; Jane M. Dewey, 'Biography of John Dewey', in Schlipp, *Philosophy of John Dewey*, pp. 1–45. The works of Ribot himself show no particular debt to or exceptional interest in Dewey.

30 D. Parodi, 'Knowledge and action in Dewey's philosophy', in *Philosophy of John Dewey*, Schlipp, pp. 229–42. See esp. p. 229. This is supported by Richard McKeon, 'Une réaction américaine sur l'état actuel de la philosophie française', in M. Farber (ed.), *L'Activité philosophique contemporaine en France et aux Etats-Unis*, Paris, Presses Universitaires de France, 1950, pp. 359–91; see esp. p. 365. David Marcell tells us that it was not until his move to Columbia, in 1904, that Dewey really began to build a reputation abroad. See D. W. Marcell, *Progress and Pragmatism: James, Dewey, Beard and the American Idea of Progress*, Westport and London, Greenwood Press, 1974, p. 200.

31 See Thomas, *John Dewey*, pp. xii and xiii. A further consideration which might be noted here is the fact that Dewey was rather diffident about the promotion of his own career. See the account of his early career in Israel Scheffler, *Four Pragmatists: A Critical Introduction to Peirce, James, Mead and Dewey*, London, Routledge & Kegan Paul, 1974, pp. 187–96.

32 Albert Schinz, 'Professor Dewey's pragmatism', *Journal of Philosophy, Psychology and Scientific Method*, vol. V, no. 23, Nov. 1908, pp. 617–28; see esp. p. 617. The article was later reprinted as part of Schinz's book *Anti-pragmatisme: examen des droits respectifs de l'aristocratie intéllectuelle et de la démocratie sociale*, Paris, Félix Alcan, 1909. See also Scheffler, *Four Pragmatists*, p. 189, who describes Dewey's academic writing as 'difficult, and fine textured'.

33 See Leroux, *Le Pragmatisme*, p. 373. Schiller's reputation may itself have served to diminish that of Peirce. See his deprecation of the importance of the American in his *Humanism: Philosophical Essays*, London, Macmillan & Co., 1903, pp. 8 and 28.

34 See below, p. 1. Mauss, in his memorial to Durkheim (*Année Sociologique*, NS, vol. 1, 1925, pp. 7–29) gives additional background material to these reasons. See also Lukes, *Emile Durkheim*, p. 485; and P. de Gaudemar, 'Les

ambiguités de la critique Durkheimienne du pragmatisme', *La Pensée*, vol. 145, 1969, esp. pp. 81–2.

35 See below, p. 1. It is interesting that James appears to agree with Durkheim here. In defending himself against his critics, in *The Meaning of Truth*, James repeatedly challenges his opponents to present a positive alternative to the views which they so decisively reject.

36 See Leroux, *Le Pragmatisme*, p. 8. Leroux gives a useful bibliography, which includes a section devoted to French commentators on pragmatism; see pp. 410–13.

37 Although Durkheim and Bergson were old acquaintances, having studied together at the Ecole Normale Supérieure, they were hardly friends, and Bergson cannot be really counted among the personal influences on Durkheim. (See Lukes, *Emile Durkheim*, chap. 2, *passim*, for a discussion of their relationship.) One further brief remark is in order at this point, however: it was precisely those qualities of subjectivism and anti-intellectualism in James's thought which both attracted Bergson and repelled Durkheim.

38 There is little point in exploring in detail the relationship between Renouvier and Durkheim in the present context, particularly since this has been adequately undertaken elsewhere. See Lukes, *Emile Durkheim*, pp. 54–8.

39 This was first published in the *Revue de Métaphysique*, vol. VI, May 1898. A translation is available in E. Durkheim, *Sociology and Philosophy* (trans. D. Pocock). Since at that time Durkheim can only have read an English-language edition of the *Principles* we might infer that he had taken some trouble to acquaint himself with James's views.

40 See Perry, *Thought and Character*, vol. I, pp. 656–7.

41 See Lukes, *Emile Durkheim*, pp. 57–8, and 296ff. The dedication of the first edition of Durkheim's *Division of Labour* was to Etienne Boutroux.

42 See Lukes, *ibid.*, pp. 57–8, 73 and 233.

43 See Perry, *Thought and Character*, vol. II, pp. 560–8.

44 Durkheim had presented a course on the sociology of religion at Bordeaux in 1894–5 (see Lukes, *Emile Durkheim*, p. 618), and had dealt with it intermittently throughout his academic career (*ibid.*, chap. 11). Another similar course was offered in 1900–1, interestingly enough, entitled 'Les formes élémentaires de la religion'. A growing interest in the topic after 1905 is indicated, not only by a further course in 1906–7, but also by a series of articles from 1906 onwards. (See Lukes, *ibid.*, pp. 580ff.)

45 See E. Durkheim, *The Elementary Forms of the Religious Life*, George Allen & Unwin, Ltd, 1915, especially the footnotes to the 'Conclusion'.

46 See Leroux, *Le Pragmatisme*, pp. 410–11.

47 See D. Parodi, 'Le Problème religieux dans la pensée contemporaine', in *Revue de Métaphysique et de Morale*, vol. XXI, 1913, pp. 511–25.

48 For full reference see above, n. 39.

49 See also p. xxxii above, regarding the interest of the *Année Sociologique* circle in the question of pragmatism.

50 An additional important field in which the continuity of Durkheim's ideas is revealed in the lectures on pragmatism is his work on sociological

epistemology. For a brief discussion, see below, pp. xxxix–xli. I intend to return in greater depth to these issues in a subsequent publication.

51 *Primitive Classification* was first published in 1908; the English edition was published in 1963, by Cohen & West Ltd, with an introduction by Rodney Needham.

52 See below, p. 89.

53 See below, p. 88.

54 See below, *ibid.*

55 See below, p. 89. Although Durkheim gives insufficient recognition to this fact, his exposition follows in many respects that of Dewey in *Studies in Logical Theory*. It is also interesting that here Durkheim seems to echo Peirce's ideas about the importance of science as a community. Of course, since little of Peirce's work on this topic was published at the time, he was unable to do so. Had he known the work of Peirce, his appreciation of pragmatism might have been rather different. See *The Collected Papers of Charles Sanders Peirce* ed. Arthur W. Burks, Cambridge, Mass., Harvard University Press, vol. vii, paras. 265 and 311, and vol. viii, paras. 51, 52 and 55, 1931–58.

56 See below, p. 90.

57 See below, p. 91.

58 See below, *ibid.*

59 Having reached this conclusion independently, I was delighted when Paul de Gaudemar sent me a copy of his article, 'Sur la théorie durkheimienne de la connaissance', in which he comes to a similar conclusion from a different approach. *Annales de la Faculté des Lettres et Sciences Humaines de Toulouse*, ns, vol. iv, no. 2, Dec. 1968, pp. 71–80. The fact that Durkheim attempts to develop a theory of ideology (although in this case in the *Rules of Sociological Method*) is also recognized in Paul Q. Hirst's *Durkheim, Bernard and Epistemology*, London, Routledge & Kegan Paul, 1975.

60 See below, pp. 48–9 and 50–1. Chap. 8 is largely devoted to the concept of 'action'.

61 See below, p. 52.

62 See below, p. 56.

63 See below, *ibid.*

64 See below, p. 57.

65 See below, p. 67.

66 See below, p. 68.

67 See below, *ibid.*

68 See below, p. 72.

69 See below, p. 73.

70 See below, p. 74.

71 See below, p. 75.

72 Hirst, *Durkheim, Bernard*, p. 83.

73 Jean Duvignaud, 'Le champ épistémologique de la sociologie à travers Durkheim', in Emile Durkheim, *Journal Sociologique*, Paris, Presses Universitaires de France, 1969; see esp. p. 16.

74 Parsons, *Structure of Social Action*, p. 442.

75 Marcel Mauss, 'In memoriam: l'œuvre inédit de Durkheim et de ses collaborateurs', in *Année Sociologique*, NS, vol. 1, 1925, pp. 7–29; see p. 10. Quoted in Lukes, *Emile Durkheim*, p. 485.

76 One of the most important contributions to date, however, is that of Dominic LaCapra, the quality of whose discussion probably depends not only on his philosophical training, but also on his evident familiarity with *Pragmatism and Sociology*. See his *Emile Durkheim*, esp. pp. 265–81.

77 Parsons, *Structure of Social Action*, p. 447.

78 Hirst, *Durkheim, Bernard*, p. 177. See also p. 169.

First Lecture: The Origins of Pragmatism

1 This is probably an allusion to the following passage in William James's *Pragmatism*, London, Longmans, Green & Co., 1907, p. 54: 'Against rationalism as a pretension and as a method pragmatism is fully armed and militant.'

2 Cf. F. C. S. Schiller, *Humanism*, London, Macmillan & Co., 1903, pp. xvii–xix; *Studies in Humanism*, London, Macmillan & Co., 1907, chap. II, 'From Plato to Protagoras', and chap. XIV, 'Protagoras the humanist'; 'Plato or Protagoras?', in *Mind*, NS, vol. XVII, Oct. 1908, pp. 518–26; 'The humanism of Protagoras', in *Mind*, NS, vol. XX, April 1911, pp. 181–96.

3 All sub-titles have been added by the editor of the French edition.

4 René Berthelot (*Un romantisme utilitaire: étude sur le movement pragmatiste*, vol. I), *Le Pragmatiste chez Nietzsche et chez Poincaré*, Paris, Félix Alcan, 1911.

5 ['The spirit of gravity', *Thus Spake Zarathustra*, *Complete Works of F. W. Nietzsche* (ed. Oscar Levy), vol. II, Edinburgh, T. N. Foulis, 1909, p. 239.] Cited by Berthelot, *Un romantisme*, pp. 36–7; from the French translation, 'De l'esprit de pesanteur', in the *Mercure de France* edition of Nietzsche's work.

6 *The Joyful Wisdom*, *Complete Works of F. W. Nietzsche*, vol. X, 1910, aphorism 112, p. 158. Cited by Berthelot, *Un romantisme*, p. 43.

7 *Ibid.*, aphorism 111, p. 157. Cited by Berthelot, *Un romantisme*, p. 42.

8 Charles Sanders Peirce (1839–1914), mathematician and chemist. [His *Collected Papers* were published by Harvard University Press, 1934–5 (vols. I–VI) and 1958 (vols. VII–VIII). References to this work are conventionally by volume and paragraph, and we will follow this system here.]

9 Charles Sanders Peirce, 'How to make our ideas clear', in *Popular Science Monthly*, vol. XII, 1878, pp. 286–302. [*Collected Papers*, vol. V, pp. 248–71 (paras. 5.388–410).]

10 Pages 39–57. The general title of the series of papers by Peirce is 'La logique de la science' ('Illustrations of the logic of science'). The first article appeared in Dec. 1878, pp. 553–69.

11 [This passage appears to be a rather loose translation of a section of Peirce's article. See *Collected Papers*, 5.394. The French text reads as follows. 'L'irritation produite par le doute nous pousse à faire des efforts pour atteindre l'état de croyance.']

12 [Peirce, *Collected Papers*, 5.398 and 5.401.]

13 [Peirce, *Collected Papers*, 5.402.]

14 It seems that Durkheim has deliberately modified the meaning of a passage on p. 293 of Peirce's [second] article in the *Popular Science Monthly*, for a reason that is easy to understand. The French translation in *Revue Philosophique*, p. 47, follows the original: '... we can ... mean nothing by wine but what has certain effects, direct or indirect, upon our senses; and to talk of something as having all the sensible characters of wine, yet being in reality blood, is senseless jargon'. In his *Pragmatism*, James uses the same example, but in precisely the opposite way, in order to prove that the notion of 'substance' is capable of a 'pragmatic application'. (*Pragmatism*, pp. 88–9.)

15 J. M. Baldwin (ed.), *Dictionary of Philosophy and Psychology*, New York, Macmillan & Co., 1st edn 1901–5, vol. II, pp. 321–2.

16 In the article 'What pragmatism is', in *The Monist*, vol. xv, no. 2. April 1905, pp. 161–81. [*Collected Papers*, 5.411–437.]

17 [Though not noted in the French text, this appears to be a reference to Peirce, *Collected Papers*, 5.407.]

18 [*Collected Papers*, 5.414.]

19 'The issues of pragmaticism', in *The Monist*, vol. xv, no. 4, Oct. 1905, pp. 481–99. [*Collected Papers*, 5.438–463.]

20 William James, 1842–1910.

21 William James, *The Will to Believe, and Other Essays in Popular Philosophy*, London, Longmans, Green & Co., 1896: French translation, 1916.

22 'Philosophical conceptions and practical results', reprinted in the *Journal of Philosophy*, vol. I, Dec. 1904, pp. 673–87, with the title, 'The pragmatic method'.

Second Lecture: The Pragmatist Movement

1 [London, Longmans, Green & Co., 1909.]

2 [New York, Longmans, Green & Co., 1907.]

3 [New York, Longmans, Green & Co., 1909.]

4 'Does consciousness exist?', in *The Journal of Philosophy*, vol. I, no. 18, Sept. 1904, pp. 477–91. [*Essays in Radical Empiricism* (Longmans, Green & Co.) was actually published in 1912, not 1910, as the French text states. It was edited posthumously by Ralph Barton Perry.]

5 'La notion de conscience', reprinted in *Essays in Radical Empiricism*, pp. 206–33.

6 John Dewey, 1859–1952.

7 In the article by H. Robet, 'L'Ecole de Chicago et l'instrumentalisme', vol. XXI, pp. 537–75. More complete bibliographies have since been published, notably in Leroux, *Le Pragmatisme*, pp. 346ff.

8 *Studies in Logical Theory*, by J. Dewey, with the co-operation of members and fellows of the Department of Philosophy, University of Chicago Press. [1903.] The first four chapters are entitled 'Thought and its subject matter'.

9 *How We Think*, Boston [D. C. Heath & Co.], 1910; French translation, 1925.

Later Dewey published many other works on the same subjects, notably, *Experience and Nature* (1925); *The Quest for Certainty* (1929); etc.

10 Addison Webster Moore, principal works: 'Some logical aspects of purpose', in Dewey *et al.*, *Studies· in Logical Theory*, chap. xi; 'Pragmatism and solipsism', in *The Journal of Philosophy*, vol. ii, 1909; *Pragmatism and its Critics*, Chicago [University of Chicago Press], 1910; 'Bergson and pragmatism', in *The Philosophical Review*, vol. xxi, 1912; etc.

11 Ferdinand C. S. Schiller (1864–1937). 'Axioms as postulates' [appeared in Henry Stuart (ed.)], *Personal Idealism: Philosophical Essays by Eight Members of the University of Oxford*, London [Macmillan & Co.], 1902 [pp. 47–133].

12 Schiller, *Humanism: Philosophical Essays*, London [Macmillan & Co.], 1903. Other articles, together with some original studies, are gathered together in his *Studies in Humanism*, London [Macmillan & Co.], 1907.

13 Published in Florence between 1902 and 1906, under the direction of Giovanni Papini and Giuseppe Prezzolini, with the collaboration of G. Vailati, M. Calderoni and others. Cf. G. Vailati ['De quelques caractères du mouvement philosophique contemporain en Italie'], in *Revue du Mois*, 10 Feb., 1907, pp. 162–85.

14 Edouard le Roy had by then published: 'Science et philosophie', in *Revue de Métaphysique et de Morale*, vol. vii [July, Sept., Nov., pp. 375–425, 503–62, 708–31], 1899, and vol. viii [Jan., pp. 37–72], 1900; 'Le problème de Dieu', *ibid.*, vol. xv [Mar., July, pp. 129–70, 470–513], 1907; *Dogme et critique* [*études de philosophie et de critique religieuse*, Paris, 2nd edn], Blond, 1907. On Le Roy, see Berthelot, *Un romantisme*, vol. iii, 1922, *Le Pragmatisme religieux chez William James et chez les catholiques modernistes*, pp. 303–8.

15 One might add also Maurice Blondel, mentioned in the preface to *Pragmatism*, p. viii. But Blondel, who gives to the word 'action' a much wider meaning than does James, has energetically dissociated himself from pragmatism. (See esp. André Lalande, *Vocabulaire [technique et critique de la philosophie*, Paris, Presses Universitaires de France], 5th edn, p. 784n.).

16 See Bergson's introduction to the French edition of *Pragmatism*, pp. 1–16.

17 W. James, *Pragmatism*, p. 5. [Although this passage appears in inverted commas in the French text, it is a paraphrase rather than a quotation from James.]

18 The complete title is *Pragmatism: A New Name for Some Old Ways of Thinking. Popular Lectures on Philosophy*, by William James.

19 At the beginning of his book (*Un romantisme*, vol. 1, p. 3), Berthelot says that pragmatism is like the cloud which Hamlet shows to Polonius through the window of the Castle of Elsinore, which sometimes resembles a camel; at other times a weasel; and at others, a whale. [The reference to 'an American writer' is plainly to A. O. Lovejoy's 'The thirteen pragmatisms', *Journal of Philosophy*, vol. v, 1908, pp. 5–12 and 29–39; reprinted in *The Thirteen Pragmatisms, and Other Essays*, Baltimore, Johns Hopkins Press, pp. 1–29, 1963.]

20 The same remark has been made in relation to Dewey and the Chicago School

by Leroux, *Le Pragmatisme*, p. 206. As for Schiller, he excuses himself, at the beginning of his *Studies in Humanism*, for 'the discontinuity of the form' in which he has presented his thought. (The book is, in fact, a collection of articles.) (See p. vii.)

21 *The Meaning of Truth*, pp. 51–2. See also *Pragmatism*, pp. 46–7.
22 And also Peirce. See *Studies in Humanism*, p. 5n. [It seems to be stretching a point to interpret this reference as Schiller's recognition of James's 'mastery'. The leadership of James (and Dewey) is probably more openly acknowledged in Schiller's note, *Studies in Humanism*, p. 19.]
23 See *Pragmatism*, p. 5, where James designates Dewey as 'The founder of pragmatism himself'.
24 See *Pragmatism*, second lecture, pp. 43–81.
25 [*Ibid.*, p. 45.]
26 In *Pragmatism* (p. 11) James presents a sketch of the characteristics of the rationalist and the empiricist.The rationalist is shown as being dogmatic, the empiricist as a sceptic.
27 Notably in 'Plato and his predecessor', in *Quarterly Review*, Jan. 1906. This was reprinted [in an expanded version] in his *Studies in Humanism*, chap. ii, with the title 'From Plato to Protagoras' (pp. 22–70).
28 James, *The Meaning of Truth*, p. 57.
29 The whole of the third lecture, in *A Pluralistic Universe*, is devoted to Hegel.
30 See *Pragmatism*, p. 226.
31 See *A Pluralistic Universe*, p. 101. [The reference is to Joachim, *The Nature of Truth*, Oxford, 1906, p. 22.]
32 J. Dewey, *Studies in Logical Theory*: 'the further work of thought is one of supererogation', pp. 36–7; 'futilely reiterative', p. 47. [The first of these passages is slightly misquoted in the French text.]
33 See *The Meaning of Truth*, p. 80. Cf. also *Pragmatism*, p. 235.
34 Here begins, in our two versions, a passage in which the sequence of ideas does not seem to us to be perfectly clear. We have reconstituted it to the best of our ability.

Third Lecture: Truth and Human Knowledge

1 Schiller, *Studies in Humanism*, chap. ii, p. 58.
2 *Studies in Logical Theory* [Chicago, University of Chicago Press, 1903], chap. vi, p. 141. This fourth chapter is not by Dewey himself, but by one of his collaborators, Simon Fraser McLennon. For Dewey's own views, cf. chap. iv, and especially pp. 71–2.
3 We have reproduced here almost exactly the text of one of our two versions, although the other, which is more fragmentary, follows it very closely. We have contented ourselves with underlining the last sentence, which is common to both versions.
4 [*Pragmatism*, pp. 231–3. The French text incorrectly makes reference to a passage in *The Meaning of Truth*.]
5 Schiller, *Studies in Humanism*, p. 128.

6 *Ibid.*, p. 7.
7 See James, *The Meaning of Truth*, p. 153; Schiller, *Studies in Humanism*, chap. III, 'The relations of logic and psychology'; 'Psychology and knowledge', in *Mind*, vol. XVI, 1907, pp. 244–8; Dewey, *Studies in Logical Theory*, pp. 14–15 and 185ff. [This last reference is, in fact, not to one of the essays by Dewey himself, but to Willard C. Gore's 'Image and idea in logic'.]
8 James, *Meaning of Truth*, p. 58.
9 See esp. James, *Meaning of Truth*, p. 182 [cf. pp. 198–9]; Schiller, *Studies in Humanism*, p. 73, pp. 204ff (chap. VIII) ['Absolute truth and absolute reality'].
10 With respect to 'things' see below, the Fourth Lecture.
11 Schiller, *Studies in Humanism*, chap. VII, para. 8, pp. 191–2.

Fourth Lecture: Criticism of Dogmatism

1 [Durkheim's discussion does not mention Schiller at this point, but he is in fact paraphrasing Schiller's discussion of Spencer. Schiller, *Studies in Humanism*, chap. IX, pp. 225–7.]
2 Durkheim is alluding here to Schiller's critique of the 'appearance–reality' antithesis, as it is found in the works of Bradley, and his disciple A. E. Taylor. See esp. *Studies in Humanism*, pp. 239ff.
3 *The Meaning of Truth*, pp. 92–3; cf. *Pragmatism*, p. 252 and [253–5].
4 See W. James, *The Will to Believe* [London, Longmans, Green & Co., 1896. See esp. the first three chapters].
5 Obviously the commentary here is expressing Durkheim's own thought, and not only that of the pragmatists. See below, the Fourteenth Lecture.
6 *Pragmatism*, pp. 258–9.
7 Durkheim is summarizing here chap. IV of *Pragmatism*.
8 In our two versions the word 'contiguous' is used. In reconstituting this lecture we have adhered to James's text. [See *Pragmatism*, pp. 133–4.]
9 Durkheim seems to be interpreting rather freely here James's *Pragmatism*, pp. 140–1.
10 James, *A Pluralistic Universe*, p. 34. Cf. *ibid.*, pp. 324ff.
11 *Pragmatism*, p. 260.
12 See, on this point, the Twentieth Lecture.

Fifth Lecture: The Criticism of Conceptual Thought

1 See the three studies 'Percept and concept' in his posthumous work, *Some Problems of Philosophy*, New York and London [Longmans, Green & Co.], 1911, chaps. IV, V and VI, pp. 47–112.
2 James, *A Pluralistic Universe*, p. 257.
3 *Ibid.*, p. 263.
4 *Ibid.*, pp. 230–2.
5 See Charles Renouvier, *Essais de critique générale*, first essay [*Traité de logique générale et de logique formelle*], vol. I, Paris, Armand Colin, 1912,

pp. 42–9. James himself eulogizes Renouvier in *Some Problems of Philosophy*, p. 165n. [Cf. also chap. xi *passim*.]

6 See *Some Problems of Philosophy*, chap. v, and esp. pp. 81–3, 87–8, etc. [Cf. also James, *A Pluralistic Universe*, pp. 234ff.]

7 *A Pluralistic Universe*, p. 262.

8 *Ibid.*, pp. 250–1. The argument here is very close to that of Bergson. Cf. also pp. 237–43, when James declares that before Bergson, 'rationalism has never been seriously questioned' (p. 37); he then, 'challenges its theoretic authority in principle' (p. 243) – referring to conceptual or intellectualist logic.

9 *Ibid.*, p. 257.

10 *Ibid.*, pp. 258–9.

11 *Ibid.*, p. 246.

12 *Ibid.*, p. 253.

13 *Ibid.*, pp. 255–6.

14 *Ibid.*, p. 237. Cf. James, *The Meaning of Truth*, p. 247.

15 See below, the Twentieth Lecture.

16 James, *A Pluralistic Universe*, p. 244 and pp. 247–8.

17 *Ibid.*, p. 246.

18 In the note that completes the Sixth Lecture, at the end of *A Pluralistic Universe*, James endeavours to defend Bergson for having himself used 'a system of concepts' to give us a more profound view of reality than that of the rationalists. [This note is potentially rather misleading, in that in the English edition of James, the 'note' in question appears on pp. 338–43.]

19 See James, *Principles of Psychology* [London, Macmillan and Co., 1980], chap. ix, 'The stream of consciousness'.

Sixth Lecture: The Secondary Aspects of Pragmatism

1 James, *A Pluralistic Universe*, pp. 278–9.

2 *Ibid.*, pp. 271 and 279–80.

3 James, *Essays in Radical Empiricism*, pp. x, 42ff, 59, 70, 94, 104ff, 117ff.

4 *A Pluralistic Universe*, p. 280. [A rather fuller definition of 'radical empiricism' is, in fact, given by James in *Essays in Radical Empiricism*, pp. 41ff.]

5 *Essays in Radical Empiricism*, pp. 43 and 103.

6 *A Pluralistic Universe*, p. 238; *Essays in Radical Empiricism*, p. 162.

7 [Octave Hamelin, *Essai sur les éléments principaux de la représentation*, Bibliothèque de la philosophie contemporaine, Félix Alcan, 1907.]

8 *A Pluralistic Universe*, p. 47; *Essays in Radical Empiricism*, p. 208.

9 [Durkheim uses the word *débraillée* here, which we have rendered as 'untidy'. He appears to have in mind a passage from *A Pluralistic Universe* (pp. 325 and 328) in which James refers to a 'strung-along' conception of the universe.]

10 Durkheim is not here referring to the *Essays in Experimental Logic* [Chicago, University of Chicago Press], which appeared in 1916, but to the *Studies in Logical Theory*, already cited. As for the work mentioned by A. W. Moore, this

is his *Pragmatism and its Critics*, Chicago [University of Chicago Press], 1910. (Chap. viii of this work had appeared under the same title in the *Philosophical Review*, May 1905.)

11 Dewey, *Studies in Logical Theory*, pp. 3 and 44ff.

12 Cf. *Studies in Logical Theory*, p. 1. 'No one doubts that thought, at least reflective, as distinct from what is sometimes called constitutive thought, is derived and secondary. It comes after something and out of nothing, and for the sake of something. No one doubts that the thinking of everyday practical life and of science is of this reflective type. *We think about; we reflect over.*' [Emphasis supplied by the French editor.]

13 Cf. John Dewey, *How We Think*, Boston, D. C. Heath & Co., 1910, pp. 7 and 9–13.

14 *Pragmatism and its Critics*, chap. v, p. 92.

15 See above, p. 8.

16 *Essays in Radical Empiricism*, p. 4; the entire article entitled 'A world of pure experience', pp. 39ff. [Also pp. 93–4 and 226.]

Seventh Lecture: Thought and Reality

1 As a matter of fact, in his *Principles*, James begins by accepting that dualism is necessary to psychology as a hypothesis, without prejudice to the rights of the metaphysician. In a later chapter, however, he states that it is 'a totally wanton assumption' to believe that 'a thought, in order to know a thing at all, must expressly distinguish between the thing and its own self' (vol. i, p. 274). Against the theory which maintains that sensory qualities will be first perceived 'in the mind', and only then projected outwards, he puts forward the following: 'The first sensation which an infant gets is for him the Universe. And the Universe which he later comes to know is nothing but an amplification and an implication of that first simple germ' (vol. ii, p. 8). Subsequently, he observes that reality has no distinct context of awareness: 'The way in which the ideas are combined is a part of the inner constitution of the thought's object or context' (vol. ii, p. 286). In the last chapter of his *Textbook* [*Psychology: Briefer Course*, London, Macmillan & Co.] 1892, he recognizes that 'it is hard to carry through this simple dualism' according to which 'the world first exists, and then the states of mind; and these gain a cognizance of the world which gets gradually more and more complete' [pp. 464–5]. Finally, in his article, 'The knowing of things together', published in *The Psychological Review* [vol. ii], March 1895 (reprinted in part in *The Meaning of Truth*, chap. ii), he states plainly that things are nothing more than the rational or possible experiences of our minds, or of the minds of others.

2 James, *Essays in Radical Empiricism*, p. 29.

3 *Ibid.*, p. 218. [James's original text is, in fact, in French, of which this is our translation. It is a part of his address to the Fifth International Congress of Psychology, in Rome, 30 April 1905. Published in the *Archives de*

Psychologie of the same year, this article was quite important in helping to bring James to the attention of a French readership.]

4 *Ibid.*, p. 30.

5 James, *Principles of Psychology*, vol. I, pp. 134–8.

6 James, *Essays in Radical Empiricism*, p. 233. [James's original text is in French. See above, n. 3.]

7 *Ibid.*, p. 211. Cf. p. 11.

8 *Ibid.*, p. 10.

9 *Ibid.*, pp. 12–14, and 196–7; cf. *The Meaning of Truth*, p. 49n.

10 *Essays in Radical Empiricism*, p. 233. [James's original text is in French. See above, n. 3. The emphasis here is supplied by Durkheim, and not by James himself.]

11 *Ibid.*, pp. 213–16.

12 *Ibid.*, pp. 15–16.

13 *Ibid.*, p. 23.

14 *Ibid.*, pp. 219–20. [James's original text is in French. See above, n. 3. James is closely paraphrased in this passage, much more than the quotation marks indicate.]

15 See the Fifth Lecture. Cf. also *Some Problems of Philosophy*, p. 81 [pp. 80–3]. Ralph Barton Perry, the editor of *Essays in Radical Empiricism*, remarks however that James 'recognises' concepts as forming 'a coordinate realm' of reality. [The quotation is from James's *The Meaning of Truth*, p. 42, n. 4. This is cited by Perry, along with p. 195 of the same work (n. 1); *A Pluralist Universe*, pp. 339–40; and other references.]

16 James, *The Meaning of Truth*, p. 73.

17 Schiller, *Studies in Humanism*, p. 211.

18 James, *Pragmatism*, p. 222.

19 *Ibid.*, pp. 75–6. [Durkheim appears to be paraphrasing James, rather than quoting the original, in spite of his inverted commas. I have restored the Jamesian original.] Cf. Schiller, *Studies in Humanism*, essay V, para. IV, p. 154: '... "true" and "false" ... are the intellectual forms of "good" and "bad"'.

Eighth Lecture: Knowledge as an Instrument of Action

1 James, *The Meaning of Truth*, p. 156. Cf. also *Essays in Radical Empiricism*, p. 197: 'So long as we remain on the common-sense stage of thought, object and subject *fuse* in the fact of "presentation" of sense-perception.' [The French text incorrectly gives this reference as to *The Meaning of Truth*.] This idea is clearly apparent in James's chapter on Bergson (*A Pluralistic Universe*, chap. VI, see esp. pp. 250–1, 260–4, etc.). Cf. also the very old distinction in James's work between 'knowledge about', or indirect knowledge, and 'knowledge of acquaintance', or direct knowledge and familiarity (*Principles of Psychology*, vol. I, p. 221; *The Will to Believe*, p. 85; *The Meaning of Truth*, p. 11 and pp. 103–4; *Essays in Radical Empiricism*, pp. 53–4, etc.) and the frequent allusions in James to the 'philosophy of identity' of the idealists, which he

121

rejects, but for which he seems to experience some attraction. (*The Meaning of Truth*, p. 214; *Essays in Radical Empiricism*, pp. 134, 197, 202, etc.). [The French text incorrectly gives these last references as to *The Meaning of Truth*.]

2 This reservation on Durkheim's part is understandable if one refers to his *Elementary Forms of the Religious Life*, pp. 15–16 and esp. pp. 437–9, where Durkheim is at pains to show that concepts are not just general ideas, but representations *sui generis*, which stand in the same relation of opposition to the empirical as does the social to the individual. Cf., in addition, appendix ii below.

3 James, *A Pluralistic Universe*, p. 217; cf. *Pragmatism*, p. 208.

4 James, *The Meaning of Truth*, p. 82.

5 James, *Principles of Psychology*, vol. i, p. 472.

6 *The Meaning of Truth*, pp. 112–13. Cf. *ibid.*, pp. 16–7; James, *Some Problems of Philosophy*, chap. iv; 'The import of concepts', and esp. p. 64: 'Had we no concepts we would simply live by "getting" all successive moments of experience, as the seasick sea-anemone on its rock receives whatever nourishment the wash of the waves may bring. With concepts we go in quest of the absent, meet the remote, actively turn this way or that, bend our experience, and make it tell us whither it is bound.'

7 Bergson had developed his *schéma dynamique* in his article on 'intellectual effort' in *Revue Philosophique*, Jan. 1902. (Reprinted in his *L'Energie spirituelle* [Paris, Félix Alcan, 4th edn, 1919] chap. vi.)

8 See esp. *The Meaning of Truth*, pp. xvi, 138–42 [the quotation is from p. 140; and 252–7]; *Essays in Radical Empiricism*, p. 67, etc.

9 *A Pluralistic Universe*, pp. 247–8.

10 See above, p. 32.

11 This is the difference already noted above (p. 45 n. 1) between 'knowledge of acquaintance', and 'knowledge about'.

12 *Pragmatism*, pp. 127–8 and 265ff; *Essays in Radical Empiricism*, pp. 17ff.

13 *The Meaning of Truth*, p. 140.

14 *Ibid.*, pp. 80–1.

15 *Ibid.*, p. 89. [The passage in the French text appears to be a paraphrase of this portion of James's argument.] Cf. *Pragmatism*, pp. 217; *The Meaning of Truth*, pp. 190–7; *Studies in Radical Empiricism*, p. 247 [and p. 252ff]. Schiller has also written: 'If a feeling of satisfaction did not occur in cognitive processes the attainment of truth would not be felt to have value. In point of fact such satisfactions supervene on every step in reasoning' (*Studies in Humanism*, p. 83). Cf. finally, A. W. Moore's discussion of Royce in Dewey *et al.*, *Studies in Logical Theory*, pp. 361–72.

16 *The Meaning of Truth*, p. 191.

17 James himself expounds this objection, *The Meaning of Truth*, pp. 93ff.

18 In his article, 'What pragmatism means by practical', *Journal of Philosophy*, 13 Feb. 1908, pp. 85–99; (reprinted in his *Essays in Experimental Logic* [Chicago, University of Chicago Press, 1916], chap. xii).

19 *The Meaning of Truth*, pp. 192–7.

Ninth Lecture: The Pragmatist Criteria of Truth

1 James, *Pragmatism*, p. 213.
2 James, *The Meaning of Truth*, p. 192.
3 *Pragmatism*, pp. 201–2.
4 *Ibid.*, p. 201; cf. pp. 243ff.
5 *Ibid.*, p. 64; cf. *The Meaning of Truth*, pp. 200–6.
6 *Ibid.*, p. 218; cf. pp. 201 and 205; also James, *The Will to Believe*, pp. 95–7.
7 *Pragmatism*, p. 205; cf. pp.²219–20.
8 *The Meaning of Truth*, pp. 92–3 and 204–5.
9 *Pragmatism*, pp. 207–8.
10 See the Fourth Lecture. Cf. also Schiller's *Studies in Humanism*, essays v, vii and xix, particularly pp. 425–6: 'We really *transform* them [i.e. reality, truth] by our cognitive efforts ... Now this is a result of enormous philosophical importance. For it systematically leads the way to the persistent but delusive notion that "truth" and "utility" somehow exist apart, and apart from us ... "Reality" is reality for us, and known by us, just as "truth" is truth for us.'
11 *Pragmatism*, p. 211.
12 *Ibid.*, p. 218.
13 *Ibid.*, pp. 173–84.
14 James, *The Will to Believe*, p. 118; *Pragmatism*, pp. 243 and 249; F. C. S. Schiller, in *Personal Idealism* [ed. Henry Stuart, Macmillan & Co., 1902. The reference is to Schiller's essay 'Axioms as postulates'], p. 60; Schiller, *Studies in Humanism*, p. 433.
15 This idea has principally been developed by Schiller; see his *Studies in Humanism*, pp. 427 and 444–5. In his 'Axioms as postulates', para. 6., he had already affirmed that it is our minds which bestow on this shapeless matter the harmonious outline of a cosmos [Stuart, *Personal Idealism*; cf. also para. 7].

Tenth Lecture: Constructing Reality and Constructing Truth

1 Schiller, *Studies in Humanism*, p. 446.
2 *Ibid.*, para. 2, p. 426.
3 James, *Pragmatism*, p. 256.
4 Dewey, *Studies in Logical Theory*, p. 9; cf. pp. 41–2; also *Essays in Experimental Logic*, pp. 17–18. [The edition of the French text has added a reference to Dewey's *Experience and Nature*, Chicago, Open Court Pub. Co., 1926, pp. 31ff. This, of course, cannot have been available to Durkheim.]
5 See above, p. 38.
6 One is aware at this point that, for his part, Durkheim sees things quite differently. For the pragmatists there is, after all, a continuity between instinctive and reflective consciousness. For Durkheim, that is where the whole distance which divides the individual from the social lies.
7 *Studies in Humanism*, essay iii, para. 9, p. 90; cf. essay xvi, para. 9, .361: '... to abstract from the personal side of knowing is really impossible'.

8 In addition to the references already cited on p. 18 cf. also James, *Pragmatism*, p. 248; Schiller, *Studies in Humanism*, pp. 96 and 354; Dewey, *How We Think* [Boston, D. C. Heath & Co., 1910], pp. 563–67.

9 *Pragmatism*, p. 61.

10 *Studies in Humanism*, essay VIII, para. 6, p. 213.

11 James, *The Meaning of Truth*, pp. 268–71.

12 *Pragmatism*, p. 170.

13 Schiller, *Studies in Humanism*, essay V, section III, p. 153: 'Society exercises almost as severe a control over the intellectual as over the moral eccentricities and non-conformities of its members.'

14 James frequently emphasizes the phenomenon of the conflict between beliefs: see esp. *Pragmatism*, pp. 77–9, and p. 108; *The Meaning of Truth*, p. 205.

15 *Pragmatism*, p. 257.

16 *Ibid.*, p. 259.

Twelfth Lecture: Pragmatism and Religion

1 See esp. Dewey, *Outlines of a Critical Theory of Ethics*, Ann Arbor [Register Pub. Co.], 1891; 'Moral theory and practice', in *International Journal of Ethics*, Jan. 1891 [vol. I, pp. 186–203]; *The Study of Ethics: A Syllabus*, Ann Arbor [Register Pub. Co.], 1894; *Ethics* (with the collaboration of [James] H. Tufts, New York [Henry Holt & Co.], 1908; 'The bearings of pragmatism upon education', in *The Progressive Journal of Education* [Dec. 1908, vol. I, no. 2, pp. 1–3; Jan. 1909, vol. I, no. 3, pp. 5–8; and Feb. 1909, vol. I. no. 4, pp. 6–7]; 'Maeterlinck's philosophy of life', in *Hibbert Journal* [July], 1911 [vol. XI, pp. 765–78]; etc. It is only later that Dewey devotes himself to questions of education, and to the philosophy of democracy. [Two editorial remarks seem to be called for in connection with this remark of Durkheim's, which appears to illustrate the relative lack of familiarity in depth with Dewey's work, in comparison with his intimate knowledge of James's writings. First, it is not true that Dewey 'only later ... devotes himself to questions of education'. His first articles in this area appeared in 1885, and he maintained an active interest in this question throughout the period covered by Durkheim's note. See Milton H. Thomas, *John Dewey: A Centennial Bibliography*, Chicago, University of Chicago Press, 1962. Secondly, it is by no means clear, in the early years of his career, that Dewey would have regarded himself as a pragmatist. It is probably incorrect to apply the label to him before about 1900. See H. S. Thayer, *Meaning and Action: A Critical History of Pragmatism*, Indianapolis, The Bobbs-Merrill Co. Inc., 1968, pt 2, chap. 3]

2 Esp. in Moore, *Pragmatism and its Critics*. [One might mention also James's essay, 'The moral philosopher and the moral life', in his *The Will to Believe*, cf. 1903.]

3 W. James, *Varieties of Religious Experience* [The Gifford Lectures, 1901–2, London, Longmans, Green & Co.], 1902. A French translation by Abauzit appeared in 1906 (Alan & Kündig, Geneva).

4 *Ibid.*, p. 30. Cf. also pp. 334–5: 'It is very important to insist on the distinction

between religion as an individual personal function, and religion as an institutional, corporate, or tribal product. But in this course of lectures ecclesiastical institutions hardly concern us at all.'

5 *Ibid.*, pp. 499–500. [The French reference appears to be incorrect here. See also, however, pp. 491ff.]

6 In the first part of his book, lectures III–VII.

7 One might compare this classification with that given by Durkheim himself, in his *Elementary Forms of the Religious Life*, bk III: 'The negative cult' (ascetic rites); 'The positive cult' (sacrifice, imitative rites, representative or commemorative rites); 'Peculiar rites and the notion of sacredness'. The two classifications clearly have nothing in common.

8 *Varieties of Religious Experience*, pp. 489–90.

9 *Ibid.*, p. 519. [The French text gives the following rather loose reading of James: 'Le pragmatisme est la meilleure attitude à l'égard de la religion.']

10 *Ibid.*, p. 326. [The French text gives the following rough paraphrase of James: 'deux ou trois formules précises et irrévocables'.]

11 *Ibid.*, p. 327.

12 *Ibid.*, p. 331.

13 See *ibid.*, lectures XI–XIII [esp. pp. 272–325].

14 *Ibid.*, p. 356.

15 *Ibid.*, pp. 356–7.

16 [*Ibid.*, p. 358.]

17 *Ibid.*, p. 377.

18 See James, *ibid.*, lecture XVIII; 'Philosophy'.

19 See James, *ibid.*, lectures XVI and XVII; 'Mysticism'.

20 This is once again James's distinction between 'knowledge of acquaintance', and 'knowledge about'. [See above, pp. 45–6.]

21 The last part of lecture XIX and the conclusion, esp. pp. 498ff.

22 *Ibid.*, p. 455.

23 *Ibid.*, p. 507.

24 *Ibid.*, p. 388. See also the last chapter of *The Will to Believe*; 'What psychical research has accomplished', and chap. XVII of Schiller's *Studies in Humanism*: 'The progress of psychical research'. Both of these deal principally with the work of F. W. H. Myers. [See Frederic W. H. Myers, *Human Personality and its Survival of Bodily Death*, ed. & abr. by L. H. Myers, London, Longmans, Green & Co., 1907. Myers already attracted the attention of both James and Schiller with his investigation of what modern psychologists would call 'altered states of consciousness'. His book has chapters on hypnotism, trances, possession and ecstasy, the disintegration of personality and so on. In this present context, the chapter on 'sleep' is of relevant interest.]

25 James, *Varieties of Religious Experience*, p. 512.

26 *Ibid.*, p. 517.

27 *Ibid.*, p. 525.

28 *Ibid.* [Cf. also James's remarks on p. 132.]

29 See in addition James's own remarks in *A Pluralistic Universe*, pp. 298–9. But

he concludes: 'For my own part I find in some of these abnormal or supernormal facts the strongest suggestions in favour of a superior consciousness being possible.'

30 *Varieties of Religious Experience*, p. 519. [The reference in the French text to pp. 525–6 would appear to be incorrect.]

31 In his *Elementary Forms* (p. 417), Durkheim had already made reference to James's book: 'Together with a recent apologist of the faith we admit that these religious beliefs rest upon a specific experience whose demonstrative value is, in one sense, not one bit inferior to that of scientific experiments, though different from them.'

Thirteenth Lecture: General Criticism of Pragmatism

1 See above, pp. 12–13. James himself seems to recognize this when he writes, for example, in his preface to *The Will to Believe* (p. xiii): 'The essay "On some Hegelisms" doubtless needs an apology for the superficiality with which it treats a serious subject.'

2 James, *Essays in Radical Empiricism*, p. 2. [This reference is incorrectly given in the French text as *Problems of Philosophy*.]

3 See above, p. 8.

4 See above, p. 42.

5 [The reference to *The Will to Believe* seems to be incorrect here. The subsequent phrases in inverted commas suggest that Durkheim has in mind chap. 6 of *Pragmatism*.]

6 Cf. Durkheim, *Elementary Forms*, p. 444: 'Attributing social origins to logical thought is not debasing it or diminishing its value ... on the contrary it is relating it to a cause which implies it naturally.'

7 Cf. *ibid.*, p. 438: 'But a collective representation ... may express this its subject) by means of imperfect symbols; but scientific symbols themselves are never more than approximate.' Cf. also *ibid.*, p. 18, where ideas 'elaborated on the model of social things' are said to be 'well-founded symbols'.

Fourteenth Lecture: The Variations of Truth

1 [James flirts with the issues, however, in his two lectures on 'Great men' in *The Will to Believe*.]

2 *Sic* in the only version available to us at this point. We must, however, retain serious reservations about the authenticity of this formulation, which scarcely seems to fit into the whole pattern of Durkheim's thought which, as is well known, was influenced by Boutroux. [Etienne E. M. Boutroux, *De la contingence des lois de la nature*, 7th edn, Paris, Félix Alcan, 1913. English trans. by F. Rothwell, Chicago & London, Open Court Pub. Co., 1920; also, *De l'idée de loi naturelle dans la science et la philosophie contemporaine*, Paris, Société française d'imprimerie et de librairie, 1913.]

3 Cf. Durkheim, *Elementary Forms*, p. 446, where society is shown as being endowed with 'creative power'. Durkheim adds that 'all creation ... is the

product of a synthesis', and such syntheses are themselves 'productive of novelties'.

4 Cf. Durkheim, *The Division of Labour in Society* [trans. George Simpson, New York, Macmillan & Co., 1933]. Chaps. ii and iii [of bk 1], in which Durkheim shows that 'mechanical solidarity' which realizes the maximum of homogeneity, stifles personality, and therefore progress: also the famous passage from *The Rules of Sociological Method*, in which he declares that crime is 'normal', mainly because a degree of elasticity is necessary for social change to be possible (p. 70).

5 Cf. Durkheim's own discussion of this issue in his essay 'The determination of moral facts', in the *Bulletin de la Société française de Philosophie*, 22 Mar. 1906, and reprinted in *Sociology and Philosophy* [pp. 35–62]. See p. 41, where he contrasts the method of philosophers, who 'construct' morality, with the sociological method, which consists in observing and explaining moral 'reality'.

Fifteenth Lecture: Truth and Utility

1 James, *Pragmatism*, p. 222.

2 James, *The Meaning of Truth*, p. 76.

3 *Pragmatism*, pp. 67–8, 234, 244–5; *The Meaning of Truth*, pp. 190ff.

4 Schiller, *Studies in Humanism*, essay viii, p. 215.

5 *Pragmatism*, pp. 216 and 245.

6 [Théodore-Simon Jouffroy, *Le Cahier vert: comment les dogmes finissent. Lettres inédites*, Paris, Pierre Poux,1923.]

7 *The Meaning of Truth* [pp. 206–12], esp. pp. 209–10. James is protesting against the assumption of 'practical' to a matter of purely personal utility.

8 *Pragmatism*, p. 222.

9 'The only experience that we concretely have, is our own personal life': James, *The Will to Believe*, p. 327.

10 James often returns to this idea of 'temperament'. See esp. *Pragmatism*, pp. 6–8: 'Temperament is no conventionally recognised reason, so he (the philosopher) urges impersonal reasons only for his conclusions. Yet his temperament really gives him a stronger bias than any of his more strictly objective premises'; also p. 35: 'Temperaments, with their cravings and refusals, do determine men in their philosophies, and always will.' Cf. also pp. 51–2, and 67–8 (where a pragmatist 'temper' is contrasted with the rationalist 'temper'); also pp. 259–60, where the 'temperamental differences' between pragmatism and monism are contrasted. See also *The Will to Believe*, pp. 210ff.

11 See above, pp. 56–7; also, *The Meaning of Truth*, pp. 266–7. 'Truth absolute, he says (i.e. the pragmatist), means an ideal set of formulations towards which all opinions may in the long run of experience be expected to converge.'

12 Schiller, *Studies in Humanism*, p. 90.

13 Cf. Durkheim, *Professional Ethics and Civic Morals*, 1950, the start of the fifth lecture (pp. 55ff) [the page reference is incorrect in the French text], where he

writes that the individual is at first 'absorbed ... into the mass of society', but that 'the further one travels in history, the more one is aware of the process of change', and that 'there is no rule more soundly established' than this progressive emergence of individual personality.

14 In *The Meaning of Truth*, pp. 184ff and 206ff, James denounces as two of the 'misunderstandings' committed by those who have not paid careful attention to the pragmatist theory of truth, the idea that pragmatism is 'primarily an appeal to action' and that it 'ignores the theoretic interest'. Cf. *The Meaning of Truth*, pp. 182 and 206–7.

15 See esp. Schiller, *Studies in Humanism*, the conclusion to the essay 'Protagoras the humanist', p. 325, and the whole of the twentieth essay, especially para. 20, p. 475.

Sixteenth Lecture: Speculation and Practice

1 This is what he calls 'etherealising' truth. See Schiller, *Studies in Humanism*, essay III, para. 19, p. 111.

2 Cf. *Elementary Forms*, pp. 234ff, where Durkheim, in opposition to Lévy-Bruhl, who at that time contrasted logical and 'prelogical' thought, stresses the continuity of 'logical development' from mythology and religious thought. See also *ibid.*, p. 428: 'But feasts and rites, in a word, the cult, are not the whole religion. This is not merely a system of practices, but also a system of ideas whose object is to explain the world; we have seen that even the humblest have their cosmology.'

3 *Pragmatism*, p. 214. See also *The Meaning of Truth*, chap. x, 'The existence of Julius Caesar'. [Durkheim seems to be using James here – out of context – to argue precisely the reverse of the point James is in fact making. The full sentence reads as follows: 'The stream of time can be mounted only verbally, or verified indirectly, by the present prolongations or effects of what the past harboured.']

4 In his article 'Pure experience and reality', *Philosophical Review*, vol. XVI, 1907, no. 2, pp. 419ff, Dewey maintains that we can actually experience the past, as conditioning our present experience.

5 See above, pp. 37–8 and 55.

6 John Dewey, *Human Nature and Conduct [an Introduction to Social Psychology*, London, George Allen & Unwin], 1922, pp. 175–80. [For obvious reasons this work cannot have been available to Durkheim.] Cf. also, *Studies in Logical Theory*, p. 154. [This later passage is not by Dewey himself, but by Myron L. Ashley.]

7 John Dewey, *The Public and its Problems* [London, George Allen & Unwin], 1927, esp. pp. 57–67. [For obvious reasons this work cannot have been available to Durkheim.]

8 Théodule Ribot, *Psychologie de l'attention* [Paris], Félix Alcan, 1889, see esp. pp. 72–3. [An English trans. appeared, as follows: Chicago, Open Court Pub. Co., 1911. See pp. 55–6. This passage depends heavily on Ribot, although the quotation in the following sentence is from Bain, cited by Ribot.]

Seventeenth Lecture: The Role of Truth

1 See below, p. 100.
2 [The concept of 'coenaesthesia' was in common use in nineteenth-century psychology, but in particular was given attention by Ribot. See above, p. xv, n. 9.]
3 Benedict de Spinoza, *Ethic: [Demonstrated in Geometrical Notes, and Divided into Five Parts* (trans. W. Hale White), 2nd rev. edn, London, T. Fisher Unwin, 1894], Part II, proposition XIII. ['The object of the idea constituting the human mind is a body, or a certain mode of extension actually existing, and nothing else.'] The part that Durkheim saw the body as playing in the individualization of the person is well known. Cf. *Elementary Forms*, p. 270: ['... in order to have separate personalities, it is necessary that another factor intervene to break up and differentiate this principle]; in other words, an individualizing factor is necessary. It is the body that fulfils this function.' On this thesis of Durkheim's, see Maurice Leinhardt, *Do Kamo: [la personne et le mythe dans le monde mélanésien*, Paris, Gallimard, 1947], pp. 210–14.
4 It is quite remarkable here that Durkheim seems to anticipate what was rather later to be called 'behaviourism', to which a writer like Dewey is very close. [The term 'behaviourism' did not become widely current until after the publication of J. B. Watson's *Behaviour: An Introduction to Comparative Psychology*, New York, Henry Holt & Co., 1914.]
5 See esp. James, *Essays in Radical Empiricism*, essay IV, pp. 123–36, 'How two minds can know one thing'.

Eighteenth Lecture: The Different Types of Truths

1 We know that in his essay 'On the determination of moral facts' Durkheim identified 'desirability' as being (alongside 'obligation') 'the second characteristic of all moral acts'. See *Bulletin de la Société française de Philosophie*, 11 Feb. 1906, p. 122. Reprinted in *Sociology and Philosophy* [pp. 35–62], see p. 45.
2 Cf. Durkheim, *Elementary Forms*, p. 418: '... this reality, which mythologies have represented under so many different forms, but which is the universal eternal and objective cause of these sensations, *sui generis* out of which religious experience is made, is society'.
3 On this parallel between religious conceptions and social structures, see *Elementary Forms*, *passim*, but esp. pp. 196–7, 285–96, 425–7 [indeed, the remainder of the 'Conclusion'].
4 Here we can recognize the two forms of social consensus which correspond to what Durkheim called, in *The Division of Labour in Society*, 'mechanical' and 'organic' solidarity.

Nineteenth Lecture: Science and the Collective Consciousness

1 Cf. Auguste Comte, *Discours sur l'esprit positif*, éd. de la Société positiviste

[Paris, 1898. English trans. by E. S. Beesley, London, William Reeves, 1903], p. 15, para. 10: 'The use of the Metaphysical philosophy in the past cannot be properly understood, especially in our day, unless we recognise that its spontaneous effect on beliefs, and, *a fortiori*, on social institutions, must always be to criticise and dissolve them. This is its very nature. It can never organise any belief or institution of its own.'

2 Auguste Comte, *Cours de philosophie positive* [Paris, Schleicher Brothers, 1907–8, 4 vols.], the first lecture. [Cuvillier gives here what appears to be incorrect page refs. The 1864 edition of the *Cours* contains the quoted passages on pp. 27–9.] 'The true means of stemming the pernicious influence by which the intellectual future seems threatened, as a consequence of the excessive specialisation of individual researches ... lies in the perfecting of the division of labour itself. It is enough, in fact, to make of the study of the general features of science an additional, grand specialism ... Such is the purpose which I have in mind for the positive philosophy, within the general system of the positive sciences proper.' [See Harriet Martineau's abridged edition (London, John Chapman, 1893), pp. 9–10.]

3 Comte, *Discourse on the Positive Spirit*, pp. 39–43, paras. 20–1: 'From this subjective point of view there is at bottom but one science, the human or, more accurately, the Social Science. Of this science our existence is at once the source and the end ... Why was it that during the infancy of Humanity the theological philosophy was the only one capable of regulating society? Because it was the only possible source of some mental harmony. It can hardly be seriously disputed that this logical coherence, once the exclusive privilege of the theological spirit, has now passed over to the positive spirit. The positive spirit therefore, must be the one determining principle of that great intellectual communion upon which all true human association must rest!'

4 Cf. Durkheim, *Rules of Sociological Method*, p. 96: 'Similarly, in proportion as the social milieu becomes more complex and more unstable, traditions and conventional beliefs are shaken, become more indeterminate and more unsteady, and reflective powers are developed. Such rationality is indispensable to societies and individuals in adopting themselves to a more mobile and more complex environment.'

5 We can perhaps catch here an echo of Comte's distinction between social statics and social dynamics.

6 There is very probably also an echo here of Boutroux, who is known to have been a major source of inspiration for Durkheim's thought.

7 [The argument of this paragraph had been set out in remarkably similar terms by Durkheim in *Rules of Sociological Method*. See pp. 79–80.]

8 We know that Durkheim always maintained that, in relation to the psycho-organic being of man, his social being is supervenient [est du 'surajouté'].

Twentieth Lecture: Are Thought and Reality Heterogeneous?

1 We know that in his *Principles of Psychology*, James himself accepts that

concepts are essential to reasoning. [The French edition incorrectly refers to vol. I, p. 329. See, however, vol. II, pp. 325–32, also vol. I, chap. XII.]

2 Cf. Durkheim, *Elementary Forms*, pp. 204, 237–9, etc.

3 Cf. Durkheim, *Sociology and Philosophy*, pp. 48 and 69–70.

4 See Durkheim's 'Introduction to the sociology of the family', in the *Annales de la Faculté des lettres de Bordeaux*, vol. x, 1888, pp. 257ff; 'La famille conjugale', in the *Revue Philosophique*, vol. XCI, 1921, pp. 1ff. [These two articles have now appeared in English translation: see Mark Traugott (ed. and trans.), *Emile Durkheim on Institutional Analysis*, Chicago and London, University of Chicago Press, 1978, chaps. 13 and 14.] See also Georges Davy, 'La famille et la parenté d'après Durkheim', in his *Sociologies d'hier et d'aujourd'hui* [Paris], Félix Alcan, 1931, pp. 103ff. [2nd edn, Paris, Presses Universitaires de France, 1950.]

5 Cf. Henri Bergson, *Creative Evolution* [trans. A. Mitchell, London, Macmillan & Co., 1911]. 'The evolution of life, worked at from this point, receives a clearer meaning ... It is as if a broad current of conciousness had penetrated matter, loaded, as all consciousness is, with an enormous multiplicity of interwoven potentialities. It has carried matter along to organisation, but its movement has been at once infinitely retarded and infinitely divided.'

6 Cf. *ibid.*, pp. 260–1: matter is 'a creative action which unmakes itself', the spray of water droplets condensed from a jet of steam: life is '... like an effort to raise the weight which falls'.

7 Durkheim often emphasized the phenomena of 'recurrence' as they have been called, or 'causal reciprocity' in the social field. See *The Division of Labour in Society*, pp. 256 and 260; but, in particular, see *The Rules of Sociological Method*, p. 95: 'The bond which unifies the cause to the effect is reciprocal to an extent which has not been sufficiently recognized.' Durkheim gives several other examples (see above, p. 91, n. 4).

8 This formulation might surprise the critics of a certain type of caricature of 'sociologism'; but it is nevertheless entirely in keeping with Durkheim's thought. Cf. *Sociology and Philosophy*, p. 55: 'While it (i.e. society) surpasses us it is within us, since it can only exist by and through us.'

9 See above, pp. 73ff.

Appendix I: Certainty

1 The appendixes are based upon notes provided by M. Marcel Tardy.

2 See above, p. 38. A very similar idea is developed by Moore.

3 [We have retained the French term here as the simplest solution to the problem of rendering Durkheim's meaning.The term *évidence* conveys Descartes' concern with 'clear and distinct ideas' which are accessible to the attentive mind. See, on this point, R. Descartes, *The Principles of Philosophy*, in *The Philosophical Works of Descartes*, Elizabeth S. Haldane and G. R. T. Ross (eds.), Cambridge University Press, 1967, vol. 1, p. 219; also 'Reply to objections: II', in *ibid.*, vol. 2, pp. 43ff.]

4 See above, pp. 69–70. [The French is somewhat ambiguous here, reading: 'Il y a un relativisme de la vérité qui s'impose historiquement.']
5 See above, the beginning of the Fifteenth Lecture.

Appendix II: Concepts

1 Cf. above p. 32.
2 See above, the Third and subsequent Lectures.
3 Cf. Durkheim, 'Détermination du fait moral', in the *Bulletin de la société française de philosophie*, 11 Feb. and May 22, 1906. Reprinted in *Sociology and Philosophy*, pp. 35–79.
4 See above, the Nineteenth Lecture.

Bibliography

(Note: Although throughout the text care has been taken to provide references to the editions cited in the French original, in this Consolidated Bibliography the references are to the English editions of works where these exist. Hence articles by Durkheim, in the periodical literature, appear here usually in the form of items in collections of essays.)

Anon., Review of *Archives de Philosophie de Droit et de Sociologie juridique*, 1938, in the supplement 'Périodiques', *Revue de Métaphysique et de Morale*, vol. 46 (no. 3, July 1939), p. 545.

Aron, Raymond, *Main Currents in Sociological Thought*, vol. II, London, Weidenfeld & Nicolson, 1967.

Baldwin, J. M. (ed.), *Dictionary of Philosophy and Psychology*, 2 vols., New York, Macmillan & Co., 1st edn, 1901–5.

Bergson, Henri, *Creative Evolution* (trans. A. Mitchell), London, Macmillan & Co., 1911.

Bergson, Henri, *Mind Energy* (trans. H. Wildon Carr), London, Macmillan & Co., 1920.

Berthelot, René, *Un romantisme utilitaire: étude sur le mouvement pragmatiste*, vol. I, *Le Pragmatisme chez Nietzsche et chez Poincaré*, 1911; vol. II, *Le Pragmatisme chez Bergson*, 1913; vol. III, *Le Pragmatisme religieux chez William James et chez les catholiques modernistes*, 1922, Paris, Félix Alcan.

Boutroux, Etienne, *The Contingency of the Laws of Nature* (trans. F. Rothwell), Chicago and London, Open Court Pub. Co., 1920.

Boutroux, Etienne, *Natural Law in Science and Philosophy* (trans. F. Rothwell), New York, Macmillan & Co., 1914.

Boutroux, Etienne, *William James*, London, Longmans Green & Co., 1912.

Brickman, W. W., 'John Dewey's foreign reputation as an educator', *School and Society*, vol. LXXX (22 Oct. 1949), pp. 257–65.

Clark, Terrence N., 'Emile Durkheim and the institutionalisation of sociology in the French university system', *Archives Européennes de Sociologie*, vol. IX (no. 1, 1968), pp. 37–71.

Clark, Terrence N., *Gabriel Tarde on Communication and Social Influence*, Chicago, University of Chicago Press (Heritage of Sociology Series), 1969.

Bibliography

Comte, Auguste, *Cours de philosophie positive*, 4 vols., Paris, Schleicher Brothers, 1907–8.

Comte, Auguste, *A Discourse on the Positive Spirit* (trans. and ed. by E. S. Beesley), London, William Reeves, 1903.

Coser, Lewis, *Masters of Sociological Thought: Ideas in Historical and Social Context*, New York, Harcourt Brace Jovanovich, 1977.

Davy, Georges, *Sociologies d'hier et d'aujourd'hui*, Paris, Félix Alcan, 1931. (2nd edn, Paris, Presses Universitaires de France, 1950.)

Descartes, R., *The Philosophical Works of Descartes*, 2 vols. (trans. and ed. Elizabeth S. Haldane and G. R. T. Ross), Cambridge University Press, 1967.

Dewey, Jane M., 'Biography of John Dewey', in Paul A. Schlipp (ed.), *The Philosophy of John Dewey*, New York, Tudor Publishing Co. Ltd, 2nd edn, 1951, pp. 1–45.

Dewey, John, 'The bearings of pragmatism upon education', *The Progressive Journal of Education*, vol. I (no. 2, Dec. 1908), pp. 1–3; vol. I (no. 3, Jan. 1909), pp. 5–8; vol. I (no. 4, Feb. 1909), pp. 6–7.

Dewey, John, *Essays in Experimental Logic*, Chicago, University of Chicago Press, 1916.

Dewey, John, *Experience and Nature*, Chicago and London, Open Court Pub. Co., 1925.

Dewey, John, 'From absolutism to experimentalism', in G. P. Adams and W. P. Montague (eds.), *Contemporary American Philosophy*, vol. II, London, George Allen & Unwin Ltd, 1930, pp. 13–27.

Dewey, John, *How We Think*, Boston, D. C. Heath & Co., 1910.

Dewey, John, *Human Nature and Conduct: an Introduction to Social Psychology*, London, George Allen & Unwin, 1922.

Dewey, John, 'Maeterlinck's philosophy of life', *Hibbert Journal*, vol. XI (July 1911), pp. 765–78.

Dewey, John, 'Moral theory and practice', *International Journal of Ethics*, vol. I (Jan. 1891), pp. 186–203.

Dewey, John, *Outlines of a Critical Theory of Ethics*, Ann Arbor, Register Pub. Co., 1891.

Dewey, John, 'Psychology and knowledge', *Mind*, vol. XVI (1907), pp. 244–8.

Dewey, John, *The Public and its Problems*, London, George Allen & Unwin, 1927.

Dewey, John, 'Pure experience and reality', *Philosophical Review*, vol. XVI (no. 2, 1907), pp. 419ff.

Dewey, John, *The Quest for Certainty*, New York, Minton, Balch & Co., 1929.

Dewey, John et al., *Studies in Logical Theory*, Chicago, University of Chicago Press, 1903.

Dewey, John, *The Study of Ethics: A Syllabus*, Ann Arbor, Register Pub. Co., 1894.

Dewey, John, and Tufts, H., *Ethics*, New York, Henry Holt & Co., 1908.

Durkheim, Emile, *The Division of Labour in Society* (trans. George Simpson), New York, The Free Press, 1964.

Durkheim, Emile, *The Elementary Forms of the Religious Life* (trans. J. W. Swain), London, George Allen & Unwin Ltd, 1915.

Bibliography

Durkheim, Emile, *The Evolution of Educational Thought: Lectures on the Formation and Development of Secondary Education in France* (trans. P. Collins), London, Routledge & Kegan Paul, 1977.

Durkheim, Emile, *Journal Sociologique*, Paris, Presses Universitaires de France, 1969.

Durkheim, Emile, *Moral Education: A Study in the Theory and Application of the Sociology of Education* (trans. E. K. Wilson and H. Schnurer), New York, The Free Press, 1961.

Durkheim, Emile, *Pragmatisme et Sociologie*, ed. Armand Cuvillier, Paris, Librairie Philosophique J. Vrin, 1955.

Durkheim, Emile, *Professional Ethics and Civic Morals* (trans. C. Brookfield, ed. H. N. Kubali), London, Routledge & Kegan Paul, 1957.

Durkheim, Emile, *The Rules of Sociological Method* (trans. S. A. Solovay and J. H. Mueller), Chicago, University of Chicago Press, 1938 (republished by The Free Press, New York, 1964).

Durkheim, Emile, *Sociology and Philosophy* (trans. D. F. Pocock), London, Cohen & West Ltd, 1953.

Durkheim, Emile, and Mauss, Marcel, *Primitive Classification* (trans. Rodney Needham), London, Cohen & West Ltd, 1963.

Duvignaud, Jean, 'Le champ épistémologique de la sociologie à travers Durkheim', in Emile Durkheim, *Journal Sociologique*, Paris, Presses Universitaires de France, 1969, pp. 7–26.

Gaudemar, Paul de, 'Les ambiguités de la critique durkheimienne du pragmatisme', *La Pensée*, vol. 145 (1969), pp. 81–8.

Gaudemar, Paul de, 'Sur la théorie durkheimienne de la connaissance', *Annales de la Faculté des Lettres et Sciences Humaines de Toulouse*, NS, vol. IV (no. 2, Dec. 1968), pp. 71–80.

Giddens, Anthony (ed.), *Emile Durkheim: Selected Writings*, Cambridge University Press, 1972.

Ginsberg, Morris, *On the Diversity of Morals*, London, Heinemann, 1956.

Gurvitch, Georges, 'Hyper-Empirisme dialectique: ses applications en sociologie', *Cahiers internationaux de sociologie*, vol. xv (1953), pp. 3–33.

Hamelin, Octave, *Les Eléments principaux de la représentation*, Paris, Félix Alcan, 1st edn, 1907, 2nd edn, 1925.

Hamelin, Octave, *Essai sur les éléments principaux de la représentation*, Bibliothèque de la philosophie contemporaine, Paris, Félix Alcan, 1907.

Hamelin, Octave, *Le Système de Descartes*, Paris, Félix Alcan, 1911.

Hawthorn, Geoffrey, *Enlightenment and Despair: A History of Sociology*, Cambridge University Press, 1976.

Hirst, Paul Q., *Durkheim, Bernard and Epistemology*, London, Routledge & Kegan Paul, 1975.

House, Floyd N., Review of G. Gurvitch, *La Vocation actuelle de sociologie*, *American Journal of Sociology*, vol. LX (no. 2, 1954), p. 198.

Hughes, H. Stuart, *Consciousness and Society: The Reorientation of European Social Thought, 1890–1930*, London, McGibbon & Kee, 1967.

James, Henry (ed.), *The Letters of William James*, 2 vols., London, Longmans Green & Co., 1926.

Bibliography

James, William, *Essays in Radical Empiricism*, London and New York, Longmans, Green & Co., 1912.

James, William, 'The knowing of things together', *The Psychological Review*, vol. II (March 1895), pp. 105–24.

James, William, *The Meaning of Truth*, London and New York, Longmans, Green & Co., 1909.

James, William, *A Pluralistic Universe*, London and New York, Longmans, Green & Co., 1909.

James, William, 'The pragmatic method', *Journal of Philosophy, Psychology and Scientific Method*, vol. I (Dec. 1904), pp. 673–87.

James, William, *Pragmatism*, London and New York, Longmans, Green & Co., 1907.

James, William, *Principles of Psychology*, London, Macmillan & Co., 1890.

James, William, *Psychology: Briefer Course*, London, Macmillan & Co., 1892.

James, William, *Some Problems of Philosophy*, London and New York, Longmans, Green & Co., 1911.

James, William, *The Varieties of Religious Experience*, London and New York, Longmans, Green & Co., 1902.

James, William, *The Will to Believe, and Other Essays in Popular Philosophy*, London and New York, Longmans, Green & Co., 1896.

Joachim, Harold H., *The Nature of Truth: An Essay*, Oxford, Clarendon Press, 1906.

Johnson, Allen and Malone, Dumas (eds.), *Dictionary of American Biography*, 21 vols., New York, Charles Scribner & Sons, 1928–37.

Jouffroy, Théodore-Simon, *Le Cahier vert: comment les dogmes finissent. Lettres inédites*, Paris, Pierre Poux, 1923.

LaCapra, Dominic, *Emile Durkheim: Sociologist and Philosopher*, Ithaca, N.Y., Cornell University Press, 1972.

Lalande, Pierre André, *La Raison et les normes*, Paris, Hachette, 1948.

Lalande, Pierre André, 'Sur une fausse exigence de la raison dans la méthode des sciences morales', *Revue de Métaphysique et de Morale*, vol. 15 (Jan. 1907), pp. 18–33.

Lalande, Pierre André, *Vocabulaire technique et critique de la philosophie*, 5th edn, Paris, Presses Universitaires de France.

Leinhardt, Maurice, *Do Kamo: la personne et le mythe dans le monde mélanésien*, Paris, Gallimard, 1947.

Leroux, Emmanuel, *Le Pragmatisme américain et anglais*, Paris, Félix Alcan, 1923.

Le Roy, Edouard, *Dogme et critique* (Etudes de philosophie et de critique religieuse), 2nd edn, Paris, Blond, 1907.

Le Roy, Edouard, 'Le Problème de Dieu', *Revue de Métaphysique et de Morale*, vol. XV (1907), pp. 129–70 and 470–513.

Le Roy, Edouard, 'Science et philosophie', *Revue de Métaphysique et de Morale*, vol. VII (1899), pp. 375–425, 503–62 and 708–31; vol. VIII (1900), pp. 37–72.

Bibliography

Lovejoy, A. O. *The Thirteen Pragmatisms, and Other Essays*, Baltimore, Johns Hopkins Press, 1963.

Lukes, Steven, *Emile Durkheim: His Life and Work*, London, Allen Lane, 1973.

McKeon, Richard, 'Une réaction américaine sur l'état actuel de la philosophie française', in M. Farber (ed.), *L'Activité philosophique contemporaine en France et aux Etats-Unis*, Paris, Presses Universitaires de France, 1950, pp. 359–91.

Marcell, D. W., *Progress and Pragmatism: James, Dewey, Beard and the American Idea of Progress*, Westport and London, Greenwood Press, 1974.

Martindale, D., *The Nature and Types of Sociological Theory*, London, Routledge & Kegan Paul, 1961.

Martineau, Harriet, *The Positive Philosophy of Auguste Comte*, 2 vols, 'freely translated and abridged', 2nd edn, London, John Chapman, 1875.

Mauss, Marcel, 'In memoriam: l'œuvre inédit de Durkheim et de ses collaborateurs', *Année Sociologique*, ns, vol. 1 (1925), pp. 7–29.

Moore, Addison Webster, 'Bergson and pragmatism', *The Philosophical Review*, vol. xxi (1912), pp. 397ff.

Moore, Addison Webster, *Pragmatism and its Critics*, Chicago, University of Chicago Press, 1910.

Moore, Addison Webster, 'Pragmatism and solipsism', *The Journal of Philosophy, Psychology and Scientific Method*, vol. vii (1909), pp. 378–83.

Moore, Addison Webster, 'Some logical aspects of purpose', in John Dewey et al., *Studies in Logical Theory*.

Myers, F. W. H., *Human Personality and its Survival of Bodily Death* (ed. and abr. by L. H. Myers), London, Longmans, Green & Co., 1907.

Nietzsche, Friedrich W., *Complete Works of F. W. Nietzsche* (ed. Oscar Levy), 18 vols., Edinburgh, T. N. Foulis, 1909–15.

Parodi, Dominique, 'Knowledge and action in Dewey's philosophy', in Paul A. Schlipp (ed.), *The Philosophy of John Dewey*, New York, Tudor Publishing Co. Ltd, 2nd edn, 1951, pp. 229–42.

Parodi, Dominique, *La Philosophie contemporaine en France*, Paris, Félix Alcan, 3rd edn, 1925.

Parodi, Dominique, 'Le Problème religieux dans la pensée contemporaine', *Revue de Métaphysique et de Morale*, vol. xxi (1913), pp. 511–25.

Parsons, Talcott, *The Structure of Social Action*, New York, The Free Press, 1949.

Peirce, Charles Sanders, *The Collected Papers of Charles Sanders Peirce*, vols. i–vi (ed. C. Hartshorn and P. Weiss); vols. vii and viii (ed. Arthur W. Burks), Cambridge, Mass., Harvard University Press, 1931–58.

Perry, Ralph Barton, *The Thought and Character of William James*, 2 vols., Boston, Little, Brown & Co., 1936.

Plato, *The Dialogues of Plato* (trans. and ed. B. Jowett), Oxford, Clarendon Press, 4th edn, 1953.

Renouvier, Charles, *Essais de critique générale*, first essay, *Traité de logique générale et de logique formelle*, vol. i, Paris, Armand Colin, 1912, pp. 42–9.

Bibliography

Ribot, Théodule, *The Psychology of Attention*, Chicago & London, Open Court Pub. Co. & Routledge & Kegan Paul, 1911.

Robet, H., 'L'Ecole de Chicago et l'instrumentalisme', *Revue de Métaphysique et de Morale*, vol. xxi (1913), pp. 537–75.

Russell, Bertrand, *Philosophical Essays*, London, George Allen & Unwin Ltd, rev. edn, 1966.

Scheffler, Israel, *Four Pragmatists: A Critical Introduction to Peirce, James, Mead and Dewey*, London, Routledge & Kegan Paul, 1974.

Schiller, Ferdinand C. S., 'Axioms as postulates', in Henry Stuart (ed.), *Personal Idealism*.

Schiller, Ferdinand C. S., *Humanism: Philosophical Essays*, London, Macmillan & Co., 1903.

Schiller, Ferdinand C. S., *Studies in Humanism*, London, Macmillan & Co., 1907.

Schinz, Albert, *Anti-pragmatisme: examen des droits respectifs de l'aristocratie intellectuelle et de la démocratie sociale*, Paris, Félix Alcan, 1909.

Schinz, Albert, 'Professor Dewey's pragmatism', *Journal of Philosophy, Psychology and Scientific Method*, vol. v (no. 23, Nov. 1908), pp. 617–28.

Schlipp, Paul A. (ed.), *The Philosophy of John Dewey*, New York, Tudor Publishing Co., 2nd edn, 1951.

Spinoza, Benedict de, *Ethic: Demonstrated in Geometrical Notes and Divided into Five Parts* (trans. W. Hale White), 2nd rev. edn, London, T. Fisher Unwin, 1894.

Stuart, Henry (ed.), *Personal Idealism: philosophical essays by eight members of the University of Oxford*, London, Macmillan & Co., 1902.

Thayer, H. S., *Meaning and Action: A Critical History of Pragmatism*, Indianapolis, Bobbs-Merrill Co. Inc., 1968.

Therborn, Göran, *Science, Class and Society: on the Formation of Sociology and Historical Materialism*, London, New Left Books, 1976.

Thomas, Milton H., *John Dewey: A Centennial Bibliography*, Chicago, University of Chicago Press, 1962.

Traugott, Mark (ed.), *Emile Durkheim on Institutional Analysis*, Chicago and London, University of Chicago Press, 1978.

Vailati, G. 'De quelques caractères du mouvement philosophique contemporaine en Italie', *Revue du Mois* (10 Feb. 1907), pp. 162–85.

Watson, J. B., *Behaviour: An Introduction to Comparative Psychology*, New York, Henry Holt & Co., 1914.

Weise, Leopold von, in *Kölner Zeitschrift für Soziologie*, vol. iv (1954, no. 2), p. 289.

Wolff, Kurt H. (ed.), *Emile Durkheim: 1858–1917*, Columbus, Ohio, Ohio State University Press, 1960.

Wright, Mills, C., *Sociology and Pragmatism: The Higher Learning in America*, New York, Oxford University Press, 1966.

Index

Index

Index

identity (principle of) 29, 32, 94
ideology xxxvi
illusion 21–2, 78–9, 101
image(s) 4, 28, 40, 45–6, 82, 99–100, 103–4
imagination 42–3, 100
individual 103, 107
  i. and the social xix, xxxviii, 68, 84–5,
    86–7, 97, 103, 107
  i. and truth xx, 67, 75–6, 91–2, 97
  see also Durkheim
individualism see intellectual
  individualism
institutions xiv, xviii, 70
Instrumentalist School 9, 38
intellectual individualism xx, 91–2
intellectualism 30, 31, 59
  see also Bergson

James, William xi, xiii, xviii, xxi, xxiii,
  xxvi, xxvii, xxviii, 8, 9, 16, 23, 34, 78,
  92
  Does Consciousness Exist? 39, 41, 65
  Essays in Radical Empiricism 8
  Meaning of Truth xxv, xxvii, 8, 10, 11,
    16, 23, 33
  Pluralistic Universe xxi, xxv, xxvii, 8,
    28, 32
  Pragmatism xxv, xxvi, xxviii, xxxvii, 8,
    10, 19, 23, 24, 25, 59
  Principles of Psychology xxvii, xxxi, 32,
    40, 43
  Psychology xxv
  Talks to Teachers xxv
  Varieties xix, xxv, xxvi, xxvii, xxxii,
    xxxiii, 60–1
  Will to Believe xxv, 7, 66
  his attack on dogmatism 11–14, 22–7
  on concepts Lecture 5 *passim*, 35, 46–8
  denies the duality of human
    experience 4, 8, 33, 39, 42–4, 64, 120
  as a founder of pragmatism 7, 8, 9
  links logic and psychology 18, Lecture 7
    passim, 54
  on religious experience 7, Lecture 12
    passim
  on sensation and knowledge Lecture 8
    passim
  spread of his ideas in France xxv–xxix,
    xxx
  'strung-along' universe xxi–xxii, 27, 35,
    119
  on thought as an active process Lecture 7
    passim, 54
  on truth xx, xxxvii, 11–12, 13, 15–16,
    Lecture 3 *passim*, Lecture 4 *passim*, 45,
    Lecture 9 *passim*, 54, 73, 75
Janet, Paul xvii

Jouffroy, Théodore-Simon 74
judgements 2, 23, 44, 56, 76, 94, 97
  see also truth as necessary judgements

Kant, Immanuel xiii, xl, 2, 12–13, 34
  his theory of truth xiii, 13, 16–17, 102
knowledge xv–xvi, xvii, xix, 47, 55, 82,
  121
  conditions for the appearance of k. 38,
    43–4
  k. in relation to action 43–4, Lecture 8
    passim, 77, 79–81
  scientific k. Lecture 19 passim
  sociology of k. xviii, xxxiii–xxxiv
  see also experience, rationalism,
    sensation

La Capra, Dominick 114
Lalande, André xvi–xvii
law 24, 94
Leibnitz, Gottfried W. von 12–14, 19, 40,
  88
Leroux, Emmanuel xxxi
Le Roy, Edouard 9
life-force (*élan vital*) xv, 95–7
logic 3, 4, 18, 29, 31–2, 37, 44, 54, 57, 58,
  59, 102
logical utilitarianism xiv, xxxviii, 72, 73–4
Lovejoy, Arthur O. 10

Martindale, Don xxiii
Maublanc, René xxii
Mauss, Marcel xi–xii, xxii, xxxiii
  his assessment of the importance of *P. &*
    S. xiii, xl
Mead, George Herbert xxiii
metaphysics xvi–xvii, xxviii, 30–1, 59, 71,
  89
method 10, 11, 57, 58, 60, 72
mind(s) 13–14, 50–1, 56, 77
  m. in communication 25–6, 88, 91–2
  the diversity of m. 19–20, 22, 24, 69, 92
monads 13, 19, 40, 88
monism (and pluralism) 25–6, 36, 43
  pragmatism as a disguised m. xxii, 43
Moore, Addison W. 9, 38, 60, 78
  Pragmatism and its Critics 37
morality xix, 3, 26, 60, 67, 70, 72, 77, 94,
  101–2, 127
  see also Durkheim, science, truth
myth (mythology) xxi, xxxiv–xxxv, xxxvi,
  76, 77, 84, 86–8, 90–1, 94, 101
  see also religion, truth

necessity 52–3
Nietzsche, Friedrich W. 2–4
novelty 21, 23–4, 78

Index

Index

pragmatism as an attack on s. xv, 1, 64
functions of speculative thought 38, 50, 76, 92
Spencer, Herbert 21–2, 94
Spinoza, Benedict de 35, 82
'strung-along' universe see James
subjectivity (-ism) xxxviii, 41, 45, 48, 61, 99

thought xiv, 17, 37–9, Lecture 7 passim, 54, 55, 59, 65
'ambulatory' nature of t. 47
heterogeneity of t. and reality Lecture 20 passim
representation and t. Lecture 7 passim, 84
the world constructed by t. 54, 65
see also action, Bergson, Dewey, reality, speculation
tolerance 20, 71, 92
truth xix, xx, 3, 7, 13, 17, 22, 44
t. and action xiv, xxxvii, 44, 45, 51–2, 67
t. as constructed 54–6, 57, 72, 74, 83
'copy' theory of t. 11–12, 15–16, 27, 28, 45, 51, 66, 85, 92, 93
t. as disconcerting or painful xiv, xxxviii, 74
dogmatic theory of t. 11–14, 19–20, 23
expedience and t. 44, 73, 75
idealistic theories of t. xiii, 12
t. and morality xiv, xxxviii, 13, 44, 67, 73, 87, 98
mythological t. xv, xxxv, xxxvi, 86–8, 90–1
t. as necessary judgements 2, 28, 56, 73
the obligatory character of t. xiv, xxxviii, 2, 16–17, 68, 73, 84, 98
t. as 'personal' or 'impersonal' xxxvii–xxxviii, 3, 12, 13, 15, 16, 17, 18, 21, 56–7, 69, 74, 75, 87, 88, 91–2

pragmatism as a theory of t. 10, 11–14, Lectures 3 and 4 passim, 37, Lectures 9 and 10 passim, 59, Lecture 15 passim, Lectures 17 and 18 passim
rationalism and the theory of t. 11–14, 16, 19, Lecture 4 passim, 52, 97
t. and satisfaction xiv, xxxvii, xxxviii, 48–9, 50–1, 55, 56, 122
sociological theory of t. xiv, 57, 67–8, 70–2, Lecture 18 passim, 86–8, 92, 97–8
pragmatism 'softens' the t. xvii, xxxviii, 64, 66–7
'it is the useful that is true' 50, 72, Lecture 15 passim, 87
the variability of t. xiv, xvii, xxxviii, 18–20, 21, 23–4, 25, 64, 66, 68, Lecture 14 passim, 87
verification xxxvii, 16, 48, 51–2, 57, 86, 91, 105
see also action, Bergson, Dewey, Durkheim, James, Kant, religion, Schiller, science

universe 13–14, 21, 34, 57, 63, 74, 88, 94
pragmatism as a theory of the u. 10, 11, 25, 59
the u. as unfinished 23, 53, 94
see also James
utilitarianism xiv, 11, 72
see also logical utilitarianism
utility 3, 44, 78
see also truth

values xvi–xvii, xix, xxii, 44, 55, 64, 73
verification see truth

Wolff, Kurt H. ix, xxiv

Zeno 29–30